MUIR & MIRRIELEES

The Scottish Partnership that became
a Household Name in Russia

HARVEY PITCHER

Swallow House Books
CROMER

First published in 1994
by Swallow House Books
37 Bernard Road, Cromer, Norfolk NR27 9AW

The moral right of the author has been asserted

A catalogue record for this book is available
from the British Library

ISBN 0-905265-03-3

Printed in 11/12pt Times Roman by
Broadgate Printers, Dunkirk, Aylsham,
Norfolk NR11 6SS

Contents

Acknowledgements

I am most grateful to John Bagenal, great-grandson of Alice and Andrew Muir, for his kindness in making available all the Muir family papers and photographs in his possession, and to his wife, Patience, for the large amount of research and correspondence that she undertook so cheerfully on my behalf. My task was also made easier by the late J.Herbert Brett (husband of Margaret, younger daughter of Meta and Stuart Hogg), who in 1974 collected and transcribed a large number of papers for a Muir Family Compendium. Information about the Muir Chemical Works at Degunino was kindly passed on to me by the late Varia Lane (daughter of Kenneth Muir) and her son, Andrew. The contributions made by Beauchamp Bagenal, Kate Havinden, Eileen Muir, and members of the Brett and Richmond families, were also much appreciated.

To Faith Robinson, great-granddaughter of Jane and Archibald Mirrielees, I am very much indebted for the loan of Mirrielees family papers and photographs, especially the Family Record compiled by her grandmother, Maida Bernard, and the unpublished biography of Henry Bernard, *A Spiritual Odyssey*, written in 1960 by his daughter, Una Bernard Sait. For this vital introduction to the Mirrielees family archive I have to thank Rosemary Hearn, granddaughter of Sir Frederick Mirrielees.

Information on the history of the Philip family was taken from the booklet, 'A Fifeshire Family: The Descendants of John & Thomas Philip of Kirkcaldy', compiled in 1980 by the late Peter Philip, grandson of Walter Philip's elder brother, John. In obtaining material about Walter, I was greatly helped by his granddaughter, Edomé Broughton-Adderley, and by Chloë Dobree, great-granddaughter of John Philip, who on a visit to South Africa consulted the papers left by Peter Philip to the University of Cape Town Libraries (archivist, Leonie Twentyman Jones), which included Walter's letter of January 1863 from St Petersburg to his brother John in Cape Town.

To Geraldine Hills, daughter of Frederick Cazalet, I am very grateful for providing me with extensive biographical details about the Cazalet family, and for lending me various Muir & Mirrielees business papers, including an invaluable copy of the Specification for the new building of 1908.

Among Russian friends who assisted me I must give special thanks to Professor Vladimir Kataev of Moscow University, who collected a wealth of information from Russian sources, including all the material describing the Muir & Mirrielees fire of 1900; Sergei Romaniuk, for producing several indispensable references to Muir & Mirrielees from his encyclopaedic knowledge of the history of Moscow's buildings, and for providing me with some unusual illustrations; and the late A.A.Demskaya, for passing on information and photographs relating to the architect, R.I.Klein.

To Dr Catherine Cooke I feel particularly grateful, not only for the keen interest that she took in the book from the outset, but for giving liberally of her time to rephotograph a dauntingly large number of original photographs and illustrations. The colour postcard of Muir & Mirrielees used on the front cover was kindly lent by Aidan White.

At Cambridge University Library I was able to consult the archives of the British & Foreign Bible Society (including the correspondence between John Paterson and Archibald Mirrielees) in the charge of Alan Jesson, and at the School of Oriental and African Studies, University of London, the archives of the London Missionary Society (archivist, Rosemary Seton). Kathleen Cann, formerly archivist of the B.F.B.S., never failed to produce all the information I needed, and kindly gave me her comments on a draft version of Chapter 2, while Kate Perry, archivist of Girton College, Cambridge, provided interesting material relating to Meta Muir's time at Girton. I also take the opportunity of thanking the following archivists and librarians: Mrs Isobel Couperwhite (Watt Library, Greenock), Jo Currie (Edinburgh University Library), Mrs C. J. Hopkins (Trinity College, Oxford), Mrs P. Judd (Pembroke College, Cambridge), Martin Rady (Mill Hill School), Miss A. Terre (Cultural Services Division, Ealing London Borough) and Mary Williamson (University of Aberdeen).

Finally, I wish to thank the following good friends in Britain and Russia who helped me in a variety of different ways: David Allan (Greenock), Dr John Appleby, Nic Barlow (photograph of 42 Holland Park), Professor S.Batalden, A.Yu.Bazilyevich, John Bowles (National Library of Scotland), Professor R.F.Christian, Richard Davies (Leeds Russian Archive), Professor Paul Dukes, James Forsyth, Grace Garrett, Veronika Gern and Mira Pumpyanskaya (especially for their help in enabling me to find a Moscow publisher), the late Michael Glenny, Professor Evelyn Harden (currently preparing for publication an annotated edition of Anna Whistler's Russian diaries), Professor Peter Henry, A.Kazakov, Henry Kelly, Timothy Knox, Hellen Matthews, Patrick Miles, Kathleen Berton Murrell, Lydia Polinovskaya, Emmie Polotskaya, Laura Raybould, Eric & Sue Robinson, Valentina Ryapolova, Nina Sheeran, Yurii Skobelev (Curator, Chekhov House Museum, Yalta), Stuart Thompstone, Polly Walcot-Stewart and Michael Welch.

Illustrations

Front cover: pre-1917 colour postcard of Muir & Mirrielees
(inset: l to r: Archibald Mirrielees, Andrew Muir, Walter Philip)

i: Muir & Mirrielees 'logo'

Foreword

On the last day of March 1990, newly arrived in Moscow, I was standing with my camera in the gardens opposite the Bolshoi Theatre. The weather was far from ideal for taking photographs: sudden flurries of snow alternated with longer periods when the sun shone fiercely and cast deep shadows across the buildings. But there always seemed to be people taking photographs in this part of the city, whatever the conditions. It was a Saturday afternoon, and nearby a Russian family party, perhaps visiting Moscow for the day, was posing self-consciously against a backdrop of the Bolshoi's huge entrance columns. It was not, however, the famous Theatre that I had come to photograph. I was concentrating on another building just to its right, very different in style, though also distinctive: Central Universal Stores or TsUM, Moscow's second largest department store, known before the Revolution as Muir & Mirrielees, and to the resident British community as M & M's.

My interest in Muir & Mirrielees came about through a series of happy chances. In the early 1970's, on moving to the seaside resort of Cromer to concentrate on writing, I was intrigued to discover living in the next street an elderly retired schoolteacher, Emma Dashwood, who had spent the years from 1910 to 1919 working as an English governess in Russia. Though a gifted storyteller with an excellent memory for detail, she had never had an opportunity to talk to anyone at length about her Russian experiences, and found in me a perfect audience: someone not only eager to listen to all her Russian stories, but who positively encouraged her to recall the colour of the dress that she was wearing on a particular occasion or the food that she was served at a particular meal. In the Russian families where she was employed, Emma Dashwood was known as 'Miss Emmie'. To my surprise I discovered that there had been thousands of these English governesses, and I tried to give an impression of their colourful experiences in my book, When Miss Emmie was in Russia *(1977).*

One thing leads to another. Among those who read Miss Emmie *and wrote to me was Harry Smith, living in Canada. In 1847 his grandfather, Richard Smith, had gone out to St Petersburg from Greenock to assist in the construction of the first Russian railways, and in 1856 he started the Smith Boiler Works in Moscow. Harry had devoted his retirement to compiling a detailed history of the Smith family in Russia, and of the small forgotten expatriate community to which they belonged, the Moscow British. As a young boy he remembered being taken by his mother on shopping expeditions to M & M's, followed by a light lunch in their restaurant, and I included a brief description of the shop in my book,* The Smiths of Moscow *(1984). And among those who wrote to me after reading* The Smiths *was John Bagenal, whose great-grandfather, Andrew Muir, had been the Muir of Muir & Mirrielees. The Muirs had been diligent letter-writers in an age when letter-writing was still a cultivated art; many of their letters had been preserved and gave a remarkably full picture of their family life. They had lost contact with the Mirrielees family many years before, but enquiries eventually led me to Faith Robinson, whose grandmother, Maida Bernard, née Mirrielees, wife of the British Chaplain in Moscow in the 1880's, had compiled a Family Record no less detailed than that of Harry Smith.*

It became clear at the outset that M & M's, the retail shop, was only the most visible part of a much larger historical canvas. The department store in Moscow dated from the second half of the 1880's, but the business itself had started life as a wholesale concern in St Petersburg in 1843. Underlying them both, however, was a story of more human dimensions: of two Scottish families whose fates had become finely interwoven over several generations as a result of their involvement with Russia.

The story began with Archibald Mirrielees (1797-1877), an ambitious young man from Aberdeen, who arrived in St Petersburg in 1822, and in 1843 founded an import business there under his own name. The Muirs entered the story a year later when Jane, the daughter of a wealthy Greenock merchant, married Archibald as his third wife and accompanied him to Russia. How that matrimonial partnership worked out is a central theme in Part One of Muir & Mirrielees. *The families first became commercial partners in 1852, when Jane's younger brother, Andrew Muir (1817-99), joined the firm; the name, Muir & Mirrielees, was adopted after he became senior partner in 1857. Part Two focuses on Andrew's career, marriage and family. His wife, Alice, was the widow of William Philip, a Scottish missionary in South Africa, and it was their son, Walter Philip (1845-1919), who became the third and last head of M & M's. By the second half of the 1880's the firm had transferred its operations from St Petersburg to Moscow, and in 1891 it became a purely retail concern. Muir & Mirrielees soon established itself as a household name throughout the Russian Empire: Chekhov went there to buy his hats and his writing-paper, ordered furniture from them for his new house in Yalta, and named two of his dogs after the founders. The life-story of Walter Philip and the history of the department store are inseparable: together they form the subject of Part Three.*

While I was researching and writing the book, two themes began to stand out. The first was that of motivation. What kind of men were they, these three

Scottish merchants? What drove them on? Was it only the urge to make money? The answers varied considerably in each case, as did the fates that awaited them as individuals. The other theme, which emerged more unexpectedly, was that of the second generation. What happens to the sons who are obliged to follow in their father's footsteps and enter the family business – supposing that they are reluctant to do so, or in various ways unsuitable?

Though not planned as such, Muir & Mirrielees *forms the third part of an Anglo-Russian trilogy, along with* Miss Emmie *and* The Smiths of Moscow. *All three describe British people living in Russia, and interacting in various ways with Russian life, between 1820 and 1920 – whether as governesses, boilermakers or merchants. To describe anyone as Anglo-Russian (or Scoto-Russian) may mean different things. It can refer to the children of mixed marriages, but intermarriage was not very common, and more frequently it is used of families like the Smiths, who belonged to a well-established community of British people in Russia. The Smiths had retained their British nationality and outlook, but adopted Russia as their permanent home: they were born, lived and died there, with only occasional visits to Britain. The governess who went out to Russia not intending to stay more than a year or two, but liked it so much that she stayed on for life while continuing to attend the British Church every Sunday, might also claim full Anglo-Russian status. But although Archibald Mirrielees and Andrew Muir took a very active part in the life of the British community in Russia, they retired to England as soon as their working lives were over, so that their stories are 'Anglo-Russian' in a wider sense than those of their predecessors.*

By 1920 the British community in Russia had ceased to exist. Within Bolshevik Russia it was quickly forgotten. Members of the community, for their part, could not forget Russia, but what remained uppermost in their minds was the cruel fate that had overtaken them: on returning to Britain, many of them found themselves destitute and forced to depend on charity. The bitterness of being thrown out of their adopted country so coloured all their memories of Russia that the good times were obscured, but now that the bitterness has evaporated, it is possible to see that those who felt most bitter were very often the ones who had become most fond of Russia and its people. The unusual depth of British feeling for Russia has been a recurrent theme throughout the trilogy.

After my visit to TsUM on that first Saturday afternoon, I spent a further three weeks in Moscow and Yalta. During that time I found myself frequently being asked by Russian acquaintances about the subject of the book I was writing. When I replied that it was 'about TsUM', their reaction was one of barely concealed mirth: why bother to write about their familiar old department store? It came as something of a shock to Russians to learn that the store's founders were from Scotland. They are more inclined to think of Scotland as the setting for Walter Scott's colourful historical romances, still very popular with Russian readers, or as the mountainous, mist-shrouded country that the Russian Romantic poet, Lermontov, whose distant ancestors were Scottish, liked to think of as his spiritual home. But there was always a more prosaic Scotland, a Scotland of practical, hard-working, enterprising people, like the Scottish engineers who became renowned all over the world, and it was to that other Scotland that such men as the boilermaker Richard Smith, and the merchants, Archibald Mirrielees and Andrew Muir, belonged.

When I first began collecting material in the mid-1980's, the publication of a book like Muir & Mirrielees *in the Soviet Union was quite unthinkable: only those who harboured unhealthy longings for the old regime could possibly be interested in such a subject. By 1990 all that had changed, and Russia's immediate pre-Revolutionary past, once a prohibited area to all but a few of the Party faithful, was being explored with intense curiosity. I had always dreamed of having a book published in Russia. Now the timing and subject seemed right, and I submitted a proposal to the well-known publishing house, Moscow Worker.*

Shortly before I was due to leave Russia, I visited the publishers with a Russian friend. Crossing a crowded entrance-hall, we took the lift to the fourth floor of a six-floor building and walked along an absurdly wide corridor lined with pot-plants. Our contact had chosen this moment to go on holiday, but my friend assured me that we should meet a lady who knew all about my proposal. She was wearing dark glasses and looked flustered. The Germans had just sent a large consignment of paper, but where could they find transport to bring it from the airport? She had obviously never seen my proposal before. In the intervals between making and receiving frantic telephone calls, she at last finished reading it. 'I like the subject very much... but we'd need to print at least 120,000 copies and charge a high price, so I'm afraid... But have a word with the deputy editor of our History of Moscow section.' She rang his office. No reply. She rang other offices. When all seemed lost, he walked in, apparently by chance. He read the proposal through in one go. 'Yes, we'd like to do it,' he said. 'We'll translate it here. Our readers are very interested now in that kind of subject.'

On my return to England I decided to write two versions of the book, one with Russian readers in mind and the other for English readers. The Russian version was published in February 1994. Here is the English version.

H.J.P.

Piety and Profit

Archibald Mirrielees (1797 – 1877)

1

From Aberdeen to St Petersburg

The names trip lightly off the tongue: Muir and Mirrielees. Muir is no problem. According to *The Surnames of Scotland*, it indicates residence beside a moor or heath, and not surprisingly, it is one of the commonest Scottish surnames. It transliterates easily into Russian as *Myur*, requiring four letters in the old Tsarist spelling, but in modern Russian, only three.

Mirrielees is a very different matter. It derives from Merrilees, the name of an estate and hamlet now merged in the estate of Binns, West Lothian. *The Surnames of Scotland* lists six possible spellings; Mirrielees is not one of them. When young Archy Mirrielees landed at Calais in 1873, the French official asked him his name.

I said 'Mirrielees'. Again he asked *'Votre nom, s'il vous plaît?'* I said it again. He seemed puzzled. I suppose he had never heard such a name before. After a pause he asked *'Anglais?'* to which I said 'yes' and he seemed to think this quite sufficient excuse for having a queer name, for he immediately said: *'Passez'*!

Few names can have been more consistently and variously misspelt. To be fair, those who first meet the name in its Russian form of *Meriliz* can be forgiven for thinking that it must have been Merrilees in the original. There was less excuse for the former Jane Muir, who, ten days after her marriage to Archibald Mirrielees, was still unable to sign her married name correctly. Anna Whistler, 'Whistler's Mother', a close friend of the family in St Petersburg in the second half of the 1840's, never spells the name the same twice running in her diaries. But the most bizarre misspelling occurs in *The Centennial History of the American Bible Society* (1916), which refers to a Bible Committee in St Petersburg whose members included a certain Mr Miricles.

Archibald *Mirrielees*, then, was born in Aberdeen on 7 September 1797, one of the ten children of John Mirrielees and Jessie Gordon. There were two sets of twins in the family, Archibald being one of the second set; his twin brother died in infancy.

The ancient burgh of Aberdeen derives its nickname, 'The Granite City', from the seemingly indestructible local granite used in many of its buildings, which gives the city a very distinctive appearance: solid, grey, dignified and somewhat austere, except when the sun comes out and makes the granite glisten. But the nickname also serves as a reminder that until recent times, when North Sea oil turned Aberdeen into a boom city, life there was always very hard; many had to wrest a meagre livelihood from the fishing industry; everyone knew the value of money. Not that Aberdeen ever seems to have been inward-looking. Apart from extensive trading links with other ports in Britain and all over Europe, it was also a pioneer in culture and education. By the end of the 15th century, when England had only two universities, Scotland already had four, including King's College, Aberdeen, which was unique in offering from its inception a course in medicine.

What little that is known about Archibald's time in Aberdeen derives largely from the Family Record that his youngest daughter, Maida, began to compile when she herself was seventy. Of Grandfather John Mirrielees she knew only that he was short of stature and very hot-tempered, and was looked on askance by his God-fearing neighbours, because he read such revolutionary books as Tom Paine's *The Rights of Man*. Of his wife Jessie she knew nothing at all, except that there survived in the family a pair of horn-rimmed spectacles said to have belonged to her, which could only have been used by a small woman. Archibald inherited his parents' shortness of stature and his father's quick temper. He was not very communicative about his early years, but would sometimes tell his children a little about his Spartan upbringing. For breakfast there was only porridge and milk, and if one of them left any porridge, that had to be eaten at dinner before anything else. Porridge and milk were served again for supper. This frugal but nourishing diet, Maida thought, had helped to give her father his excellent constitution.

In the early 19th century Scotland as a whole, and Aberdeen in particular, was far ahead of England in the provision of popular education. The Grammar School provided one of the best classical educations to be had in Scotland, but its fees were modest and pupils came from all classes of society. Byron first went there in 1794 at the age of six and stayed for four years. There were also many schools in the city using the Lancaster method. Joseph Lancaster was the English educationist who encouraged the principle – much favoured, among others, by Tolstoy – of involving the older pupils in teaching the younger ones. It seems likely that Archibald and his brothers attended one of these so-called 'English' schools, which catered especially for boys intending to pursue careers in commerce, and where fees, again, were minimal.

In 1813, when he was sixteen, Archibald Mirrielees felt sufficiently confident of his abilities to set off on his own for London. Many young Scots throughout the 19th century made that same journey south, seeking better opportunities and going on to acquire prominent positions in London and all over the world; but Archibald must have been more ambitious than his brothers, for he was the only one to do so. By the time that he next returned to his birthplace, thirty years later, the others had all prospered – William had been for some years an Elder of the Kirk, and was shortly to become a partner in the firm of Cattenach & Mirrielees, clothiers and tailors, of 126 Union Street – but none of them achieved the same spectacular success as Archibald.

In London he became a clerk in the counting-house of the firm of Fisher & Co. His sound Scottish education would have provided him with the prerequisites for such a job: a fair hand and a good head for figures. He had two particular recollections of his nine years in London. One was of watching Mrs Siddons act. Officially the great actress had retired in 1812 at the age of fifty-seven, but in 1819 she staged a brief comeback. No longer popular with the London critics, she had at least one enthusiastic young follower from north of the Border. Later, after his religious conversion, Archibald renounced all such worldly entertainments, and it was most unfair of him, Maida felt, to wax so eloquent about Mrs Siddons to his children when *they* were not allowed even to set foot inside a theatre. His other vivid recollection was of watching from afar the execution of the Cato Street Conspirators. Meeting in Cato Street off London's Edgware Road, the conspirators had hatched a colourful plot to murder Castlereagh and his ministers, seize the Bank of England and the Mansion House, and set up a provisional government. They were betrayed, and the five ringleaders were executed in 1820. It was the last case in England of hanging, drawing and quartering, and thousands gathered to watch the grisly spectacle.

The Scots have always been great self-educators, and Archibald was no exception. Between 1818 and 1822 he purchased many little volumes of classics, and Maida remembered as a child how she used to admire the gold tooling along their edges and backs, and loved stroking their smooth covers of yellow calf. They included the collected poems of Dryden, Pope and Cowper, Young's *Night Thoughts* and Doddridge's *Rise and Progress of Religion in the Soul*: serious reading for a counting-clerk in his twenties. These volumes, some of which survive, also suggest his lifelong love of accuracy and precise habits of mind, for on the flyleaf of each he carefully inscribed his name and the date of purchase.

In 1822 the book-buying ceased, for in that autumn Archibald Mirrielees left London and went out to St Petersburg as his firm's permanent representative. Fisher & Co. must have been very confident of their serious-minded young Scottish clerk to entrust him with such a responsible position, while the ambitious Archibald must have felt well satisfied that nine years of hard work and self-discipline had been duly rewarded.

St Petersburg, like Aberdeen, was a northern city and seaport. It, too, had its distinctive granite, used in huge quantities to construct the embankments and parapets that were intended to protect the city against the ever-present danger of flooding by the river Neva. But there the similarities ended. In contrast to ancient Aberdeen, St Petersburg was then little more than a hundred years old. European architects in the previous century had created a city that was remarkably uniform in its classical elegance and splendour. Everything was on a grand scale. 'The distances here are enormous,' Lewis Carroll wrote in his Russian journal in 1867. 'It is like walking about in a city of giants.' To cross one of its squares took several minutes. Aberdonians might take pride in Union Street, their main thoroughfare, which ran for over a mile, but in St Petersburg the Nevsky Prospect was almost three miles long. Petersburg, too, unlike Aberdeen, was not grey but colourful, for the palaces and great houses were painted in bright pastel shades that contrasted with the grey northern light that prevailed throughout the long months of winter.

Many ordinary Russians felt alienated from the Imperial magnificence and impersonal splendour of St Petersburg. Archibald Mirrielees, however, is unlikely to have experienced any such feelings of alienation. On his arrival in St Petersburg he would have found himself part of a tightly-knit resident British community, which by 1822 numbered some 2000 people. J.G.Kohl, a German who spent some years in Russia in the 1830's, wrote of the British that they were 'the only foreigners in St Petersburg who keep exclusively to their own community, and form a kind of state within a state, or at least endeavour to do so'. Peter the Great, in his campaign to westernize Russia in the early 18th century, had imported from Britain shipbuilders, naval and military personnel, engineers and doctors; later there came architects and landscape gardeners, painters and engravers, and a variety of craftsmen and skilled workers. It was Anglo-Russian trade, however, still supervised from London by the Russia Company founded in the 16th century, that accounted for the presence of the most influential and well-to-do British residents in St Petersburg. These merchants were known collectively as the British Factory, of which Kohl wrote that 'though small in numbers (there are about 800 souls), it is extremely rich, and in credit, power and opulence perhaps as important as a settlement of 20,000 individuals of any other nation'.

Nor would Archibald have had any difficulty in meeting fellow Scots. There was a note of envy in the comment made in 1805 by an English engineer, Zacchaeus Walker, about Charles Baird, then in the process of building up his industrial empire in St Petersburg, that he 'comes from the North side of the Tweed which is the best recommendation a man can bring to this city, the Caledonian Phalanx being the strongest and most numerous, and moving always in the closest union'. As this story unfolds, we shall see that the Caledonian Phalanx continued to move in the closest union in Russia for many years to come.

Some of St Petersburg's finest houses were acquired in the 18th century by members of the British Factory, and an area grew up on the left bank of the Neva which came to be known as the English Quay. By the time of Archibald's arrival, however, the Quay had become too exclusive even for the wealthy British, and Kohl later wrote that it ought to be re-named 'the Princes' Walk, for there daily the élite of the Russian Empire may be seen wearing away the granite with their princely and noble feet'. Instead, the most affluent British and American residents began to colonize the street running parallel to the English Quay, known as the Galernaya.

In the middle of the English Quay stood the English Church, opened in 1754. According to the English writer, A.B.Granville, it had 'a noble front to the river, being decorated by a colonnade, placed on a massive and well-distributed basement storey, in which are the apartments of the Revd E.Law, nephew of the late Lord Ellenborough and Chaplain to the Factory.' The entrance, properly speaking, was through a handsome gateway from the Galernaya. Inside, the church was richly decorated, with a state pew for the British Ambassador and a pulpit surmounted by the Royal Arms of England.

When Kohl visited the church in the 1830's, what struck him first was the number of young British officers there who had entered the Russian service and were wearing Russian epaulettes. Then, as he stood in the entrance, looking over the little congregation and estimating their numbers, he heard a voice behind him, saying 'Farther, farther'.

It was an elegant, but grave and severe-looking gentleman, who directed my attention to the regulations suspended from a pillar, which forbade standing in the passages, and then gave me a seat. On one occasion when the Emperor Nicholas visited this church, and stood still at the entrance, he also was addressed with the 'Farther, farther! your majesty', and shown to a seat.

Kohl was impressed by the extreme quiet which reigned over the assembly, but not by the sermon, which lacked eloquence or fervour. 'The St Petersburg preacher, moreover, propped his head sometimes on his right, sometimes on his left hand, and sometimes on both together, which would have looked indecorous in a coffee-house, but in the pulpit, and from a preacher, was in the highest degree improper and offensive.'

Of Archibald Mirrielees' religious beliefs before this time we know little, but we do know that he was a Scot, of humble origins, who had made his way in the world without benefit of patronage; so that the handsome English Church and its well-connected Chaplain, the state pew for the British Ambassador and the pulpit surmounted by the Royal Arms, are unlikely to have had much appeal for him. Fortunately, however, there was in St Petersburg an alternative place of worship, and one which was to shape the character of his whole future life.

2

The First Twenty Years

Like Archibald Mirrielees, John Paterson (1776-1855) was a Scot from a humble background. In his youth he had worked as a cabinet-maker before starting to train for the Independent ministry. In the summer of 1805, he and a colleague set off for India as missionaries, but on reaching Copenhagen, found that they could not embark until the following spring. On their first Sunday they also discovered that while the city's streets were crowded with cheerful holiday-makers, its churches were empty. Christian Denmark, they decided, needed them no less than heathen India. In 1808 Paterson moved to Stockholm, where he married a Swedish girl. By this time he had become closely involved with the work of the British & Foreign Bible Society. Founded in London in 1804 on an interdenominational basis, the Society had one simple objective: 'To encourage the wider circulation of the Holy Scriptures, without note or comment'. In 1811 he visited Finland, hoping to arrange for the printing of a Finnish Bible and the formation of a Bible Society, but since this required the approval of the Tsarist authorities, he was obliged to visit Russia itself, where another Scot, Robert Pinkerton, was already trying to interest prominent people in the formation of a Russian Bible Society and had invited Paterson's co-operation.

The timing of this visit in the summer of 1812 could not have been more unfortunate. In St Petersburg the Minister of Foreign Creeds, Prince Golitsyn, gave him a sympathetic hearing, but reminded him politely of Russia's invasion by Napoleon. In Moscow the Governor-General granted him a brief interview, but he, too, had other things on his mind. The Patersons narrowly succeeded in leaving Moscow for St Petersburg before the gates were closed. Nine days later Napoleon and his army sighted Moscow; two nights later Moscow was in flames. In St Petersburg Paterson had already made preparations for returning to Sweden when his wife, who was expecting their second child, contracted a fever and for weeks lay helpless. Paterson occupied his mind by drawing up an address on the establishment of Bible Societies in Russia, especially one in St Petersburg, which he submitted to Prince Golitsyn for presentation to the Emperor. With Napoleon in retreat, Alexander was on the point of rejoining the army, but postponed his departure until he had examined the scheme. He gave it his approval, and early in 1813 the St Petersburg Bible Society was inaugurated with great pomp and ceremony. This public triumph was overtaken by private tragedy, however, for Paterson's wife and her newborn child both died soon after.

Paterson remained in St Petersburg and in the next few years developed the publishing capacity of the Russian Bible Society, as it was renamed, to a spectacular degree. He was essentially a man of action, driven on by the strength of his convictions, and at his best when engaged in activities requiring unlimited amounts of energy and hard work. He soon mastered the latest printing technologies and took on a hundred workmen, supervised by a master printer and bookbinder brought out from England. At Bible House huge numbers of Bibles and Testaments were printed in many different languages, while Auxiliary Societies were set up all over the Russian Empire to facilitate distribution. In 1821 Prince Golitsyn, as President of the Society, presented the Emperor on his forty-fourth birthday with a copy of the first complete edition of the New Testament in Russian, undertaken at the Emperor's request. This proved to be the high point of the Society's activities.

In 1817 Paterson married again. It was an unlikely match. Jean Greig was the only daughter of Admiral Samuel Greig (1735-88), who came from the little Scottish port of Inverkeithing. Highly esteemed by Catherine the Great and dubbed the 'Father of the Russian Navy', Greig is one of two Scots – the other being Patrick Gordon at the time of Peter the Great – who were closest to the centre of historical events in Russia. Much to the annoyance of her more worldly family, Jean became seriously interested in religion and appealed for spiritual guidance to Paterson, who had been introduced to her as one of the few 'truly pious' Christians in Russia. But this marriage was even shorter than the first. Jean threw herself into philanthropic work, including prison-visiting, but after one such visit she contracted typhoid and died in January 1820, leaving a daughter.

On his arrival in St Petersburg Paterson had quickly become convinced that the English Church was not preaching the 'pure Gospel', and decided to start his own Sunday meeting for the serious-minded. At first this was held in his own home, but then, as numbers grew, he was allowed to hold a service in the Chapel of the Moravian Brethren. In 1820, perhaps feeling the strain of his commitments after his wife's death, he persuaded the London Missionary Society to send out a resident minister, and in December the Revd Richard Knill (1787-1857) arrived in St Petersburg.

Mr Knill was an Englishman. A former missionary in India, he had been recommended to the bracing influence of a northern climate (though it is hard to think of St Petersburg as 'bracing'). His arrival caused a considerable stir among the British community. In 1822, as Paterson wrote in the notes for his autobiography, Mr Norris, a leading critic of the Evangelicals, circulated in St Petersburg a pamphlet in which he made a furious attack on the Russian Bible Society and Mr Knill's little church, supporting his allegations by 'a silly letter' from the Revd Mr Law, which, according to Paterson, 'contained so many calumnies and palpable falsehoods that it was almost impossible to believe that it had been written by a person on the spot and especially by a Minister of the Gospel'. Paterson's reply was circulated in the following year, and since Law took no further action, Paterson felt that he had carried the day. But although the open bickering stopped, the differences between the two places of worship remained: differences that were as much to do with background and social class as with religious belief.

Mr Knill was clearly an inspiring preacher and evangelizer. On his arrival in St Petersburg he made a list in his journal of the names of full members of their church. It consisted of about twenty men and twenty women. Within a few months, however, full membership doubled and the general congregation increased even more. It does not seem surprising that Archibald Mirrielees, newly arrived in St Petersburg and on his own, a serious young Scot seeking like-minded friends, should have been attracted to Mr Knill and his congregation. His conversion probably took place some time in 1823. There can be no doubt that he always regarded it as far and away the most significant event in his life.

What kind of beliefs and attitudes was he embracing?

In spite of Mr Knill's inspired teaching, the overall numbers of his congregation remained small by comparison with the English Church. To be able to think of themselves as a beleaguered minority was always, however, a strong part of their church's appeal; they cultivated their own exclusive vocabulary and forms of address, always referring to each other in letters as 'our dear Mr Mirrielees' or 'our good friend Mr Gellibrand'. In his journal Knill writes: 'Make us a holy and consecrated band! Though despised by many, may we be rich in faith.' This faith was based on a vivid awareness of sin, on the possibility of attaining salvation through a personal experience of conversion, and on a belief that the guiding hand of Providence was to be detected in all things. They were despised (and often ridiculed) because they self-consciously cultivated pious virtues and made no secret of their disapproval of the worldliness of others. For themselves they set the highest standards. Mr Knill writes of having been requested by some of the members that a Mr Prince might no longer be considered a member of their church, because of his 'unsuitable walk and conversation'. This intensely serious view of life prompted them to undertake numerous good works and to denounce such frivolities as theatre-going and Sunday afternoon tea-parties. They were also convinced that no other form of Christianity was truly valid. To these beliefs and attitudes Archibald Mirrielees remained loyal until his death. They not only dominated his own life, but profoundly affected the lives of those closest to him.

*   *   *

On the night of 18 November 1824 there was a gale in St Petersburg of such unusual violence that in Knill's words, 'the iron roof of the Bible House was rolled up like a sheet of paper and carried into the air'. The flood that followed on the next day was the most spectacular and disastrous in the city's long history of flooding. The streets, Knill wrote in a letter four days later, 'were occupied by ships & boats & watch-houses & floating trees & even coffins from the cemeteries...' These 'coffins from a flooded cemetery' also appear floating along the streets in Pushkin's famous description of the flood in *The Bronze Horseman*, but whereas in the poem the people see the flood as a manifestation of God's wrath and await their punishment, Knill characteristically exclaims: 'Oh, what would I have given for an angel's voice, and an eagle's wings, to flee and tell the drowning peasants of the Lamb of God.' The Knills must have been among the lucky ones occupying an upstairs apartment, unlike 'dear Mr Mortimer, the Moravian minister', who was obliged to move in with them temporarily. Relief subscriptions were organized, and Archibald Mirrielees contributed 200 roubles: a considerable sum, showing that he must have already been prosperous as well as philanthropic.

A little over a year later, another event occurred in St Petersburg that Archibald sometimes recalled: the Decembrist uprising. Compared to the Cato Street Conspiracy, this was a very gentlemanly affair. A group of officers and noblemen, eager for constitutional reforms, took advantage of the period of confusion that followed the death of

Alexander to try to seize power in St Petersburg. The coup was badly organized and suppressed within a day. Archibald remembered turbulent scenes in the streets, while the Knills, returning that night to St Petersburg, found large heaps of something piled up on Senate Square. They turned out to be dead bodies, of bystanders more than of participants. Five of the ringleaders were shot by order of Alexander's successor, his younger brother Nicholas – under Alexander there had been no death penalty – and many others sentenced to hard labour or exile in Siberia.

These events also spelled the end of the Russian Bible Society. It had always depended heavily on the personal support of Alexander. Even before 1825 there had been a reaction among conservatives, who feared that the distribution of more than half-a-million copies of the New Testament in Russian to the masses might seriously undermine the authority of Church and State. The suspicion that in some places the conspirators had met in the guise of a Bible Society committee further hastened the Society's downfall. In August 1826 its activities were suspended, although the Imperial ukase did not specifically prohibit the sale of existing stocks of Scriptures at the Society's Russian depots. John Paterson was granted a generous pension for life by Nicholas and decided to return to Scotland.

Fear of incurring the wrath of the Holy Synod inhibited Mr Knill from attempting to distribute any bibles for a couple of years, but then a chance event made him realize that because of the sizeable Finnish population in St Petersburg, there was an immediate demand on his doorstep for bibles in Finnish. These he began to sell for a rouble each, and it was not long before he was setting off 'with a light heart to the dear old Bible House', where the keeper told him that the copies of the New Testament in Russian were rotting away. He determined to circulate them. One of those whose help he enlisted in this task was Archibald Mirrielees. So began an association with the British & Foreign Bible Society that lasted until Archibald's death forty-eight years later, for he attended a Committee meeting at the Society's headquarters in London only two days before he died.

An atmosphere of high drama surrounds the operations carried out by Mr Knill's little flock in disposing of the sacred volume. Although they might not be violating any law, they were certainly defying the wishes of the Holy Synod. In the winter of 1829-30 two of their number were arrested for circulating New Testaments and tracts. One, described by Knill as 'an English physician member of my little

Church', was given twenty-four hours' notice to leave the country. 'This so alarmed us,' Knill writes, 'that we did not know what to do; my name was associated with the affair in a certain degree, as I had supplied them with the Scriptures, and they belonged to my congregation. This they stated at their examination. I therefore expected to be seized every hour, and prepared for the event.' Nothing happened to Knill, but the other person arrested, British-born Captain Drury, an officer in the Russian Army with Russian nationality, was sent to prison. Some months later, after his release, he was attending a levée, and 'on his name being announced, the General arose and kissed him, and then introducing him to the officers said: "Here, brothers, is Captain Drury, the first officer of our army who was ever imprisoned for doing good".'

It was through the Bible Society that Archibald Mirrielees made the acquaintance of George Borrow (1803-81). Of all the Society's agents employed all over the world none caught the popular imagination more than Borrow, best known as the author of two autobiographical novels, *Lavengro* (1851) and *The Romany Rye* (1857), and two travel books, *The Bible in Spain* (1842) and *Wild Wales* (1862). As a young man, he possessed enormous mental and physical energy. According to one (apocryphal?) story, the clergyman who found him waiting on the Society's doorstep at a very early hour on the day of his first interview, asked him nervously whether he had slept well. 'I am not aware that I fell asleep on the road,' Borrow replied. 'I have walked from Norwich to London' (a distance of 115 miles). Amused eyebrows were raised in Norwich, his home city, when it was learned that Borrow, who had failed to make a literary career for himself in London and seemed to be most at home in the company of gypsies – that he of all people had been taken on by that sober-minded organization, the British & Foreign Bible Society. Borrow's bumptiousness did not indeed go down well at first with the Society, but, gifted linguist that he was – he had been recruited largely on the strength of having read the Bible in thirteen languages – he soon picked up the required vocabulary of pious humility.

Borrow described his seven years working for the Society as the best and happiest of his life. It was his peculiar genius, as *The Bible in Spain* makes clear, to be able to convert the apparently unexciting task of printing and distributing bibles into a romantic drama full of challenge and suspense and strange encounters with the most colourful individuals. The well-known Spanish years (1835-1840) were preceded by two years in St Petersburg, where Borrow harnessed all his energies and succeeded brilliantly in the tasks set him by the Society. Before going out, he had spent six months teaching himself Manchu, and his first task was to help the Scottish missionary, William Swan, transcribe a Manchu Old Testament manuscript. In April 1834, when Archibald Mirrielees was about to leave for London, the completed transcript was entrusted to him for delivery to the Society. The other task, for which Borrow had sole responsibility, was to supervise the printing of a Manchu translation of the New Testament. There were many obstacles to overcome. 'I have spared neither myself nor my own money,' Borrow reported to the Society. 'I have toiled in a close printing-office the whole day, during 90° of heat, for the purpose of setting an example, and have bribed people to work whom nothing but bribes would induce to do so.' What Borrow preferred not to reveal, according to Archibald Mirrielees, was that the bribes had been in the form of vodka. He was hoping to distribute the Testaments himself from Kiakhta on the Russo-Chinese border – a challenge that fired his romantic imagination – but the Russian government refused him a passport and he had to return to England with the books in September 1835. In that same year he achieved another remarkable first, when he published his own translation into English of poems by Alexander Pushkin.

*　　　*　　　*

In addition to his patronage of the Bible Society, the Emperor Alexander took a keen interest in the Society of Friends, having first met the Quakers during his visit to England in the summer of 1814. In 1817, following a request from Alexander, Daniel Wheeler was chosen by the Society to go out to superintend drainage and agricultural works on land outside St Petersburg, while in 1820 Sarah Kilham responded to an invitation to start a school in St Petersburg for poor girls on the Lancastrian model. It was in the city centre, and when the great flood arrived in November 1824, she had no time to send her pupils home but was forced to dispatch them all upstairs, while she waded about down below for three quarters of an hour salvaging provisions, including a store of flour which enabled her to bake cakes for the children during their confinement.

Sarah was from Sheffield. Her stepmother, Hannah Kilham, a pioneer in West African education, had two nephews in St Petersburg, William Spurr, who was in business, and his younger brother Henry, sons of a Sheffield Master Cutler. Early in 1826 William was taken dangerously ill. His father and sister Sarah came out to St Petersburg, but he died before their arrival. During their visit Archibald Mirrielees, a friend of William's, fell in love with Sarah Spurr, and that summer he travelled to Sheffield to ask her parents to agree to an engagement. He was twenty-nine, his prospects were excellent, he shared the same religious beliefs as the Spurrs, and his character was beyond reproach; and if the parents demurred in any way, which seems unlikely, he could also, as Jane Muir discovered many years later, be very persuasive.

Having successfully accomplished his mission, Archibald returned to London in the first week of October en route for St Petersburg. Unknown to him, John Paterson was also returning to St Petersburg to wind up his affairs after the abolition of the Russian Bible Society, so they were able to share a cabin. A freak wave nearly washed Paterson overboard, but he had a Providential escape. Later, he made his own characteristically practical contribution to the couple's future happiness, for when in the spring he was packing up to leave, he not only gave Archibald the best of his furniture, but also bequeathed to him his trusted Russian servant, Mary. The marriage of Sarah Newbould Spurr and Archibald Mirrielees was celebrated in Sheffield Cathedral on 14 February 1828. A son, William Spurr Mirrielees, was born at the very end of the year, and a daughter, Sarah Jane, followed in 1830.

On 28 September 1830 Mr Knill received a letter from Mr Mirrielees, 'dated sixty versts from St Petersburg, where he is performing quarantine; many are detained there, and many more at the next station'. Archibald must have been returning from Moscow, where cholera was rampant. In spite of all precautions, it was only a matter of time before Petersburg, too, was engulfed by the epidemic. Early in June 1831 the Knills, like all those who could afford to do so, moved out of the airless capital to a summer residence provided for them by a generous American member of his church, William Ropes. Mr Knill was to spend Sundays only in St Petersburg. When news came that cholera had broken out, he decided at once that he ought to be permanently with his flock, but as regards his wife and three small sons, Samuel, John and Joseph, the issue was 'not so plain'. They determined, however, to commit themselves into the Lord's hands and not to be separated. The first member of the flock to be struck down was Mrs Chapman, mistress of another Lancastrian school of which Mr Knill was the superintendent. Archibald Mirrielees and his great friend, William Gellibrand, hurried to her aid, but to no avail. She was buried in the ground expressly appointed for the victims of cholera, where the scene, Knill writes, was 'truly awful'; Mrs Gellibrand took the orphaned daughter to live with them. Morning service on 28 June was thinly attended: some were sick, some watching, others afraid to venture out. On the Tuesday, Joseph was seized with symptoms resembling those of cholera – 'yet we fondly thought that children were exempt'. As they watched at Joseph's bedside, there came a cry from another quarter: 'Johnny is seized!' Within hours Johnny died and was placed in Mrs Chapman's grave.

My beloved wife, who had rallied all her strength to nurse her lovely children, immediately sank and was confined to bed. The next morning dear Mrs Mirrielees took our eldest child to reside with them. On Saturday about midday Joseph expired. I was now unable to support myself any longer: both body and spirits were exhausted. I took to my bed... We have had seven doctors... three silent Sabbaths... We are now in the country, but I hope to be able to preach next Sunday. The High and Holy One has not forsaken us. None of our particular friends who live near us have been afflicted. They have been incessant in their attentions. Whom the Lord loveth He chasteneth. He has pruned off two boughs from us at a stroke, but our prayer is that it may render us more fruitful.

In May 1832 Mr Knill visited England at the request of the London Missionary Society. He was hoping to make use of the visit to raise funds for the building of a new church to be used exclusively by his congregation, who were still having to share the small Moravian Meeting House – nicknamed 'the snuff-box', as the use of snuff by the German brethren was so widespread that the room had to be thoroughly ventilated (not very pleasant in winter) before the British congregation could enter. In the event, however, he did not return to Russia, and raised only £300 of the £1000 the congregation had expected. So they had to do their own fund-raising, the American merchant, William Ropes, and his son, being especially active. At last, in August 1839, Archibald Mirrielees was able to write to John Paterson: 'When I left home our New Chapel was one third raised and dear Gellibrand writes me that all goes forward satisfactorily. I trust we shall be able to open it free of debt.' The official dedication of the British & American Congregational Church (or Chapel, as it is usually called) took place on 24 August 1840. An unpretentious, functional building right next to the Ministry of Posts, it is seldom mentioned in the guide-books. Thus, Bastin's French-language guide to St Petersburg of 1866, having described the English Church as 'one of the most beautiful Anglican churches to be seen in the whole of Europe', dismisses the Chapel with the words: 'Since it contains nothing remarkable, we shall not describe it here.'

The Mirrielees family had emerged unscathed from the cholera epidemic of 1831. Like other members of the flock, Archibald had disregarded personal safety to visit the sick, reading from the Bible and praying with them. Cholera was not the only threat to health, however. In February 1833 he wrote to John Paterson in Edinburgh:

The past two months have been a time of great sickness & death here – more so I believe than has ever been experienced before. The deaths among the English amount to about fifty of all ages, and our own little Circle has not been exempt. Typhus fever prevailed very much six weeks since, and since then a kind of influenza, in many cases accompanied with inflammation, has been in almost every house, and now scarlet fever is very general. Most of our friends have been afflicted in one way or other. I had something of fever hanging about me for several weeks, but am now through mercy quite restored. Last Sunday all my three little ones & three servants, including dear Mary, were on the sicklist, but by a blessing on the prompt measures adopted, they are now all about again.

The third child referred to here, a daughter, died, however, soon after, and it must have been around this time that the health of Archibald's wife, Sarah, also began to deteriorate, for Paterson recalled that in August 1834 'we had a flying visit of good Mr Mirrielees who had come over to take his wife and children back to St Petersburg. Mrs Mirrielees was greatly improved in health; but alas it did not continue and ere long she left him a widower.' This did not happen until late in 1835, Sarah having previously given birth to a daughter, Frances Elizabeth. 'My loss is indeed heavy,' Archibald wrote to Paterson, 'but I feel that that of my beloved children is still heavier – their precious Mother was peculiarly qualified to train them for God. My trust is that in His own good time He will show me what to do in regard to them.'

Was there a hint here to the Almighty? If so, it was promptly heeded, for on 9 May 1837 at South Leith, Midlothian, Archibald married again. His second wife, Mary Cullen, came from Edinburgh, her sister being married to William Swan the missionary. The doors of the

Mirrielees home in Galernaya Street were always wide open to worthy religious people – 'the dear Swans are still with us and will remain for several months yet,' Archibald wrote in February 1833 – but whether he had met Mary Cullen before his visit to England and Scotland early in 1837 is not clear. It seems possible that the business-like Archibald, having settled in his own mind – and with divine guidance – the question of who was to be the second Mrs Archibald Mirrielees, set off from St Petersburg with a plan of action clearly mapped out, and that everything was arranged during his visit, perhaps with some help from John Paterson, who knew the Cullen family well.

This second marriage was sad and short. Mary became very attached to her little stepdaughter, Fanny, and was deeply upset when the child sickened and died. Mary herself died of typhus fever in the summer of 1839. Somewhat surprisingly, at the time of her death Archibald, with his two children and a 'nephew just arrived from Aberdeen, a fine lad of fourteen', was on holiday at Reval. 'It was my intention,' he explained to Paterson, 'to have brought Mary, who was very feeble at the time we left, but it was thought best to leave her in the country with one of the other servants to wait upon her under the Doctor's care who lives close by.' There were moments, he admitted, when a feeling of isolation stole over his mind, even though he was convinced that his Heavenly Father would not lay one stroke upon him more than was needful.

*   *   *

Little information has survived about Archibald's business activities during these first twenty years, but all the indications are that he was very successful. It is possible that he gave up working for Fisher & Co. early on, but it was not until 1843 that he founded under his own name the business that later became Muir & Mirrielees. In the years up to 1837 he certainly travelled frequently between St Petersburg and London, so he may have been working for London companies as a commission agent. What we do know is that from 1837 to 1842 he gave up working on his own account, and was employed permanently in St Petersburg by the American firm of William Ropes & Company.

William Ropes had settled in St Petersburg in the spring of 1832 with his second wife and four teenage children by his first marriage. From the start he received a warm welcome from Mr Knill and the flock, and these ties were strengthened in 1834 when his eldest daughter married William Gellibrand, whose first wife had died in the disastrous winter of 1832-3.

After working at first on a commission basis, William Ropes formally announced in March 1833 his establishment in St Petersburg as William Ropes & Co., importers and exporters. In 1837 he handed over control of operations in St Petersburg to his eldest son, William Hooper Ropes, but before doing so, engaged his good friend, Archibald Mirrielees, to take charge of the internal department in the counting-room. 'Mr Mirrielees,' he wrote, 'is one of the most capable, industrious, methodical and persevering men I ever knew. William Hooper is to do the outside business as purchasing is his forte.' Later, William's second son, Joseph Samuel, having graduated from St Petersburg University with the highest honours, also joined the counting-house as an apprentice. Archibald had no difficulty in working smoothly with William Hooper, but Joseph was very sure of himself and behaved as if he owned the firm; only discipline in a large house like Baring's, Archibald thought, would improve him. Not being the kind of man who could easily tolerate indiscipline or accommodate himself to what he perceived as the imperfections of others, Archibald gave up working for William Ropes & Co. in 1842.

A year later, accompanied by his two children and their German governess, Miss Funck, he set out from St Petersburg on a long visit to England and Scotland. What happened in the course of that visit can best be viewed from a different perspective: that of the life and background of Miss Jane Muir.

3

Miss Muir of Greenock

Jane Muir spent the first thirty-three years of her life in Greenock, the Scottish port and industrial centre, which stretches out for a considerable distance along the south shore of the Firth of Clyde, some twenty-three miles west of Glasgow. Early in the 17th century, it was still a fishing village, but the Act of Union between England and Scotland of 1707 gave an impetus to its growth by opening up trade with America and the West Indies: in Greenock today you will still find an Antigua Street and a Tobago Street. By the 19th century its staple industries were shipbuilding (both warships and passenger liners), engineering, worsted and woollen manufacturing, and sugar-refining. Sugar was the chief import, ships and machinery the chief exports. The town also produced and exported engineers, including Richard Smith, who in 1856, at the age of thirty-one, started the Smith Boiler Works in Moscow. But it is with the Far East and 'the China coast' that the legendary figure of the Clyde Engineer is most closely associated. Go into a Greenock home today and you may still find the mementoes of a lifetime spent wandering in Chinese waters: a set of fragile tea or coffee cups and saucers in a glass display cabinet, a carved model of a rickshaw being pulled by a Chinaman with bent back and large broad-brimmed hat balanced precariously on his head, or, in some distant part of the house, less accessible to public view but far more serviceable, an ornately-carved blanket chest.

Greenock reached the height of its prosperity in the second half of the 19th century. The wealthy ship-owners and sugar-refiners built themselves grand mansions far away from the industrial squalor, while the brokers and merchants had to make do with more modest villas. By 1900 the town was already in decline. In the Depression of the 1930's the idle factories and shipyards at least held out some hope of future employment by their very presence; today they have all gone. Unlike Aberdeen, no North Sea oil came to Greenock's rescue. A few of the grand mansions have been put to other uses, some have been sub-divided, but most are no more. Only the opulent interior of the Town Hall still serves as an incongruous reminder of Greenock in its Victorian heyday.

The brothers James Muir (1771-1834) and Andrew Muir (1778-1849), born in nearby Paisley, were merchants who rose to prosperity on the tide of Greenock's expansion in the early 19th century. Among the most successful of their many business ventures was the Straw-Hat Factory. Mention straw-hats in Greenock today and the response is likely to be a disbelieving grin, for Greenock, like Glasgow, has the reputation of being one of the wettest places in the British Isles. That a thriving straw-hat industry once existed there is well documented, however. The Muir brothers were among those who agreed to subscribe in 1829 to Weir's *History of Greenock*, and their patronage was duly rewarded by a glowing account of their commercial activities. Straw-hat making, Weir writes,

has been carried on successfully in town, for a considerable time, by Messrs. James & Andrew Muir: and they have done much good in employing the young girls, and giving them habits of industry; while, by this means, the female part of the community have been often enabled to provide for aged parents, to assist poorer relations, and also to appear clean and genteelly dressed. Greenock is under deep obligations to these enterprising individuals; and the extent of the good they have done cannot be fully known.

They had begun manufacturing straw-hats in 1808. The pipe-straw was sent from England to Orkney, where it was plaited, and thence to Greenock to be made into hats. In 1823 they began the manufacture of Leghorn hats from rye-straw, the rye being grown on Orkney itself; while in 1824 'they invented light elastic water-proof silk hats on Leghorn bodies, which, for durability, lightness and elasticity, surpass any manufacture of silk hats that has yet been produced'. The most striking of Weir's many statistics, indicating the scale of the operation, is that although the number of workers employed at the commencement was small, 'it has annually increased, and may now be reckoned, in Orkney, at about 2000, and in Greenock, at from 200 to 300'. The profits from the Straw-Hat Factory enabled James Muir to become a partner in the Clyde Pottery Company, which began operations in 1816, manufacturing all kinds of goods, from the commonest to the finest tea and breakfast services, and generally employing about seventy people.

The Muirs' growing affluence was reflected in the house, 'Rosebank', which they purchased some time in the 1820's. The old centre of Greenock was dirty and overcrowded. In 1832 more than a thousand people died in the cholera epidemic that had spread from Europe, and the cemetery looked more like a battlefield. The West End of town, however, contained at that time only a couple of dozen houses dotted about in more or less open country. 'Rosebank' was on rising ground not far from the shore and had a fine uninterrupted view across the Firth of Clyde. A small part of the property had been turned into a separate dwelling for Andrew Muir and his wife, who were childless, while the main part was lived in by James Muir and his large family.

In 1910 Maida Bernard (née Mirrielees) visited 'Rosebank', then being altered, and was allowed by the workmen to look over the house in which her mother Jane, James Muir's daughter, had grown up. It had nine or ten bedrooms, four sitting-rooms, a library with deep recesses for books, and an oval drawing-room of which her mother had often spoken, with tall windows looking out over a large garden. The history of 'Rosebank' parallels that of Greenock itself. It was said to have been built in 1805 at the time of Greenock's rising prosperity. Already in 1843 we find Jane Muir complaining that the new houses on the low road will spoil their view, while in the mid-Victorian period, as the town expanded rapidly to the west and an impressive new esplanade was built, 'Rosebank' was soon engulfed by the villas of the prosperous middle classes. It remained a family home until 1901, when a process of sub-dividing began. Today, as Nos. 25 & 27 Forsyth Street, it consists of six separate households, and is located in what estate agents call 'a central position'.

The obvious affluence of the Muirs in Greenock is in sharp contrast to the Spartan upbringing of Archibald Mirrielees in Aberdeen. When one turns to the Muirs' religious outlook, however, the scene becomes familiar again, especially since John Paterson is once more a dominant figure. Having finally returned from Russia in 1827, Paterson settled in Edinburgh and at once threw himself into vigorous preaching and campaigning. He spent some weeks in Greenock in the winter of 1829-30 and a longer time in the summer, lodging with Andrew Muir. His preaching, he writes, was 'greatly blessed for awakening not a few', including 'the family of James Muir, all of whom joined the church. It was a stirring time. While it lasted perhaps not fewer than 100 were brought under deep concern, several of whom however disappointed our hopes, and even of those who joined themselves to the church a few drew back and walked no more with the people of God. About 60 were added to the church, the greater part of whom remained faithful.' In November Andrew Muir wrote to Paterson: 'We are all well at "Rosebank", and as a church we are still holding on and living together in peace & harmony... I am visited regularly by enquirers, last

Saturday there were 15 at my house... the 2 who come to me on Friday evening cannot come on Saturday, one of them is a Street Scavenger and the other is a founder.' The doors of 'Rosebank', like those of the Mirrielees home in St Petersburg, were also wide open to worthy religious people passing through the city, with the result that it was nicknamed 'Missionary Hotel'. And while Archibald and his fellow-believers were collecting funds to build their new church in the 1830's, so, too, were the brethren in Greenock, James Muir subscribing £200. The George Square Congregational Church, still in existence today, was opened on 6 September 1840.

By that time only Andrew Muir was still alive. James, the elder brother, died on 20 December 1834, and was survived by his second wife and the seven children of his first marriage. At the time of his death only the eldest daughter was married and living in Canada. The elder son, James, took over the running of the Straw-Hat Factory, which was later transferred to Glasgow and then Luton, traditional centre of hat-making. The management of the Clyde Pottery Co. passed to Andrew Muir, who was joined by James' younger son, also Andrew – later to make the biggest Muir contribution to Muir & Mirrielees. Presumably Andrew senior must have possessed some business acumen, but he seems to have been best remembered in the family for his absent-mindedness. As he was constantly losing umbrellas, he took to using a red one, which became known in Greenock as 'Mr Muir's umbrella' and was restored to its owner whenever found. One Sunday a sensation was caused in church when he walked up the aisle to his pew with this striking object over his head. He might also be seen walking backwards when lost in thought.

The third evangelical divine to influence the lives of the Muir and Mirrielees families, along with John Paterson and Richard Knill, now appears on the scene: Dr Ralph Wardlaw (1779-1853). If Paterson was a man of action, practical and energetic, robust and down-to-earth as a preacher, but intellectually somewhat limited, his friend Wardlaw was a more thoughtful man, the author of hymns and tracts, and from 1811 Divinity Professor at the Congregational Seminary in Glasgow. In the second half of the 1830's his chapel was the point of intersection in the lives of a large number of people associated with this story, including the four unmarried daughters of James Muir, who seem to have transferred their religious allegiances after their father's death from the local church in Greenock to the undoubtedly more fashionable chapel in West George Street, Glasgow, over which Dr Wardlaw presided.

At the chapel Margaret, the second sister, attracted an ardent admirer in Matthew Lethem, who became a frequent visitor to Greenock. A shy youth and even in later years never a fluent talker, he worshipped Margaret with silent devotion until one day, among the gooseberry bushes in the garden at 'Rosebank', he plucked up the courage to propose. Margaret turned him down flat. Not only that, she left soon after on a long visit to her married sister in Canada. When she reached Liverpool on her return voyage, the uninviting prospect of the long journey to Greenock lay ahead of her, but there, waiting at the docks, was the faithful Matthew. Such persistence finally received its reward, and the marriage took place in Dr Wardlaw's chapel on 10 July 1839. Not long after, the Lethems moved to London, where they bought No.2 Manor Villas in the northern suburb of Holloway.

Jane Isabella Muir, 'Miss Muir' after the marriage of her elder sister, was born on 21 December 1810. She probably received most of her education at home, though for a time she attended an Academy at Liverpool. When John Paterson succeeded in awakening 'not a few' in Greenock, including the family of James Muir, Jane was at the impressionable age of nineteen, and she retained a strong evangelical faith for the rest of her life.

Two letters survive that give us a good impression of Jane Muir before her marriage. They were written on 29 September and 12 October 1840 to her younger brother, Andrew, at 'Rosebank', from the fashionable English health resort of Leamington Spa, where she and her Greenock friends, the Martins, were on holiday. Jane has her tongue firmly in her cheek when she informs Andrew that she has taken two tumblers of the Water 'this morning for the first time to cure a pimple that was just *threatening to appear on my forehead* – and lo, at this hour (one o'clock PM) – it has entirely vanished'. She is sorry to have to say that

there is not much that looks very attractive among our *own species* at Leamington. There are plenty of plain looking old ladies, & spruce well dressed old gentlemen, & pale-faced maidens (among whom *I* am quite a wonder) & a few exquisites who saunter up & down the Parade looking at the ladies. The only people we know are from 'poor old dirty' [i.e. Greenock], I mean the Aytons. We could not help a smile & bow of recognition in Leamington, however unknown we may be to each other in Greenock. Yet undazzling as the company for the most part may appear, we have only to look into the Pump room or library lists to find there is here notwithstanding a pretty considerable sprinkling of Lords Ladies Marchionesses Barts. Honls. Generals & so forth. A good many ladies ride on horseback, but what we remark most is the great number of beautiful equipages, from them alone we must conclude there are many people of consequence here, and we sometimes think from the extreme politeness of the shopkeepers & that class generally, that *we* who look as most of the people around us, are occasionally taken for *Marchionesses* or even *Duchesses*, indeed *Mrs Martin* is so afraid of this mistake being made to her *cost* that we have not been able to get her into a single shop since she came.

Andrew is to tell his brother James that 'the most fashionable straw worn here is *Leghorn*, by next year I should think they will cut out everything else'; while as for Andrew, by this time manager of the Clyde Pottery Co., it would be quite worth his while to make a pilgrimage to Warwickshire for the express purpose of beholding the beautiful china to be seen everywhere. One shop almost opposite them in the Parade

has a most magnetic influence on the strollers up & down particularly of the fair sex. There we go often, to look at the exquisite little ornamental baskets, trays, etc., of open wicker work, adorned with flowers & paintings of every description. Warwick Castle is of course a favourite subject and it is surprising to see what a fine effect it has, even on a china tray, with its noble towers encompassed with the richest foliage, & with its picturesque river & bridge in the foreground. But by far the most perfect painting I ever saw on china was at the Warwick curiosity house. When I asked in my delight 'what it was?' & 'where it came from?' they repeatedly told me '*Safe*' (perhaps it does not spell so). I understood it referred to some *place*, but did not like to shew my ignorance by asking where *Safe* was? Foolish pride you will say. They had in the same room a small tray full of *little ladies* of the Elizabethan age, covered, of course, with a glass case. An air of expression & humour the little creatures (an inch & a half long) had about them, reminded me strongly of Hogarth who had he been a Potter would have made just such ladies & gentlemen. The lace ruffles & trimmings of their dresses, stood out in perfection, in exact proportion to the size of the figures & positively all of china ware.

Andrew must have begun his reply with some elaborate compliments, for on 12 October Jane writes:

You commenced your last letter with such a magnificent flourish of trumpets that but for the uncertain sound those instruments are apt to give, I might have been tempted to think of myself more highly than I ought to think. The *policy* of such a preface however, must be undoubted, for although one's throat may not be so wide as to swallow the *whole*, enough gets down to smooth the way for all that follows, of which you will be convinced when I tell you, that your own letter amused & pleased me so much that I had no sooner read it, than I wished by sending a reply to entitle myself to another...

I give you great credit for the solution you offer respecting the mysterious 'Safe' china. It was odd that we happened to pay another visit to the place where it is seen, the very day I got your letter and one of the very first discoveries we made was the truth & verity of your supposition. They have the finest specimens imaginable both of the ancient & modern china of the celebrated manufacture of *Sevres*. The little ladies I mentioned are natives of *Dresden* and I was somewhat startled to find they had *grown* about *twò inches* since our last visit. I rather think this strange phenomenon is only to be accounted for, by a kind of bewilderment that came over my bump of *size*, & all my other faculties in visiting that perfect chaos of curiosities.

Jane and the Martins were about to move to new lodgings. Their windows would directly overlook the home of a most amiable looking young clergyman, to whom Eliza, the Martins' daughter, had lost her heart, so that an elopement might be imminent.

The lively tone of these letters makes it easy to understand why Jane was so popular. Tall and slim, with a good figure and natural complexion, she attracted attention wherever she went. According to her youngest sister, Mary, she had a flair for anticipating the fashions, and if she thought them becoming to her, adopting them at once. Among the younger female attenders at Dr Wardlaw's chapel, the sight of 'Miss Muir' sailing along to her pew in a simple but elegant lilac muslin dress inspired feelings of profound worship; the mere mention of her name was enough to bring sentimental tears to their eyes. One can sympathize with Mary, who resented all the attention that her elder sister received when they were out together, and wished that Jane were 'less conspicuous'. On receiving a proposal from one of Jane's many rejected suitors, she replied indignantly that she did not care to take her 'sister's leavings'.

Jane's animated manner and vivacious personality ensured her a full and varied social life. Two particular friends were her namesakes, Mrs Jane Fairrie – the Fairries were big sugar-refiners in Greenock – and

Jane Paterson of Edinburgh, John Paterson's daughter. She was used to leading a life of her own, and had certainly visited other fashionable resorts apart from Leamington. She had also been on a visit to her married sister in Canada and had an adventure, for on the way out her boat was wrecked on an island, but without loss of life.

There was a more serious side to Jane, however. Like her father, who read widely (and not only books of which the brethren would have approved), she loved literature and was well read. Writing in May 1843 to Andrew, by then trying his luck in business in Canada, she tells him that she is reading with great delight some of Macaulay's *Critical and Historical Essays*, which are all the talk of London; gives him a detailed account of lectures she has been attending on mesmerism and phrenology; and does not ignore 'the great topic of the day', the church. This was the time of the 'Disruption', when 477 Scottish ministers broke away from the Established Church, and Mr Fairrie, who had attended the meetings of the newly-established Free Assembly, 'was in such raptures when he came back that they could get nothing from him but one continued flourish of trumpets'. She has also discovered in herself an unsuspected artistic gift: the ability to draw what she calls 'memory miniatures', likenesses of people drawn not from life, but from the impression of them in her mind.

By that time, Jane was the only one of the four sisters living at 'Rosebank'. Augusta, the third sister, was on an extended visit to Canada, while Mary was living permanently in London with her married sister, Margaret, and her husband, Matthew Lethem. Uncle Andrew's wife had died in 1840, and Jane was keeping house for him. Her uncle, however, had plans of his own. In October 1842 another member of the Wardlaw 'set', Ann Eliza Bell, spent three or four very happy days with Miss Muir at 'Rosebank' and wrote afterwards to her sister: 'There is some prospect of the old man getting *married*!! & in that case Miss Muir would also go to London & live with her sisters. He (old Mr Muir) got himself engaged a month or two ago to a young lady *only forty*! years younger than himself but her friends acted shamefully at the making of the marriage settlements, & so it was blown to the winds, but he is *determined* to have a wife, & Miss M thinks he will succeed ere long.'

Miss M was right. Andrew Muir, merchant, silk mercer and haberdasher, married Isabella Fox at Helensburgh on 30 January 1844. 'What do you think,' wrote Ann Eliza, 'old Andrew Muir has got married again and is even now on his marriage jaunt, he is married to a dear young friend of mine, Miss Fox. She is only 25 & he is 65, I cannot understand her at all, for it really seems true that she is attached to him. In consequence of this marriage Miss Muir is off to London to live with Mr & Mrs Lethem.'

Another sequence of events had already been set in train, however, that was to have a very different outcome, as Jane explained in a long letter to Andrew in Montreal, written from the Lethems' home, Manor Villas, on 18 June 1844. After describing the guests they are entertaining to dinner that evening, she goes on:

I have just one small scrap of news this time, that I am sure will interest you, and it is, that I am going to be *married* at last!!! You won't believe your own eyes I am sure, but I say again, it is *perfectly true*. I could not help following so good an example as Jane Paterson's – so I am going to be *third wife* to a dear *little* man on whom I shall have the power to *look down* when ever it suits my purpose – tho' joking apart I do *look up to him* at *present very much*, & feel that in bodily dimensions *only* the measurement is somewhat in my favour. Did you hear me speak of Mr Mirrielees? He is the man.

They had become acquainted during the autumn of 1843 in Edinburgh, where they met at several dinner parties. Archibald's second wife had been an old friend of Jane's, so 'poor dear Mary' provided a fruitful topic of conversation. Afterwards they spent two or three days under the same roof at Dr Paterson's, and it was then, says Jane, that 'the mischief was done' – at least so far as Mr Mirrielees' feelings were concerned. Later Archibald would tell his children how impressed he had been by this fine, handsome woman, who dressed so beautifully, and how he remembered her specially in a certain 'yellow' gown (the scornful quotation marks are those of his daughter Maida, who obviously did not think much of her father's colour sense), 'crossing the street and looking like a Queen'. It is strange that John Paterson should once more play such a conspicuous part in Archibald Mirrielees' private life, but if there was a match-maker at work, it seems more likely to have been his daughter. Nothing further happened during the winter, which Archibald spent visiting various friends, but early in the spring he came to London 'in prosecution of his object'; Jane, however, was chiefly with Mrs Fairrie then, and matters did not advance much. In May he came again, but 'still there was no damage done with me. I did not take in the idea at all.' And why, after all, should this high-spirited young woman, used to leading an independent life, be attracted to the idea of marriage to a widower considerably older than herself, with two children – now aged fifteen and thirteen – and a governess in tow, and living, of all places, in Russia? Archibald was to be more persuasive on paper, however, than in person.

On leaving towards the middle of May he wrote me a long letter, a kind one (of course) and a much superior one in many respects to any I ever had on *that subject*. Something in it, and in many peculiar circumstances of my position, both mental & personal, startled and compelled me into a *serious* consideration of the proposal – some correspondence took place. I gave my whole soul to the consideration of my duty under all the singular circumstances (too long to tell you of) which seemed to point me to a decision favourable to Mr M's wishes. Things cleared up more & more, yet my old habit of resistance was *strong* in me, but I felt like a blind person, whom God had taken by the hand, & was leading irresistibly on in a way of *His*, & *not of my*, choosing – I stumbled & struggled hard against His leading and yet was carried on as it were by an invisible power – last Friday Mr M who had gone to Scotland, returned to add his *visible & physical* influence to the matter, and what between the force of faith in things *not seen*, and the compulsion of human love which was forced upon *all my senses*, the fearful word, which must give a new cast and colouring to my whole future life, was at last squeezed out of me. Nothing else or less than all this could have softened my stony heart – and now that the *word has gone out* I feel as composed & happy about it as possible. I see as I never did so distinctly about any thing else, that it has all been done *for me* by a higher power. I feel assured that Mr M is just the sort of husband I need – I doubt if any *bachelor* ever could be a *warmer* lover. I put perfect confidence in all his vows & promises, I believe him to be one of the best and most consistent of Christian men – and I mean to try if I can to be a wife worthy of so much love & goodness.

Now dear Andrew, is not all this *very fine & satisfactory*? I know you will laugh heartily at it as the production of my heart & pen, for you had no doubt given me up as hopeless – and no wonder. The worst of it, and indeed the only bad, or really trying thing about it is that I must go to Russia (fearful). I shall not say a word more about that. I dare not let myself think of leaving the few I love here, or of perhaps not seeing for years others I dearly love further off.

Although he was six years her junior, Jane clearly set considerable store by Andrew's good opinion, and may have found it easier to confide in him than in her sisters. She goes on to give a surprisingly frank assessment – only possible at this juncture in her life – of her future husband's situation and character:

I believe he is tolerably well off as to circumstances, but he spends money freely both on religious objects & domestic comforts – no small matter to me as of all men on earth, I could not endure a scrub. About money matters I suppose you will hear more again, as Matthew [Lethem] is, to me most annoyingly determined that he & James shall look to my temporal interests in this matter. Mr M is just 46 – twelve years older than myself – he is a restlessly active little man – generally well informed, a rather sharp, clever sort of man, and if not what would be called *very polished* neither is he defective, having much knowledge of the world and sufficient ease & confidence to conduct himself with propriety among *any* class of people. He is from Aberdeen originally (& at Petersburg *22 years*) & has a number of respectable relatives there – as well as the devoted attachment of both his former wives' friends – and that of a very pleasant select circle of Christian people in St Petersburg. So you see my dear Andrew I have every reason to be most thankful to God for his great goodness to me, after all my naughtiness in many ways, and especially in refusing not a few good men before – of which however I always was satisfied, and am now entirely confirmed in the faith that none of them were the men for me!

Jane was married from Manor Villas on 21 July 1844, the service being held at the Holloway Congregational Church which the Lethems attended.

Was this 'all fine and satisfactory', as Jane claimed? One person who later thought not was her daughter, Maida. When she had reached an age to think about such things and her head was full of romantic notions, she wondered how her mother could possibly have fallen for an elderly widower, and asked her outright whether she had really been 'in love'. Her mother laughingly replied that some of her younger girl friends had asked her the same question at the time, and had warned her against marrying a Bluebeard. Then, more seriously, she added: 'I had a great esteem for your father. I knew he was a really good man, and such esteem is the best foundation for love.'

Maida was not satisfied. She felt then, and continued to feel long after she had ceased to be a romantic teenager, that esteem was not enough; something warmer was needed. 'Mother was not at all a susceptible girl I fancy, and I believe never fell in love, though she became a devoted wife to our father.'

4

Married to Mr M

Archibald and Jane Mirrielees spent a short honeymoon in England, beginning at Windsor, and then set off in August 1844 for Bad Kissingen. This was a German equivalent of Leamington Spa, and had been chosen by Archibald for the not very romantic reason that he hoped its waters might help to relieve a long-standing stomach complaint. The newly-weds were accompanied by Archibald's daughter Sarah – 'a very sweet amiable little girl,' according to Jane, '& a clever creature too, a complete German scholar with knowledge of Russ, English & French at the age of thirteen and a half, not pretty but not much the reverse either' – and by Sarah's German governess, Miss Funck. Sarah must have welcomed Jane's arrival, as did Miss Funck, for five years earlier, at the age of forty-eight, that pious lady had had grave doubts about the propriety of entering the service of a widower. William Mirrielees, whom Jane found 'rather a nice boy', stayed behind to enrol for an Arts degree at Edinburgh University.

It was Jane's first visit to Europe. Their daily routine, she admitted to her sister Margaret, was uneventful – 'fresh arrivals and departures, a new dish at the table d'Hote, a worse dinner than usual or the making of another acquaintance, are matters which tho' deeply interesting to us, you could hardly be expected to appreciate' – but she enjoyed long walks in the surrounding countryside, and observing her fellow visitors: gay ladies and handsome men of all nations, including a great many military men who 'come here to get their livers limbered up'. They became quite intimate with Captain Miles, 'a sad rattle', who sought Jane's advice about finding a wife: whatever other charms the lady might possess, she 'must be able to pay her own Mess bill & Milliner's bill, as he has no more than enough to support himself'. Neither Miss Funck nor Mr Mirrielees was sensible of much change from the waters – if anything, Jane thought, they looked worse – but as the doctor was careful to point out, no benefit could be expected until the course was over. A kinder husband than Mr M was nowhere to be found. 'He spares nothing to give me every gratification. He is much more cheerful habitually when we are alone than you would suppose from his manner in the company of others.' But, she adds, 'what I feel most is the want of letters from friends'.

As she prepared to embark on married life in St Petersburg, Jane was approaching the age of thirty-four. It was a late time of life at which to uproot herself. She had always dreaded the thought of Russia; the prospect was fearful; she would not say a word about it. 'They promise me tea worth drinking when I get to Petersburg, and almost everything else in perfection, including *snow, frost & despotism.*' The thought of separation from family and friends was extremely painful. However much she might have gained in love and friendship as a result of her marriage, 'the loss of *one line* from your pen,' she tells Andrew, 'or of that of any of my dear sisters will not be the less felt by me. On the contrary, the circumstance of my going to a foreign land will make me more than ever dependent on the kindness & regularity of your letters.'

Nor did Jane take to Russia. If only one of her unmarried sisters could come out to visit her! In August 1845 she tells Margaret that Mr M – sensitive, it seems, to his wife's feelings – had taken such a fancy to Augusta from her letters that he was quite impatient to know her better and wished that she and Mary would come out together. Mary did come in the spring of 1846 and in February Jane was anticipating her visit 'with very great comfort & pleasure, though I have no expectation that she will like this country. *I* never shall like it either, though I hope always to live as I do now, in perfect contentment & happiness here, at least so long as it is my appointed home, and so far as my husband's present views go, he has no idea of ever living elsewhere.' Even in Kissingen, she had realized that Archibald was 'exceedingly fond' of Russia (where he had, after all, spent most of his adult life). Jane fortified herself with two lines from *Paradise Lost*, which she quotes both to Margaret and Andrew: 'The mind is its own place, and in itself / Can make a heav'n of hell, a hell of heav'n.' The unspoken equation of Russia with hell tells its own story.

In material terms Jane suffered no hardships. Archibald, as she had rightly supposed, was not 'a scrub'. The spacious apartment at No.1 Galernaya was in the midst of the British and American community, conveniently placed for access to friends and all the amenities of city life. Her large domestic staff was supervised by a very competent Swedish housekeeper, who spoke both English and Russian, as did John Paterson's former servant, the devoted Mary. This was a mixed blessing, since the need to learn Russian might have helped to break down Jane's feeling of alienation. As for the cold of winter, she suffered nothing from it herself, 'being well provided with furs & a warm house', but, always sensitive to the sufferings of other people, she could not see how those less favoured could exist 'in anything short of a state of absolute bodily misery'. She goes on to describe to Andrew, with a pencil sketch, the kind of 'Shube' that gentlemen wear,

which literally covers them from the crown of the head to the sole of the foot, for the collar turns up one half or the whole just according to the weather & is a complete defence for the ears & head. It is true a man in such a coat, looks much more like a Bear on its hind legs, than our intellectual biped, but that is nothing especially as the ladies in *their* Shubes (covered with satin though they may be) are only meet comparison for their ungraceful mates. The gentleman's Shube is covered with a good dark cloth, and according to its quality lasts a life time – more or less. Rich people pride themselves very much on the value of their furs. When the Duke of Wellington visited Russia the Emperor sent him to the frontier a cloak of sable which cost £5,000! Those in use by such as my husband cost about £25.

In the summer they moved out to a datcha at Peterhof, and it is here, writing to Margaret on 10 August 1845, that Jane appears as happy as she ever would be in Russia. 'We have another exquisite morning – except some thunder showers the weather has been delicious ever since we came out. The air is so thoroughly warm notwithstanding an almost constant little breeze that we imitate the example of the people around us & walk out (except in the evening) just as we sit in the house with no bonnet or shawl, but only a parasol.' Jane had very recently given birth to her first child, Mary Frances, named in memory of Archibald's second wife, Mary, and the little stepdaughter, Frances Elizabeth, of whom she had been so fond.

She has not yet begun to wear the pretty things you sent her, she must learn to behave a little more like a young lady first. When she is in a hurry to get to my breast, she pulls & tears at every thing she can get hold of. I don't however expect her to mend much in this respect, and I am quite alarmed for my collars, they have a poor prospect when they will be exposed to the tender mercies of the little lady... We have a little basket carriage in which she sometimes sleeps in the open air, a thing much approved of here, but she sleeps very little indeed in the daytime.

The letter was interrupted when Jane heard her dear husband stop at the gate. In addition to 'the happiness of his own presence', he brought the longed for budget of letters, overflowing with warm and delightful congratulations. Jane wished that all the dear friends who had spoken so fondly of her precious darling and herself, 'could see us both at this moment – myself thro' God's goodness *so well*, the dear lambie so sweet & good (I won't say pretty)'. Clearly, one of the most agreeable parts of becoming a mother was that all these good wishes made Jane feel so closely in touch once more with 'home'.

In the following February she tells Andrew how delighted they both are by their little girl's growing intelligence.

She has a strong will of her own and is a very particular observer, she must touch, taste, & handle, all she sees, but nothing so much as those articles which are necessarily prohibited. Both her Papa and Mamma feel they will have a decided character to deal with but one that will probably repay all their pains. She seems to inherit a good Scotch constitution, which is to me a great blessing.

These words were sadly ironical, for Mary Fanny died before reaching her first birthday from water on the brain (hydrocephalus). The condition was not then well understood, and Jane blamed herself for being too proud of her precocious baby and overtaxing her mental faculties. These feelings of guilt help to explain why this first child remained so obstinately in her memory, even though she raised five more healthy children. After her own death one of her 'memory miniatures' of the dead baby was found, which not even Archibald had seen before. Mary Fanny's death dealt her an emotional blow from which she found it hard to recover.

In April 1847 there came another crisis. Early spring was always a treacherous time of year in St Petersburg : one day the temperature might rise well above freezing-point, the next it dipped far below. Another epidemic struck the city, this time of grippe or influenza. Dr Rogers, a Scottish physician who served the British and American community, could not remember a more virulent outbreak. He himself was a victim. Sarah was the first of the Mirrielees family to be struck down. Fortunately Jane, who was several months pregnant, still had her sister Mary with her, but they became so exhausted from watching at the bedside of the delirious Sarah that it was decided to call in a *Soeur de Charité*. Anna Whistler, the Mirrielees' American friend and neighbour on the Galernaya, had had four cases in her own family. All were well on the road to recovery, but then she received a distress note from the Mirrielees household: Sarah was no better, Mrs Mirrielees had taken to her bed, the *Soeur de Charité* had become so ill she had

had to leave, two of the servants were down with influenza and two more had left. For Anna Whistler, always anxious to perform good works, this was a heaven-sent opportunity, and she wasted no time in volunteering for a night's bedside vigil. Sarah and Jane eventually recovered, and on 6 September 1847 Jane gave birth to a daughter, Augusta, named after her own sister Augusta, by common consent the cleverest of the four, who was already seriously ill and died of consumption at Manor Villas on 26 November.

The British & American Chapel, now in the charge of the Revd Thomas Ellerby, was the source of all Archibald and Jane's social activities. Here was to be found that 'very pleasant select circle of Christian people', which Archibald had recommended to Jane as one of Petersburg's chief attractions. Decidedly exceptional was the occasion at the datcha one Sunday in the summer of 1845, when their landlady invited them to a grand entertainment on her birthday: 'she is a most amusing character,' Jane wrote, 'her vivacity is quite enlivening, her language is the most complete confusion of tongues I ever met with, she often introduces four in one sentence.' It does not sound the kind of occasion that Archibald would have found appropriate to the Sabbath (even though the Russian Sabbath included Saturday evening and Sunday morning, but not Sunday afternoon), and nothing similar is described in Jane's later letters. More characteristic of her social life were the sewing circles for charity and religious meetings held regularly at the Mirrielees home. Archibald continued to entertain many worthy religious people passing through St Petersburg, and a special interest was taken in English governesses, many of whom went straight to the Mirrielees home on their arrival. Just how invaluable such a reception was can be appreciated when one recalls Kohl's description of governesses arriving from all over Europe: 'Exhausted by sea-sickness, saddened by home-sickness, frightened by the bearded Russians who greet their eyes in Cronstadt, and pierced through and through by the chill breath of a St Petersburg May, they issue from their cabins, pale, timid, and slow, anxiety and white fear upon their lips, and despair in their eyes.' Not surprisingly, many of these governesses never forgot the welcome they received from the kind-hearted Jane, and remained friends of the family for life; two of them were married from the Mirrielees home.

Jane had to admit that God had given her 'such kind friends here'. Prominent among them were the Gellibrands, William Hooper Ropes (who had married a niece of the first Mrs Gellibrand and had nine children) and the Whistlers. Major George Washington Whistler was an American railway engineer who arrived in St Petersburg in 1842 to take charge of the construction of the railway line from St Petersburg to Moscow. In the autumn of 1843 he was joined there by his second wife Anna, their two young sons, Jimmie and Willie, and Debo, his teenage daughter by his first wife. If the railway dominated Whistler's thoughts, Anna's were full of religion. On Sunday mornings she took the family to the English Church over which Mr Edward Law still presided. Morning services there were always crowded, but why not services later in the day? Those wealthy Englishmen, she decided, must have been infected by the Russian love of Sunday visits and parties. The Church also had a magnificent new organ, yet its services struck her as cold and half-hearted. Her own brand of Anglicanism was much closer to the religion of the Chapel, which the Whistlers also attended. The Church might claim a thousand members, but had no Sunday school, whereas Mr Ellerby's congregation of two hundred had a regular attendance of forty Sunday scholars. And why did the Church do nothing to bring the word of God to Russia's benighted millions? Mrs Gellibrand had been handing out tracts to soldiers for three years. Anna determined to follow suit. Her two sons, who had picked up some Russian, were engaged as helpers. The results seemed to justify Anna's faith, but neither she nor Mrs Gellibrand realized that Russian serfs and soldiers prized any bit of paper that could be used to hold their tobacco or as stuffing in their boots.

Of the Mirrielees family Mrs Whistler approved wholeheartedly. At their home she could be sure that the proceedings would not become too worldly, whereas at the Laws' house not only the daughters, but even Mr Law himself, often entertained visitors with a selection from their surprisingly large repertoire of popular Russian songs. The friendship between the families came to an end with the premature death of Major Whistler in 1849, but was renewed in England some years later.

In 1849 Jane Mirrielees was able to realize a long-cherished dream of spending the summer in England and Scotland. She was accompanied by her stepdaughter Sarah, at nineteen a helpful companion, by her own infant daughters, Augusta and Margaret, and two Russian nurses, one of whom, the wet-nurse, was kitted out in the traditional costume and headdress peculiar to her profession. From the Lethems' home in London Jane took her little party up to Dunoon, where she hired rooms near her former Liverpool friends, the Millers. Dunoon was across the water from her old friends in Greenock, and merry times were had in both places. Archibald joined her in mid-August. He was most anxious that Jane should have her portrait painted while she was in Britain. The Millers liked to encourage young artists, and it was at their house, 'Ardencraig', that Jane sat to Mr Robertson of Liverpool. His attractive portrait shows her sitting in an armchair with her voluminous skirts spread out around her; her dark hair is parted in the middle and smoothed over the ears; her long oval face is calm and her eyes serious. In a sketch by the same artist she is wearing a lace cap and mittens, although she was still only thirty-eight. The young artists were also very eager to paint the Russian wet-nurse. It was not the girl's face that attracted them – on the contrary – but her picturesque garb. The Millers' teenage daughter was persuaded to pose in it, but not before she had cried bitterly at the indignity of being made to put on a Russian peasant woman's clothing.

One purpose of the visit was to help build up Jane's strength. From Dunoon she wrote that she was deriving great benefit from the fine air and the moderate use of hydropathic measures: 'I have had the dripping sheet between 5 and 6 every morning, have worn the wet bandage all day, had a sitz bath in the afternoon & have taken a tumbler or two of water more than formerly a day.' She had resisted more extreme measures, since she had only weakness to overcome. 'My appetite has greatly improved, my back & limbs have got stronger, my colour fresher & I only want a little more flesh on my bones to be quite myself again.' She and Archibald returned to the Lethems for the last part of their stay, finally leaving on 11 October. Afterwards, Margaret reported to Andrew that Jane 'was not at all so strong as we wished to see her', but this was not surprising after all the 'visiting, shopping and knocking about' that she had done during the previous months. It had been due entirely to *their* good management

that the children improved greatly and Augusta especially could scarcely be recognized as the same child. Mr M had a sadly spoiling way with his children – and also a nurse they have in St Petersburg – it is most grievous when people are so mistaken as to act in this way – Jane was fully alive to the evil, and wished very much to take out a nurse from this country – but could not hear of a suitable one in time – I hope that she still will have one out in the spring. She is not nearly so decided in her management as you would expect from her natural character & I think gives Mr M far too much of his

own way, and he has been so much accustomed to rule that some wives who
are blessed with easy good humoured husbands as I am would think Mr M a
little despot in his way, at the same time he is so benevolent and fond...

Unfortunately, the second sheet of this letter has not survived, so that
we do not learn the full extent of Archibald's redeeming qualities, but
Margaret's picture of him as a benevolent despot is clear enough.
Maida Mirrielees, reading this letter many years later and
remembering her father as 'a decidedly severe parent', was surprised
to learn of his 'sadly spoiling way' with children, albeit very young
ones. She, too, had often asked herself why her mother, by all accounts
a high-spirited young woman used to exercising considerable freedom
of judgment and action, should have allowed herself to become such a
submissive wife. The explanation, she thought, was on the one hand,
that her mother never took to the St Petersburg climate, was drained of
her natural vitality by the repeated cycle of childbearing and
convalescence, and never overcame her grief at the loss of Mary
Fanny; and on the other, that her father had such a dominating
personality and was so 'accustomed to rule' that he took it for granted
that all household decisions were to be referred to him. How often in
her childhood did Maida remember her mother saying: 'We must see
what Papa says about this'.

Moreover, as a devout Christian, Jane fully accepted the Victorian
belief that wives should obey their husbands. Religion, perhaps, was
responsible more than anything for introducing the element of pious
submission into Jane's outlook. It was a religious impulse that had
made her accept Archibald's proposal in the first place, and the
strength of his convictions seems to have weighed heavily upon her.
The loss of Mary Fanny intensified her own religious feelings. After
the death of his two boys Mr Knill had reminded himself that 'whom
the Lord loveth He chasteneth'. Death must be accepted; punishment
was sent for a purpose. Archibald, having buried two wives and two
children before he met Jane, had also had frequent recourse to this
kind of philosophy. After the death of her daughter, Jane, too, found
herself in desperate need of it, as this remark to Andrew makes clear:
'If we believe that "God is love" we know that He afflicts not willingly
but for our good and I have truly experienced that nothing has the
effect so much of drawing the heart to Him as the taking from us of
those we loved & prized most on earth.'

*   *   *

No letters have survived between 1849 and 1857, when Archibald and Jane left Russia. For Jane these were difficult years. Any benefit in health or morale that she might have derived from her long summer holiday was quickly dissipated. She must have become pregnant even before leaving England, for on 3 June 1850 she gave birth to her first son, Archibald Muir Mirrielees. Another son, Frederick James, followed on 7 December 1851. On 31 March 1853, at the age of forty-two, she gave birth for the last time and was so ill afterwards that her life was despaired of. The minister was hastily summoned to perform the baptism, since the child was not expected to live, either. The choice of name seemed an irrelevance; when asked what the child was to be called, Jane replied: 'Matilda'. Mother and daughter both survived, however, and before long Matilda was permanently abbreviated to Maida. Not until years after her mother's death did Maida discover the reason for what had always seemed to her the eccentric choice of Matilda. Visiting St Peter's in Rome with her Uncle Andrew, she was quite taken aback when he pointed out to her the statue of Matilda, Countess of Tuscany, and explained that Jane had always had a great admiration for this dauntless defender of the Popes of her day.

Looking back on her mother's life in St Petersburg and the way in which she was weighed down by ill health, Maida later wrote: 'I fear that my birth was the last straw; she did not recover normal health for several years; I sometimes feel that I never ought to have added to her burdens by being born! But those were the days when wives just had to submit to having as many babies as Nature (or, as was then often said, God) sent to them, and to endure all that meant without the aid of any anaesthetic!'

Maida was just four when her parents left St Petersburg, so that her early memories were of trifling occurrences, but, as she says, 'rather characteristic' of Russia.

Walking with the nurse one winter's day along the English Quay near what seemed to me a high wall (which I afterwards knew as a low parapet) and wearing a little quilted bonnet, I was suddenly aware that my cheek was being rubbed with snow and I was hurried home with a small white patch (a frost-bite) still visible on its rosy surface. Our two footmen who seemed to me enormously tall were great friends of mine; Fyodor, the livelier of the two, used to lift me up and carry me on his shoulder, to my great delight. I remember kneeling on my high chair at a meal in a long dining-room reluctantly eating rice pudding (a pet aversion of mine in those days) when one of the footmen came in looking very serious to tell my mother, who had ordered the sledge, that the coachman was too drunk to drive it.

The happiest of all Maida's memories of her first home was of the hour before bedtime spent daily with their mother in front of a big open fire – an unusual luxury in those days when stoves were the universal method of heating in Russia. Maida used to be cuddled up on her mother's lap while round them were grouped the four older children. There was a never-ending and entrancingly interesting story of the doings of a certain Johnny and Mary, and Maida, while listening, liked fingering her mother's lace collar, or playing with the half hoop of diamonds and another of emeralds which she always wore above her wedding ring, or gazing at the details on her cameo brooch. On Sundays Mother told them stories from the Bible.

Another pleasant memory of the Galernaya days was of frequent visits to their father's counting-house on an upper storey. They always knew that he would open a certain drawer in his desk and offer them some delicious pear-drops shaped like fishes. In the next room the clerks' stools loomed high above Maida's head. How was it possible for anyone to sit at such a great height? All of a sudden she found herself lifted up and perched on one of them, which made her feel very proud.

In the Family Record Maida describes her father's company, founded in 1843, as 'a wholesale business importing sewing cottons, laces and many other kinds of British manufactures'. The trade-mark that he used on his cotton-reels was a boar's head, which also appears at the top of his personal notepaper. His business soon prospered, largely, Maida understood, 'because of his absolutely honourable methods of conducting it. Truth and honesty in business were rare in those days in Russia.' The Old Believers, the large sect which had split from the Orthodox Church in the 17th century, likewise prospered in business, for their scrupulous honesty ensured that other Russians willingly entrusted them with money. So prosperous did Archibald become that at some time in the late 1840's or early 1850's he gave the enormous sum of 30,000 roubles (£3000) to the Moscow doctor-philanthropist, Fyodor Petrovich Haas, to help him in his work on behalf of convicts and of poor people unable to afford medical treatment.

Jane's fears, expressed at the start of her marriage, that Archibald intended to spend his whole life in Russia were probably groundless. Retirement is unlikely to have been a subject that he felt obliged to discuss with her. It would be pleasing to think that his wife's delicate health was the decisive factor, but as Maida points out, her father was a man who always planned well in advance, and he had made up his mind that on reaching the age of sixty, in 1857, he would retire and live in England.

The question arose: who was to be his successor?

The obvious candidate was his eldest son William. But Archibald had had other plans for William, literally from before the time of his birth. Soon after his first wife's death, he asked John Paterson to agree to be nominated as one of his children's guardians, so that if anything happened to him, they would remain 'in the charge of those who I feel assured will seek first for them the Kingdom of God, and who will do all that depends upon them to train my precious boy for a Missionary to the Heathen, to which service his now glorified Mother united with me in dedicating him before he was born and often since, provided the Lord enclined his heart towards the work and bestowed the requisite talents'.

Talented William certainly was. After interrupting his degree course from 1846 to 1849, he graduated in 1851 as a Bachelor of Arts (a degree not usually associated with Scottish universities, and awarded at Edinburgh only from 1842 to 1858), and completed the higher degree of Master of Arts in 1852. His father then wished him to train for the Congregational ministry, so he studied at St John's Wood College in London and began to preach. Passionately interested in art, music and literature, he was never at ease among the unrefined people whom he met preaching, and feeling drawn towards the educated circles of the established church, asked permission from his father to be ordained in the Church of England. He would have made an excellent country parson, Maida thought, training a choir and living largely among books. But Archibald refused. Too used to accepting the rule of his despotic father, William does not seem to have questioned the decision. He returned to St Petersburg in the summer of 1856 and entered the business, a life for which he was quite unsuited.

In the mean time, however, Archibald was training as his successor a more suitable candidate: his brother-in-law, Andrew Muir, who had the advantage of being much older than William (thirty-five when he arrived in St Petersburg in 1852) and with considerable mercantile experience behind him. Archibald seems to have taken a genuine interest in the welfare of all Jane's family. Andrew served an apprenticeship from 1852 to 1857, and was then ready to take over control of the business with William Mirrielees as his junior partner.

The name, Muir & Mirrielees, must have been adopted at this time. In 1857 Andrew Muir acquired the official status of merchant of the First Guild in St Petersburg, as did William Mirrielees two years later. The whole operation is a good example of the Caledonian Phalanx in Russia 'moving always in the closest union'.

Soon after Andrew's arrival in St Petersburg, political relations between Russia and Britain became increasingly strained. Among the few people in Britain trying to prevent a war were the Quakers. In a last-minute bid to avert catastrophe, three of them, led by Joseph Sturge, decided to take a message from the Society of Friends direct to the Emperor Nicholas, in which they recalled the close links that had existed before 1825 between the Society and the Emperor's elder brother, Alexander, and urged him to act in accordance with Christ's gospel of peace on earth and goodwill to all men. The deputation had introductions to Mr Gellibrand and Mr Mirrielees, from whom they received a very warm welcome; Archibald showed them round the Lancastrian school in which he took a special interest, and entertained them to dinner. Though impressed by the Quakers' sincerity, Nicholas was not swayed by their arguments. They returned to England to a chorus of abuse and ridicule, though perhaps, as Richenda Scott writes in *Quakers in Russia*, 'the final judgment of history will be that the Quaker deputation spoke with the small, cool voice of common-sense, which was drowned in the feverish clamour of hysteria and the sombre, stirring roll of the drums'. Britain and France declared war on Russia a month later, in March 1854.

During the next two years the Russian authorities placed no restrictions on British residents. In St Petersburg life and business went on as before. The closest they came to the war in the Mirrielees household was when Archibald entertained some of the British surgeons travelling to or from the Crimea, and poor Jane had to listen to their harrowing accounts of operations performed close to the battlefield without any anaesthetic, or of standing knee-deep in blood amputating one limb after another.

Throughout the war the entire business of the British & Foreign Bible Society in North Russia was concentrated in the hands of Archibald Mirrielees, who by this time had obviously gained the complete confidence of the Russian authorities. 'Men's minds,' he reported to the Committee in London in March 1855, 'are more or less agitated at the present time and we may hope are more than usually open to your influences.' He distributed religious literature to both sides with complete impartiality. Sixty English prisoners-of-war had reached Voronezh, and thirty more wounded were expected. A considerable sum of money had been raised by the British residents in St Petersburg for them; 'I added some useful reading for the poor fellows.' A fortnight later he sent 500 'Sclavonian' (Church Slavonic) testaments to wounded Russian soldiers through Grand Duchess Hélène, and in September another 500 through the private Chancery of Her Majesty the Empress. In March 1856, as the war came to an end, he formed a small Agency, including Andrew Muir, to conduct future operations of the Society and its American counterpart. Russia, he felt sure, was 'about to enter a new era in regard to the development of its vast resources...of greater liberality of views... and liberty of action for the spreading of Divine truth.' He intended his son William to be his successor in St Petersburg 'in the grand work of spreading the word of God'.

In April 1857 Archibald and Jane Mirrielees left Russia for good with their five young children. Before their departure, daguerreotypes of two family groups were made, from which photographs were later taken. Archibald is in one group with Maggie and Fred, Jane in the other with Gussie (Augusta), Archy and Maida.

Gussie and Maggie, now aged nine and eight, have the same dark hair and central parting as their mother, and Maggie, the younger of the two, looks distinctly pretty. Archy, not quite seven, and Fred, five-and-a-half, are in tartan outfits with lace collars and lots of buttons; Fred's lace pantaloons are showing beneath his pleated tartan skirt. The youngest child, Maida, four years old on 31 March, had been looking forward eagerly to the occasion. Describing herself later as 'a vain little monkey', she recalled crying with vexation because her curl papers were not taken out until the very last moment. As a result, tight sausage curls hang down from her central parting and frame her round face. Her feet in white socks and black slippers barely touch the ground, and she wears a low-necked, wide-skirted, frilly white dress, from beneath which peep her lace pantalettes. Already she looks a determined little soul, as indeed she was: a great propper-up of other people.

As for Jane, she is still elegant in black velvet with a lace collar and cameo brooch, long lace cuffs, and a lace cap on her still dark hair; but her shoulders droop forward, there is a dull look in her eyes and about her mouth, and her hands are clasped together in an attitude of resignation. Of her own mother, who had died a year after giving birth to her eighth child, Jane seldom spoke, but there was one remark of hers

1. St Petersburg, the English Quay, with English Church on left: pre-1917 postcard

SAINT-PÉTERSBOURG PENDANT UNE INONDATION.

2. St Petersburg during a Flood, from *Les Mystères de la Russie* by Fredéric Lacroix (Paris, 1845)

3. *(above)* 'Rosebank', the Muirs' old home at Greenock, as it is today

4 & 5. Jane Mirrielees with *(l to r)* Maida, Archy and Augusta; Archibald Mirrielees with Maggie and Fred: photographs made from daguerreotypes of 1857

that she was fond of recalling. 'Oh Jeannie, Jeannie,' her mother would say to her, 'you wild lassie! Will you ever grow up into a sensible woman?' To Maida, romping about with her brothers while her mother reclined on an invalid couch, these words seemed puzzling: how *could* her mother ever have been a 'wild lassie'? With the passage of time, she was able to look back on the whole course of her parents' life from a wider perspective, and one can understand why the letter that her mother wrote to Andrew on the eve of her marriage always seemed to Maida 'a human document full of almost painful interest'.

Looking at the photographs, one might guess that Jane was the older of the two, whereas Archibald was approaching sixty, and Jane not yet forty-seven. Archibald's expression is still firm and challenging, and his legs are crossed with jaunty self-confidence. Here is a man who can look back to the time when he had to eat up his porridge from breakfast before being allowed to start his dinner, and know that he has made a success of his life. Ambition, industry and perseverance meant that he had scaled many rungs on the Victorian social ladder. But here is a man who is also looking forward, who feels that his life's work is not yet done. Like his mentor, John Paterson, Archibald was a man of action, not introspection – 'a restlessly active little man', to quote Jane's letter to Andrew. Retirement from business left him free to concentrate all his energies on religious activities, especially his work for the Bible Society, and on regulating the conduct of himself and all those round him in accordance with his deeply-held religious convictions.

5

Joining the Family Business

In 1860, after some time in Europe, the Mirrielees family went to live on a private estate at Upton Park, Slough. Their house, of red brick with white copings, was ugly, Maida recalled, but very large: even with its full complement of seven members of family, a governess, and five servants, it still had two spare rooms. In winter it was made more comfortable by the use of stoves on the Russian pattern in addition to open fireplaces. For children the park itself was the chief attraction. In the middle of a large pond stood a densely wooded island, forming a natural playground, which could be reached by stepping-stones in dry weather, but at other times only by using a crazy old raft.

From the front of the house there was a fine view of Windsor Castle, two miles away, while in between, hidden from sight, lay Eton and the river Thames. All their visitors were eager to see the famous old buildings of the school, or to stand in the big quadrangle of the Castle, watching the comings and goings of the Royal family. Maida never forgot the sound of the minute-guns being fired after Prince Albert's funeral, nor the arrival at Slough Station of Princess Alexandra of Denmark, who was to marry the Prince of Wales. They had a houseful of visitors on that occasion, and watched the procession from a wagonette in a field. An even more colourful person to arrive at Slough Station – though *he* did not go to the Castle – was Garibaldi, whose cause the Mirrielees family, as good liberals, supported with enthusiasm. Maida was lifted on someone's shoulder and gazed with awe and admiration at the picturesque figure in scarlet shirt and long grey cloak, walking along the platform with a slight limp from a wound received in the good cause. Next winter they were all wearing garibaldis, red blouses that bulged over at the waist.

On 3 April 1861 Sarah Jane Mirrielees, Archibald's daughter by his first wife, was married from the house at Upton Park to Lewis Cazalet, a widower of thirty-two with two children. Maida Mirrielees was one of the bridesmaids. The Cazalets had been in Russia since the time of Catherine the Great, when Lewis's grandfather, Noah Cazalet, started a rope factory in St Petersburg. How delighted Maida was when her future brother-in-law, though twenty-five years her senior, invited her to call him 'Lewis'! He was very tall and handsome, with a slight foreign accent that only added to his charm, but what gave the finishing touch to his romantic appeal was that his left arm was in a sling. A few months before, three of his fingers had been so badly frozen that they nearly broke off, and it was seven years before they returned to normal. Two of the children of this marriage, Willie and Fred Cazalet, were later to occupy important positions with Muir & Mirrielees.

For the wedding the house was filled to overflowing, but seldom was it entirely without visitors. Many were friends from Russian days. The Ropes family arrived in batches. One of the Ropes boys was killed fighting for the North in the American Civil War; Archibald's nephew, John, was also fighting for the North. Jane's sympathetic nature vibrated not only to the horrors of the war itself, but to the plight of the Lancashire cotton workers, made idle by the impossibility of obtaining cotton from the Southern States. She asked the children to give up sugar in their cocoa, handing them instead a small sum each week to be sent to the hardship fund. Mostly, however, the visitors were religious people, often connected with the Bible Society, for Archibald had agreed to serve on the Committee and went up to London for meetings once a week. In the matter of visitors, as in all others, it was Papa's will that permeated the house, so that everyone living in it came under his sway. 'The religious element in our family life,' Maida writes, 'was very marked, but found little echo in me.' Morning and evening there were family prayers. Sundays were specially boring days: all story books were tabooed; even a magazine containing a serial story was put out of sight on Saturday evening; needlework was forbidden and no music allowed except hymn singing. They had to attend two services at the Congregational chapel and listen to dull sermons. Another Sunday trial was a five o'clock prayer meeting in the library which even visitors attended, and at which they and all the absent members of the family were prayed for. Whenever Papa began talking 'piously' with visitors and giving them little copies of the gospels, Maida felt uncomfortable; she felt sure that some of the young people used to laugh at him behind his back.

Papa always insisted on regular hours and strict punctuality. While dressing, each of the children had to learn a text from the Bible – 'what a hunt we used to have for short ones' – and repeat it to him either during the pre-breakfast walk in the park (7.30 in summer and 8 in winter, weather permitting) or at breakfast. He would reprove the servants for having a meal on the table five minutes early no less than for being five minutes late. On one occasion the free-and-easy Lewis Cazalets arrived with their children from Russia. They were all kept waiting on the doorstep while Papa, watch in hand, sternly inquired: 'How is this, Lewis? You are a quarter of an hour early!' And yet the servants remained very loyal, appreciating that although he might be strict and fault-finding, he was also just and kind-hearted.

Towards his children, too, his naturally hasty temper was modified by a warm heart. Both as a husband and a father he was demonstratively affectionate, and of his children he was almost embarrassingly proud. Maida, being the youngest, was dealt with more leniently than the others, and took advantage of this at times to coax him into letting them have their own way. All the same, his 'Petty', as he called her, was rather in awe of him, and clearly remembered the feeling of relief which they all experienced whenever Papa went away for a few days. They then enjoyed an unaccustomed freedom under the milder sway of Mamma, who might sometimes look very grieved at their shortcomings, but was incapable of being hasty or cross.

Looking back much later on her early years, Maida concluded that in spite of her father's strict rule, her family background had been happy and secure. Both her parents were genuinely religious, and set before their children high ideals of conduct: great emphasis was placed on honesty and truthfulness, and there was no pretence or ostentation, no striving after social or financial advancement. One of the chief drawbacks was that their parents were so much older – in Maida's case, more like grandparents – and although they might tease Mamma and did not stand in awe of her, they were often cut off from her society by her delicate health. Also, they had too little liberty; they could rarely choose what they were going to do; it was always Papa who chose for them. Even the books that he used to read aloud in the evenings, when they all sat round the drawing-room table, the girls doing needlework, the boys fret-sawing or illuminating, were those that suited his taste, mostly biographies of worthy but very dull religious people. Only with difficulty did he realize, almost always after Mamma had pleaded the children's cause at their request, that they liked to stay away from home visiting longer than he was inclined to allow.

There had been some improvement in Mamma's health, but she was still not strong enough to go for walks with the children or to play croquet on the lawn. Then in 1864 came a fresh trial. Maida's eldest sister, Augusta (Gussie), caught scarlet-fever at her boarding-school in

Brighton and died after a short illness. When the telegram arrived at Upton Park, the children's governess burst into loud sobbing and lamentation, and Maida, thinking this the right thing to do, tried in vain to copy her. What a horrid creepy feeling she had on the day of the funeral itself, when she came downstairs and saw through the upper glass panels on either side of the front door a tall black figure standing motionless! These were 'mutes', whose duty it was to stand there for hours. When the hearse drove up, three more such figures appeared draped in long black scarves called 'weepers'. One walked on each side of the hearse, while a third preceded it carrying a big tray from which rose huge bunches of tall black ostrich feathers. Just inside the front door stood a man with a tray of black kid gloves, from which he invited each of the funeral guests to choose a pair of the right size. Augusta was buried in the churchyard at Stoke Poges made famous by Gray's elegy.

At the time of Gussie's death, Maggie was fifteen, and Maida almost eleven. Maggie and the boys were tall like Mamma, but Maida was short in stature like her father and had inherited his drive and energy. Some years later, her brother Archy wrote to her: 'I have often thought of late what a blessing it is that you at least enjoy so much good health and have such bright spirits and pray that they may long be spared to you, dear girl, for your own enjoyment and the benefit of all around you.' Maida was to devote much of her life to keeping up the spirits of other people, starting with Maggie and including Archy himself. As with her father, Maida's energy was both mental and physical. For some reason it had been decided not to teach her to read until she was six, but this was not good enough for her and she took the matter into her own hands. On her sixth birthday she gave Papa a great surprise by reading him part of the first chapter of St John's Gospel, thereby earning herself the gift of a Bible, and from then on she became a voracious reader. But whenever her brothers were home from boarding-school, she also loved joining in all their outdoor activities: climbing trees, skating and sliding on the frozen pond, and playing cricket. One of her proudest moments as a child was at the age of about ten, when she caught out one of their visitors. 'I caught the ball against my chest and the blow hurt horribly, but I clutched it firmly.' The visitor happened to be an Eton schoolboy, and she enjoyed being showered with praise.

Amersham Hall School, which Archy and Fred attended, had moved from Amersham to Caversham, near Reading. There were about a hundred pupils, all from non-conformist backgrounds. When the boys arrived home at Christmas, the schoolroom, normally a dull place for Maida, became the scene of such exciting activities as roasting chestnuts or making toffee over the fire. New Year was spent with the Lethems, where the water might freeze overnight in the bedrooms because of the lack of Russian stoves, but the welcome was always warm. On one occasion Aunt Mary Muir, without Papa's knowledge, even took them to the pantomime! It was St George and the Dragon, and Maida always remembered the wildly exciting scene in which the chopped-off tail of the monster became miraculously transformed in mid-air into a small dragon and flew cheerfully away. Aunt Mary was not renowned for her fun-loving disposition, but probably liked the idea of cocking a snook at her pious brother-in-law.

One Easter holiday Archy and Fred brought a schoolfriend home to stay, who was later to figure prominently in the lives of both the Mirrielees and Muir families. On the railway platform at Slough Maida saw for the first time a rather short, thickset figure with a mass of curly dark hair and a jovial round face. Augustine, known as Austin, Birrell was the youngest child of the Revd Charles Birrell, a Scot who had gone out to St Petersburg in the winter of 1831-2 and been so impressed by Mr Knill that he gave up all thoughts of a mercantile career and returned home to become a Baptist minister in Liverpool. Birrell, as they called him – only years later did they take to calling him Austin – was to spend the short Michaelmas and Easter holidays at Upton Park, having recently lost his mother. Jane at once took him to her heart, and tried to make him sit up in a literal sense, often laying a hand in affectionate admonition on his round shoulders. On each visit the boys had a fresh batch of amusing stories to tell about their headmaster, Ebenezer West, and Birrell had a way of imitating his voice and manner, quoting passages from his extempore prayers in a sanctimonious voice, that sent them all into fits of laughter.

In St Petersburg Uncle Andrew Muir was very eager for his Mirrielees nephews to join the family business. 'It is always a trial to a mother,' Jane wrote to him in April 1866, 'to part with her boys & though I see it plainly a duty to put no hinderance in dear Archy's way if he should come to chuse Russia as his sphere I still shrink painfully from the thought of parting with *both*.' In Archy Andrew would have 'a thoroughly steady plodding well principled good boy'. This was not only his parents' opinion, but that of his headmaster. When Jane had asked Mr West if he found Archy slow, in view of his want of fluency in expressing himself, 'he answered that Archy made steady good progress & compared well with other boys of his own age – & he has no fear of difficulty in his passing good examinations.'

At Christmas of that year both Archy and Fred left school. Archy, the quieter and more studious of the two, had fulfilled Mr West's expectations by passing the University of London matriculation exam, and would have liked to go on to University, but Uncle Andrew urged that both boys be sent to Arnstadt to learn business German. Within a few months, however, he was asking for Archy to come out to Russia straight away. Archy returned home to be fitted out with clothes. He was to travel to St Petersburg with Mr Ropes.

With her son's departure imminent, Jane's anxieties increased. Archy would be seventeen on 3 June 1867. In his uncle's opinion this was 'decidedly past boyhood', but Jane disagreed. 'Archy has been almost exclusively associated with *boys*,' she wrote on 7 May. 'He is very young, & of an easy, hopeful trustful temperament. I believe his principles are sound & good but they have yet to be tested.'

A week later Jane wrote again. Both she and Mr M were feeling uneasy, because they had not given Andrew any hint of Archy's natural defects. 'Now the fact is, that he is not prompt and beforehand in what he has to do, but rather inclined to delay & put off till again what should be done at once.' Within the well-regulated life of school this tendency had not been allowed to develop, 'but now in commencing with you, it will no doubt be very important that he should be kept up to the mark in all matters of lessons or business, perhaps in saying so much I am doing him injustice, but I believe it is better to notice this matter that you may be prepared'. Jane herself came from a family of successful businessmen, and recognized that it was only 'prompt & close attention to the duty of the moment' that would make a good businessman of Archy. It was the absence of this quality which had 'so signally marred the character of his elder brother. Archy is very fond of Wm but we earnestly trust the latter will avoid any influence which may in the least tend to unsettle or weaken the full force of attention to duty on A's part.' In the mean time, William was making himself useful by giving Archy his first Russian lessons.

The moment of parting between father and son was a solemn one. Papa had been extremely ill, and only his strong constitution, and the fact that he was a model patient – more docile and easy to manage in illness than at any other time – enabled him to pull through. He was still quite ill when Archy left for Russia. Some years before, he had given up kissing his sons, who from the age of fourteen were referred to as 'the lads' and no longer as 'the boys', but on this occasion, sitting up in bed in his dressing-gown, he gave Archy his solemn blessing and kissed him.

During his first months in Russia Archy appears to have been lonely and homesick. Andrew had heeded Jane's advice about keeping him up to the mark – so much so, that Archy complained to his father, as becomes apparent from Jane's letter to Andrew of 29 January 1868. It was no wonder, she writes, that having lost the company of Fred and other lads of his own age, Archy should 'feel a great blank – as I feel assured you often did in former times, even when surrounded by people, and associations which appeared full of cheerfulness *to others*'. This moody feeling, and being led to believe

that the long business hours would probably last through the winter – the evenings (when somewhat tired) to be given to Russ – and the exercise on the ice to be only an hour when other young men were about leaving it, led to his mistake in writing to his father – which in a lad of seventeen under such circumstances seemed to us far from inexcusable, and his simple remark about his health & spirits – considering the then arrangements, & his state of mind appeared also to us the very reverse of what you thought it – '*unnatural & inappropriate*'. To place ourselves in other people's circumstances and see things clearly from their point of view as well as our own – I know is impossible, but we old people have the advantage over the young, in *trying* to do so.

She hoped that when the two boys got together, they would be 'mutual helps to each other, in many ways – and in the course of years turn out efficient helps to you also'.

Fred did not join his brother until the autumn of 1868. In the mean time – although it is impossible to be sure of the date – Archy had had a most alarming experience.

As background to the story, it is worth quoting Kohl's description of a Russian 'royal walk-about' on the English Quay.

The Emperor walks up and down upon an apparent footing of equality with his subjects around him; though these, in point of fact, stand about in the same relation to him, that a child's doll does to the Colossus of Rhodes. The Englishman buttons up his hatred of despotism in his great coat, and scarcely condescends to touch his hat when he meets the 'Giant of the North'; while to the Russian by his side, a submissive demeanour has by habit become a positive source of enjoyment.

Archy, so the story goes, was due to spend an evening after work with the Cazalets at their home in the residential suburb of Chekoosh. When he failed to turn up, they became anxious, and William Mirrielees went into the city to investigate. He discovered that Archy was being held by the police. Archy told him that as the Emperor was driving past, he had taken off his new sealskin cap (suggesting that this was his first Russian winter, that of 1867-68), then replaced it and turned to go on his way. All of a sudden he felt someone snatch the cap off from behind. He thought it was a thief and turned to grapple with his assailant, only to discover that the man was a policeman arresting him for showing disrespect towards the Emperor.

William rushed off at once to the British Embassy. The Ambassador, accompanied by William, Archy and the Chief of Police, went to see the Emperor. By a fortunate chance the latter had seen the tall young Englishman take off his cap and was able to explain what happened next. His carriage had been turned, and was about to retrace the same route at the very moment when Archy began to walk away. Of course, said the Emperor, Mr Mirrielees had not seen him pass the second time and had not been guilty of any discourtesy in failing to take off his cap. He then told the Chief of Police that he had exceeded his duty and recommended that he should go away for 'six months change of air'.

Reading between the lines of this story, Alexander II seems to have acted promptly to defuse a situation that would have done nothing to improve Anglo-Russian relations. *Had* Archy been guilty of disrespect? A gesture of youthful bravado against Russian despotism seems quite out of character. If he did turn his back on the Emperor, he probably did so inadvertently, being, as his mother had expressed it, 'a little dreamy and slow'. One thing in this very odd story seems certain: that Jane was never told. Not even in her moments of wildest apprehension could she have dreamed up such a terrifying incident. It seems possible, indeed, that all the Mirrieleeses closed ranks around young Archy, and also managed to keep the secret from Andrew Muir. He would not have been amused, either.

6

Passing of a Generation

For some years the Mirrielees family had paid an annual visit to the Gellibrands, their close friends from Russian days. Among their fellow guests in 1868 were old Mrs Whistler and her son, Jimmie, who had already acquired a reputation as an artist, although the famous portrait of his mother was not exhibited at the Royal Academy until 1872. For Jane this meeting with Anna Whistler must have been a pleasant reunion. Maida, too, found her very sweet, but did not take to Jimmie. She disliked the oily appearance of his black curls and objected to sitting next to him at table, as he had a way of hanging his head to one side and shaking it, and she felt sure that some of his pomade would land on her. As for his habit of taking up some piece of china in the long gallery, poising it on his hand, and holding forth about the superiority of Oriental art to Western, this seemed to her no more than affectation. Most irritating of all, however, he would *insist* on joining in at croquet, and then miss his turn while indulging in irrelevant talk.

With the lads away from home, the house at Upton Park was too large and they moved to Ealing. This was closer to London, and more convenient for Papa's weekly Bible Society committee meetings. The new house was known as 'Elm Trees', which, as Archy put it, 'a very little imagination could picture as a picturesque old mansion surrounded with stately spreading elms'. In reality, it was semi-detached and comparatively small, though it still had two visitors' rooms that were usually occupied. For Maida one of the happiest features of the Ealing years was the periodical appearance of Archy or Fred on a long holiday from Russia.

How we girls enjoyed those arrivals! We hailed even the peculiar Russian smell of their trunks and the clothes that came out of them, an odour compounded of the smell of leather and that of fur. Each time they returned, we had much to hear of their doings and their friends in St Petersburg. I remember the curious feeling when one of them mentioned picnics and lawn tennis on Sundays, for such Sabbath-breaking was unknown among our set in England, and we felt that even our sympathetic mother must not be told of these 'lapses'! We were glad that Archy and Fred were emancipated from our father's too rigorous control which, though it spoiled our lives to a certain extent, could still, we thought, be better borne by girls than by boys.

The difference in age between the sisters soon ceased to be important, and they became intellectual companions. After attending Miss Tailer's finishing school at Finchley, Maida would have liked to go on to the college for women that had been opened in 1869 by Emily Davies at Hitchin and later became Girton College, Cambridge, but Papa took the conventional view that home was the only place for unmarried girls whose fathers could support them. He did not object, however, to them attending lectures in London, including Huxley on Physiology and Stopford Brooke on Literature. Now over seventy, Archibald was horribly afraid that any young man who came to the house must be plotting to marry one of his daughters. A suitor of Maggie's, on leave from Bangkok, was put firmly in his place, Archibald being determined that no daughter of his should go to a country 'devoid of gospel privileges'. But he did make an exception for Austin Birrell, even confiding to Jane that Austin was the only man he could tolerate as a son-in-law. After three years in a solicitor's office in Liverpool, Birrell had taken a degree in Law and History at Cambridge, and gone into practice in Lincoln's Inn. His first visit was at the time of a Boat Race, when Archy was home from Russia. 'I can see him now,' Maida writes, 'with a straw-hat surrounded by a light blue ribbon worn at the back of his head or waved wildly as he shouted encouragement in a stentorian voice to the Cambridge crew.' On another occasion he delighted Papa with a graphic account of an open-air speech by Gladstone to a huge crowd on Blackheath Common. But most of all, he loved talking and arguing by the hour with Maggie and Maida about literature and ideas, making the most outrageous statements so as to provoke disagreement. To his sister he described the two of them as a queer mixture: girls who taught in the Sunday school and yet were keen readers of Herbert Spencer and other unorthodox writers. Eventually, in August 1878, Austin Birrell did marry Maggie Mirrielees, but by that time neither of Maggie's parents was still alive.

As Jane grew older, she became more and more apprehensive. On 21 December 1872 she celebrated her sixty-second birthday. Archy and Fred had failed to write to her in time from St Petersburg, so Archy decided to telegraph their congratulations on the day itself. To Maida he wrote: 'I should not like the despatch to cause any anxiety to the tender maternal breast and shall therefore address it to you who I think will manage to stand the shock without any evil consequences. We shall write to Mamma if possible *on* her birthday, to tell her that she is in our thoughts and has our best wishes.'

On their way back to St Petersburg in the following autumn, Archy and his trunk parted company. The trunk turned up safely later, but Jane had been suffering agonies in the mean time. 'Please thank the mater for her kind letter,' Archy wrote to Maida.

She certainly did let her imagination, winged by her anxiety 'for her dear boy's welfare', take most unwarrantable flights and we had a great laugh over the dreadful possibilities of absence of mind which the mother's vivid imagination conjured up, the climax of which was – 'the misery of waking up some years hence, in a railway express, to the fact that you have left your wife on the platform, a hundred miles behind, without money enough in her pocket to bring her after you'!!... Her over-anxiety about small matters is sometimes quite distressing and must often cause her kind heart a deal of useless worry, but I am afraid this is not to be so easily got over and is indeed one of the main arteries of her dear, self-denying, anxious, 'managing' nature!

Perhaps it is not surprising that Jane Mirrielees, having aged so much more rapidly than her husband, should have died before him. All through August 1875 she gradually faded out of life. Four-year-old Gerald Mirrielees, William's son, at a loss to understand the change in her behaviour, suggested enticingly: 'Granma, shall I tickle you?' – but got no response. Fred was already in England; Archy was summoned in time to see his mother alive. She died on 3 September at the age of sixty-five.

'Her death left a terrible blank in our lives and I can truly say that I have missed her ever since,' Maida wrote when she herself was over seventy. Poor dear Mamma! Hers had not been an easy life. 'I remember in her last years at Ealing how her dear worn face would light up as she talked of past days!' – of her carefree life, that is, in Greenock before her marriage. Aunt Mary Muir was in no doubt of what Jane had had to endure, describing her sister as 'loving and gentle and kind to all, even when sorely tried as she often was'. Aunt Mary was always sharply critical of other people, and saw no reason why Archibald Mirrielees should have a monopoly on righteousness.

Although her father had been the dominant partner, it was her mother's example, Maida believed, that more than any other had

7. Harry Bernard, husband of Maida

6. Maida Mirrielees in Russian peasant costume

8. Archy Mirrielees in 1867, aged 17

Cabinet Portrait

ELLIOTT & FRY.   55, BAKER ST. LONDON. W.

9. Archibald Mirrielees

guided her own life. 'Her never failing affection and sympathy made the sunshine of our home.' Although Archy might poke fun at Mamma's excesses, he must have been very grateful that she took his part when he first complained about Uncle Andrew's strictness. But Jane's gift of sympathy was not confined to her immediate family circle. She extended it to those who, like herself, had suffered bereavement; to those nervous English governesses arriving in Russia for the first time and emerging from their cabins 'with white fear upon their lips, and despair in their eyes'; to children, whose wishes she always knew how to anticipate with little gifts and surprises; and even to complete strangers. 'She has a wonderful facility,' her sister Mary wrote when Jane was holidaying on the Isle of Arran in 1869, 'of finding out points of sympathy with people and meeting them more than half way, and always thinking the very best of them.'

After their mother's death, the girls soon realized how much her gentle influence had smoothed over difficulties with Papa. Maggie was less fit to be his constant companion and went away on several long visits. Seeking a diversion and always eager to acquire new information, Maida began teaching herself Russian. It annoyed her that when Archy and Fred occasionally spoke Russian together or with William, she could not understand them. Papa remembered some Russian, liked listening to passages from the Russian Bible, and could help her with pronunciation; she wrote letters to Archy and Fred, which they sent back corrected; and she studied the Russian classics. Later, when she first tried out her spoken Russian in Russia itself, its old-fashioned quality gave rise to some amusement.

On 11 February 1877 Papa attended his weekly committee meeting at the Bible House in London and took his usual vigorous part in the discussion. He spent the next day quietly indoors. On the morning of the 13th Maggie and Maida had to catch a train to town for a music lesson. Maggie had already gone across to the Lethems, who had left Clyde Villa and were now close neighbours. Hearing her father in the hall, Maida ran down and helped him on with his coat. He said he was only going into the garden, kissed her, and walked jauntily down the steps while Maida returned upstairs. A few minutes later, one of the servants called out that she had seen him fall on the path. He was carried in unconscious by Uncle Matthew Lethem and a neighbour, and died before the doctor arrived. It was a happy ending for such an active man. As his obituarist wrote in the *Bible Society Reporter*: 'To be laid aside as useless was to him a distressing thought.' He was seventy-nine, and was buried at Stoke Poges alongside Jane and their daughter Augusta.

To give a fair assessment of her father Maida did not find so easy. It was a difficulty shared to a lesser degree by his Bible Society obituarist, who, while predictably extolling his numerous services and praising his steadfastness of purpose, also makes this comment on his Committee work:

He gave close attention to all subjects under discussion – formed an independent opinion, and though sometimes apparently sternly decisive in his modes of expression, yet his views were leavened with so much good sense and outspoken candour, that they never failed to secure the unfeigned respect of the Committee, even when they could not concur in the conclusions at which he arrived.

That he was a devoted husband and father, overflowing with affection, and always very generous to relations and friends in distress: of this Maida had no doubt. But he did not exhibit the peculiarly Christian virtues of gentleness and unselfishness in the way that their mother did; in Biblical parlance, he might be considered 'justified', but not 'sanctified'. A man of action, not introspection, he lacked the ability to enter sympathetically into the wishes and feelings of those members of his family over whose lives he exercised – as he thought, for their own good – such a powerful domination.

Maida acknowledged that she owed to her father a training in submitting to discipline, and in regular habits. He did his best to make his children punctual, tidy and accurate, and so impressed upon them the necessity of repaying even the smallest debt that Maida never felt comfortable when owing money. From him, too, she acquired a little knowledge of business matters; every February, when his numerous subscriptions to religious and philanthropic societies fell due, she prepared the cheques and wrote appropriate notes to accompany them. She also perfected the art of making neat parcels, for every month their magazines had to be sorted into bundles for local institutions, and if any parcel was not perfectly wrapped and tied, it had to be done again: a useful accomplishment, without doubt, but not high on the scale of human virtues. Yet one can see in Maida more of her father than she herself perhaps recognized. Nowhere are his qualities of self-discipline, attention to detail, perseverance, and altruism, more apparent than in her compiling of the Family Record: a task undertaken in old age, not with a view to publication, nor because she regarded her own life as of particular interest, but because she felt that it was important that her daughters and their descendants should be fully aware of the background from which they had come. We readers of a later generation reap the benefits of this legacy, without having had to pay a price.

Of the three architects of Muir & Mirrielees, it was Archibald Mirrielees whose fate was the most straightforward. His youthful ambition instilled in him habits of industry that lasted a lifetime. Following his conversion, religion replaced business as the most powerful force in his life, but it was his good fortune that the kind of qualities which his beliefs enjoined, such as scrupulous honesty and conscientiousness, coincided with those required to make him a successful businessman: he would no more have thought of cheating his customers than he would of cheating his neighbours. He had been disappointed in his hope that William might become 'a Missionary to the Heathen', but of his children he could feel justifiably proud; he would have felt prouder still, had he known that one of his sons would scale several more rungs on the social ladder and receive a knighthood. In retirement he had been able to devote all his energies to leading a virtuous life. At the time of his death his mind must have been quite untroubled – something that could not be said about either of his successors.

One puzzle remains. Commercial life made ardent religious believers like the Muir brothers in Greenock, or Archibald Mirrielees in St Petersburg, very wealthy; yet Christ had taught that it was easier for a camel to go through the eye of a needle, than for a rich man to enter into the Kingdom of God. True, they did not flaunt their wealth; they spent money generously on religious objects and on helping to alleviate the sufferings of less fortunate people around them; but at the end of the day they remained wealthy men. How was this contradiction to be resolved? The idea took shape in evangelical circles that prosperity was to be seen as a reward, a blessing granted by God to those who led virtuous lives. In this way it was possible to have the best of both worlds, to combine Piety with Profit.

A Born Speculator

Andrew Muir (1817 – 99)

7

'My Wandering Bachelor Life'

Andrew Muir was born at Greenock on 6 January 1817. His mother died before he was two, but with the popular Aunt Augusta next door, and five elder sisters, he did not lack female company and attention.

Maida Mirrielees says of her Uncle Andrew that 'he must have been a clever boy and, in later years, became a very studious man'. In 1892, while engaged in the task of sorting through old letters and papers, he wrote to his daughter Meta: 'You know I spent four years (9 to 13) at a boarding school at Tillicoultry & the oldest paper relating to myself is a quarter's account from the master (Browning) dated 1826. Fortunately I got a very good conduct report and had got through a good part of Eutropius' (the Roman historian). Tillicoultry is some distance from Greenock, and one wonders why he did not attend the local Grammar School: had his father decided that young Andrew was in danger of being pampered by that clutch of elder sisters? So far as is known, he received no further formal education and did not attend university, although it is hard to imagine that at any stage in his life he was not an avid reader and self-educator. Since his only brother, James, was nine years older, it may have been decided that the sooner Andrew learned to play an active part in the various Muir business enterprises, the better.

In his autobiographical notes John Paterson wrote that among those awakened by his preaching at Greenock was 'the family of Mr James Muir, all of whom joined the church'. This does not seem to have included Andrew, who was still very young at the time, and he never came to share the same religious outlook as his sisters. The letter of 1892 continues:

With the exception of one bundle of letters written by me to my brother, there are none of my own letters. This I think is a happy circumstance, as I shall not be compelled to blush at my ancient follies. The letters are mostly from my sisters. It is amazing how portentously solemn they were as young ladies. When my brother left on a voyage to New York in 1830 he was plied with letters on the uncertainty of life and exhorted in the most earnest manner to prepare for death, and to be a very good lad – a very cheerful preparation for a youth on his travels. I hope they did not disturb his mind. My uncle wrote to him a letter *to be read at sea* full of solemn warnings & studded with appropriate scripture texts. It is curious to note the change from 60 years ago. I think you and the two girls [Meta's younger sisters, Eva and Molly] were much more advanced at twenty one than my sisters notwithstanding their studious habits. They were full of religion & really in earnest, but it is easy to see that they took up the old Evangelist views without really exercising their minds on them. It was long after that criticism set in and we must needs enter an era of doubt and uncertainty. I was the only one of the family, however, who took to reading philosophy & theology and so I was cut off from sympathy with those at home, in some degree at least.

In 1830, of course, the religious fervour of the Muirs would have been at its height after their awakening by Paterson. Andrew might, however, have been influenced later by the more thoughtful and intellectual Dr Wardlaw, but there is no evidence that he ever accompanied his sisters to Wardlaw's chapel in Glasgow. It seems that in the realms of philosophy and theology he was already his own man.

After his father's death in December 1834, Andrew became manager from 1836 to 1841 of the Clyde Pottery Co. under his Uncle Andrew. In reply to Jane's letter of September 1840 from Leamington, recommending him to make a pilgrimage to Warwickshire to see all the beautiful china, Andrew described his own latest 'Neapolitan set', which he had ambitious plans to market in Edinburgh. This prompted the more cautious Jane to reflect upon her younger brother's character. 'I do hope if the set "goes down" in Edinburgh, it wont carry you with it. I fear there will be more pleasure than profit in such attempts, and that your sanguine disposition & love of improvement (most desirable qualities in themselves) may tempt you too far out of the beaten track for personal safety.'

The Muirs' association with the Pottery Co. ended in 1841, when Uncle Andrew decided to retire and find himself a young wife to take the place of the late lamented Aunt Augusta. If Andrew junior was given the option of continuing as manager of the Pottery Co., he must have declined. With his sanguine disposition he intended to seek his fortune much further from the beaten track even than Edinburgh. The Pottery Co. continued to operate in Greenock until 1905, and examples of its wares are much sought after today by collectors.

There then began what Andrew later described as 'my long, unsettled & wandering bachelor life'. He made his first business visit to the United States in 1842. A year later he sailed to Boston, and thence to Montreal, which appears to have been his base for several years. Writing to him on 26 May 1843 from 'Rosebank', Jane is full of elder sisterly concern.

You give very slight intimation of *feelings* on arriving at the place of your destination, but I could easily fancy & enter into them, for who ever took such a step as yours, forsook the land of his fathers and of all his early associations, and that *alone*, to settle in another, without a chilling desolateness of spirit? – which to be sure the novelty of the scene, & the stirring calls of business go at once to counteract, and most fortunately so. By this time I hope you are feeling a little at home, but I fear it will not be easy to get up that feeling. I can't at all fancy you sleeping in a cheerless naked looking bedroom on your large premises without a soul near you, without duly shuddering. You must not leave so much in your future letters for the imagination to pile up.

Jane continued her letter on the 31st, having heard in the mean time from Andrew.

I feel a *little* enlightened about your plan – but who will do out your room? and will you be the only person sleeping on the premises except rats? Will you spend your evenings in that place? I should think it very dull, unless you have plenty to do, or very interesting books...

It is evident my dear Andrew you will have *need of patience*, but you knew this when you went out, and the general tone of your letter does not disappoint me, for I had made up my mind not to expect much in the business way for some time to come. For my part, I am thankful you got no situation in *China* or any other of those distant places, and look forward with God's blessings on your exertions, & the necessary return of better times to Canada, to seeing you a *flourishing* merchant there in the course of a few years.

This reference to 'distant places' is ironical, since Jane herself would be setting off for Russia only a year later.

By the winter of 1845-6 Andrew was more comfortably settled. The previous year had been encouraging and he now had a business partner. 'What a pleasant account you give of *Young Montreal*,' Jane writes. 'I congratulate you on finding around you friends so much to your liking, and one especially with whom you keep house on such easy and cosy and economical terms.' But, she wonders, writing as if she had been married for many years rather than eighteen months,

what is to be done if your old housekeeper loves you so well, and makes you so comfortable, and your friend Robertson & others cheat you so completely out of all feelings of loneliness that you become indifferent to the only blessing that can secure to a poor bachelor all that is kindly and comfortable in the notion of *Home*?... for assuredly there is nothing in this world that would add so much to your happiness, and the improvement of your character in every respect, as the possession of such a wife as I would desire for you – a *good, prudent, amiable* and clever woman – I say *clever* not because that is necessary to happiness, but because I know that even with the best of hearts & intentions a stupid and ignorant woman could never interest you... remember there is danger in delay, a bachelor by the law of his nature necessarily gets more selfish every year.

Jane then moves from the general to the particular. 'There is a nice family of Wedds, with whom our London sisters are well acquainted & much pleased, who would be none the worse for a Wedding among them.' Andrew, she admits, is 'awkwardly placed for such a thing', but since he is a speculative merchant and has confidence in the judgment of his sisters, might he not consider a speculation in the matrimonial field? 'Sure I am that trusting to such prudent & deeply interested parties, you would have a thousand times better chance than many a poor missionary who is obliged to send home an order to his Society for a wife.' Not surprisingly, however, Andrew turned down this idea of a mail-order wife.

Andrew's mercantile ventures were clearly very speculative, for in the autumn of 1847, as a result of 'business troubles', we find him back in London living with his sisters and ever accommodating brother-in-law, Matthew Lethem, at Manor Villas. When Andrew returned to North America in 1849, it was not to Canada but New York, and so long as he had the prospect of getting on comfortably there, Jane and Archibald saw no point in trying to persuade him to come to Russia. By 1852, however, Andrew was ready to accept

Archibald's invitation: the prospect of joining – and perhaps succeeding – his brother-in-law, by then fifty-five, in a well-established and flourishing business, must have seemed increasingly attractive. Thus began the first commercial, as opposed to matrimonial, union between a Muir and a Mirrielees.

Forty years later, writing to his son-in-law and advising him on his future business career, Andrew summed up his Russian apprenticeship in these terms:

When I arrived in Russia, being then about thirty-five years of age, I found myself for the first time in my life, subjected to a rigid discipline & obliged to conform to very strict business methods. I had previously conducted various businesses as my own master, and had a good general experience both in manufacturing & mercantile concerns. This experience was no doubt of value, but I attribute my subsequent success to the *five years* of strict discipline which prefaced my independent action in Russia.

He concludes his advice by saying that one must 'prepare by arduous effort to enter the great world of competition as a trained athlete. This is worth, not only months, but years of drudgery.' So Archibald Mirrielees had obviously been a hard taskmaster, making the same rigorous demands upon other people as he did upon himself. The young American with big ideas of his own, Joseph Ropes, had found him too dominating and was not prepared to knuckle under. Andrew Muir cannot have enjoyed the drudgery, either, but had little choice other than to endure it.

The brothers-in-law differed, of course, not only in age, but also in origins and temperament. In contrast to the wealthy family of Greenock merchants into which Andrew Muir had been born, Archibald Mirrielees had emerged from an obscure background in Aberdeen, made his way in the world entirely by his own efforts, and become, in the words of William Ropes senior, 'one of the most capable, industrious, methodical and persevering men I ever knew'. His whole temperament would have made him averse to engaging in the kind of commercial gambles that seem to have attracted his brother-in-law; while Andrew, for his part, freely admits that he was in need of Archibald's rigid discipline. On the other hand, the older man's meticulous approach might well in the long run have proved too narrow and cautious. It needed Andrew's 'sanguine disposition' and even more, his 'love of improvement', to expand the business of

Muir & Mirrielees in the years ahead. The commercial partnership, indeed, seems to have worked better than the matrimonial one, for Andrew's life and personality were not swamped by Archibald's benevolent despotism in the way that Jane's were.

In 1857, when Archibald Mirrielees left Russia, Andrew Muir was forty years old and effectively in control of the business, for the part played by William Mirrielees was negligible. He strikes one at this stage of his life as something of a lone wolf: used to fending for himself, independent in his beliefs and opinions, and preferring the company of his own thoughts or a serious book to being very sociable. His long, unsettled, wandering life had come to an end, he had acquired a sense of purpose, and his prospects were excellent; but he had still not acquired a wife. The fates of the charming Misses Wedd had been settled long ago. His sisters were determined to find a wife for their shy bachelor brother. Putting their heads together, they decided that they knew exactly the right person.

8

William and Alice

Dr Wardlaw's chapel in Glasgow was described earlier as the point of intersection in the lives of a large number of people associated with this story. In addition to Jane Muir and her sisters occupying a pew in the main body of the building, there was Margaret's earnest young suitor, Matthew Lethem, sitting not far away with two college friends, while upstairs, in the front row of the gallery, surrounded by children and stepchildren, sat Mrs Anne Fullarton.

At the time when their lives intersected, in the second half of the 1830's, they were all quite young, even Mrs Fullarton, although she had been twice widowed. Born in 1804 as Anne McLeod, she married Walter Bell at the age of seventeen and had two daughters: Alison (born 24 October 1822) and Ann Eliza (April 1824). In 1825 Walter Bell died suddenly, and after three difficult years his widow was glad to accept an offer of marriage from Archibald Fullarton, a widower with a son, four daughters, a good income, and a spacious rented house in Glasgow's Bath Street. Between 1829 and 1835 she gave birth to two more daughters and two sons. Then in 1835 she woke one morning to find her husband lying dead of heart failure beside her. His income died with him. Drastic economies had to be made, and the servant Flora, who was illiterate but could go out shopping with a list of groceries in her head and not forget an item, became the mainstay of the household. The stepdaughters had too high an opinion of themselves to become involved with household chores, while Ann Eliza was still too young and delicate, so it was Alison Bell who had to share the domestic responsibilities with her mother. Many an evening she spent in front of a huge pile of family mending. At an early age, however, she had learned a valuable lesson. Her young sister was inclined to be restless and troublesome, and Alison was told to be patient with her and not make her cry. 'I can picture myself sitting at a small table on which I had arranged my small toys and treasures – mostly shells and pebbles from the beach. Annie would come toddling in and with one sweep send them all flying. I just held my arms tight by my side, waited till she had gone out, picked them all up, and put them back on the table. Very soon she would come in and sweep everything away again. This sometimes happened three or more times. It taught me a good lesson in self-control.'

Mr and Mrs Fullarton must have been enthusiastic followers of Dr Ralph Wardlaw, for when their second son was born in 1835, they named him Ralph Wardlaw McLeod Fullarton. Mrs Fullarton remained a deeply religious person all her life, and after her husband's death continued to take her young family regularly to the Chapel. In the second half of the 1830's her Fullarton daughters were still quite young, craning over the edge of the gallery to catch a glimpse of the tall elegant Miss Muir as she made her way to her pew; but her Bell daughters were growing up fast, and with their masses of curly fair hair were themselves the objects of admiring attention. Matthew Lethem's two college friends were Durant Philip and his elder brother, William, and it was young Durant's eye that was attracted to pretty little Alison Bell up in the gallery.

The brothers' father, the Revd Dr John Philip (1775-1851), was already a celebrity. After fourteen years as a Congregational minister in Aberdeen, he had been invited by the London Missionary Society to take on the important new post of Superintendent of Missions for the Cape of Good Hope, and from 1819 onwards was based in South Africa, where his insistence on a fair deal for the native tribes provoked much hostility among the White settlers. The post of Superintendent involved him in lengthy tours of inspection, but on arrival in Cape Town he was also invited to become minister of the Congregational Church there, so it was fortunate that his efficient wife, formerly Jane Ross of Aberdeen, could relieve him of many administrative duties. Mission House in Cape Town became a social as well as an administrative centre, where missionaries of different nationalities were entertained on their way to and from their posts of duty. It was a cheerful place, for Dr Philip, with his portly figure and resonant voice, disliked all solemn displays of piety. Of his four sons, three became missionaries. They referred to their father as 'The Governor'.

William Enowy Philip – his second name has defied explanation – was the eldest son, born at Aberdeen on 31 July 1814. At Mill Hill, the public school in North London founded by the Congregational Church, he showed no interest at all in learning. He was then enrolled at Aberdeen University to study medicine, but within a few months ran away to sea and spent the next two years sailing all over the world. At the end of 1832 he announced that he was joining the South Sea Fishing Co., as prospects of promotion were good and he would meet a decent class of men. A family friend, Mrs Montague, did not share his optimism: 'William is a pleasing intelligent gentlemanly youth. I am sorry that he is going into such a desperate service.' In January 1833 he sailed away to the South Seas as a third mate. Mrs Montague's worst fears were realized. The first and second mates were coarse and drunken. Soon after they had entered the fishing grounds, the Captain fell dead of an apoplectic fit, and they had to make for Mauritius in search of a replacement. The first and second mates began drinking even more heavily, and as they approached the dangerous Straits of Magellan, the anxious crew came to William and begged the eighteen-year-old to take command. William vowed that if he brought the ship safely through the Straits, he would devote the rest of his life to the service of God by working as a missionary. He did so, and eventually made his way to Cape Town. He never told his parents about his hair-raising adventures. It was only some years later that he related them to his wife.

Dr Philip may have wished to test his son's resolve, for over a year passed before he allowed him to go to England to start studying for the ministry. During that time William helped his father, and (without his father's approval) acquired practical knowledge by working in a surveyor's office. At college in London, he studied with feverish energy to make up for lost time, rushing through most of English literature in addition to the regular syllabus, and making excursions into French and German. In August 1836 he wrote to his mother that the London Missionary Society Committee of Examination had approved of him unanimously. 'I am to go for about two months to survey until the Glasgow Session commences, and then to that place to study "Wardlaw". This was my father's wish. They are also to allow me about 12 months at the study of Medicine and Surgery. This was my wish; and I think their present disposition is that I should, after my studies are completed, return to Africa.' He was to be joined at Glasgow University by his clever young brother, Durant, who had just left school. 'We shall have to live very hard in Glasgow,' William adds, 'and any small donations from you will be very thankfully received by both of us.'

Another young Scot who enrolled at the University at the same time was David Livingstone (1813-73). Like William Philip, he had set his heart on becoming a missionary, and like him he was intending to study both Wardlaw and medicine.

When term began on 10 November 1836, William was twenty-two, and Durant nearly seventeen. At Dr Wardlaw's Chapel they sat with their college friend, Matthew Lethem, who introduced them to the Muir family. William Philip became a frequent visitor at 'Rosebank', where Jane remembered him as an attractive young man, full of enthusiasm for fine literature; they had eager discussions over new books and read their favourite poems aloud to each other.

At church every Sunday, while William was paying earnest attention to Wardlaw, Durant was busy studying the female members of the congregation. He noticed the pretty young girl in the gallery, who reached her fifteenth birthday on 24 October 1837, and was promoted to long frocks. Two years later, having left Glasgow, he wrote to her: 'In what direction do you take your walks now? Do you go to the Kelvin? I can never think of the Kelvin without remembering the time when I was a student at Glasgow – and the odd way in which I made acquaintance with you, and William's lectures on my folly and forwardness, the difficulty with which I invited him to come to tea with you. I don't remember, however, after his first visit that there was any more difficulty.'

Alison Bell was indeed exceedingly pretty, with dark greyish-blue eyes, a lovely complexion and golden hair that hung in large curls round her head. But her chief attraction, which remained to the end, lay in her expressive features and warm responsive smile, which artists and later, photographers, failed to capture. 'The foolish man told me to smile,' she would say after a visit to the photographer's, 'but how could I smile at nothing? It would only have been a grin.'

William Philip was bowled over. He, too, was extremely good-looking. In a portrait from the period he looks more like a Regency beau than a former third mate or future African missionary.

It was only a matter of weeks before William decided that he must 'know his fate'. Mrs Fullarton was very taken with this serious and intelligent young man, and could not imagine a worthier future for her daughter than to be a missionary's wife. But Alison was still far too young. William must wait a year and not give any hint of his feelings. So he immersed himself once more in his books. He was studying theology, but also taking courses in medicine and engineering. Shortly before Christmas 1838 he asked again and was accepted. Alison was still only just sixteen.

It was William who now decreed that henceforth Alison was to be known by the then more conventional name of Alice. There was nothing conventional, however, about his attitude to the education of women. Educating Alice became an urgent priority. He may have been worried by the thought of having to introduce this pretty young thing to his formidable parents, but he also wanted to ensure that Alice did not repeat his mistake and fail to appreciate the benefits of study. Reading lists were compiled, timetables drawn up. In his letters William is a mixture of lover, spiritual adviser and schoolmaster. Alice's intellectual accomplishments did not extend far beyond the ability to write a letter in good English. She was eager and quick to learn, but there were still household duties to perform. In the summer of 1839 Mrs Fullarton decided to rent the little Manse at Sannox on the Isle of Arran for four months. William spent a week on the island in June. From Glasgow he wrote afterwards: 'I hope you did not feel as I did the morning we parted. I gazed at you from the vessel as you ran along the road and wished myself again at your side. And for long after my eyes were fixed on you and followed you till they could dimly discern a little white speck, and lost you just about that beautiful angle of the road where we sat the first time we passed that way.' He urged her to work regularly every day from 10 to 2, concentrating on mathematics – first Euclid, then algebra – or if she preferred, English composition, 'and the four hours must be spent in *close application*, there must be no musing and no interruption'. But her mother still expected her to spend at least two hours a day giving lessons to her half-sisters. It was a strenuous curriculum and took no account of the difficulty of remaining indoors in Arran on a fine summer's day. When Alice mentions that she is writing at midnight, William is alarmed: 'You must rather take time off your studies, say a quarter of an hour a day, but do not for your health's sake and my sake take from your hours of rest.'

In August William succeeded in escaping from 'this pestilential prison' of Glasgow and again visited Arran, but there must have been a lovers' tiff, for afterwards he wrote: 'You cruel little *pest*, you must never treat me as you have done, never tell me again that you will think whether you love me or another.' So Alice was not entirely submissive to her ardent schoolmaster lover. Later that month William visited Paris in pursuit of his interest in homeopathic medicine. He was introduced to Lord Elgin, who sought his opinion on a paper he had written, but William did not follow up the acquaintance: he found the paper 'by no means original'. To Alice he wrote: 'You will exclaim: "Just like you, that is the way you treat all your friends!" But my Alice what should a democrat and thorough leveller of all souls do among lords and ladies, much more flatter them? My pride is too stern to permit me to flatter what I do not respect, his rank.'

William and Alice were married in Glasgow on 8 April 1840. By this time William had been ordained, and Alice had become a full member of the Congregational Church. On 17 August they set sail from Portsmouth for South Africa. William's brother, Durant, and Alice's sister, Ann Eliza, were there to see them off. Many years later, the latter recalled how she and Durant had 'stood on the beach together watching the ship sail & when it had disappeared he simply sat down on the beach & boo-hoo'd!!' The susceptible Durant, having ceded Alice to his elder brother with a good grace, now turned his attention to her younger sister.

When William and Alice were about to land at Cape Town, Alice put on a becoming bonnet and a gay shawl, as she had not met William's parents before. The effect, however, was unfortunate. One of William's cousins waiting at the quayside overheard Mrs Philip murmur: 'Not suited to be a missionary's wife'. Later she had to eat her words. In the next few years Alice was to display in full measure all the requisite qualities: a clever pair of hands, courage and resourcefulness, an equable temper and cheerfulness in the face of adversity.

William was too averse to town life, and too independent-minded, to wish to remain in Cape Town as his father's assistant, so Dr Philip appointed him to the Mission Station at Hankey, about three weeks' journey by oxwaggon from Cape Town. He advised them to settle first at Cambria, an outstation of Hankey. Soon after their arrival, smallpox broke out. William was in great demand as a doctor, and his large supply of homeopathic remedies proved very useful; for Alice, who acted as his assistant, this was the start of a lifelong commitment to homeopathic medicine. When asked in later years whether she had not been afraid of catching smallpox, she replied: 'No, I only minded if I had to put my finger on a spot when taking a pulse'!

Letters from South Africa to the Fullartons in Scotland took three or four months to arrive and were anxiously awaited. At the mention of the word 'Africa' the boys always pricked up their ears, while Flora listened to accounts of what Alice and William were doing 'with tears in her eyes'. Mrs Fullarton had taken her new son-in-law very much to her heart. 'My dear dear William,' she writes on 28 April 1841. 'How I long to know how you are, and what you are doing.' She grieves to think that he and Alice had not been able to see in the New Year in proper style – 'No Bun, No Cake, no anything' – and also confides that she is involved in 'a rather unpleasant correspondence with Durant about an engagement he wishes to form'.

In May 1841 William and Alice moved on to Hankey itself. One of their first visitors was David (by then Doctor) Livingstone, with whom William had attended medical lectures in Glasgow. Livingstone was on his way north, and when he set off again from Hankey, William and Alice accompanied him for part of the journey. In later years, Alice would dine out on the story of how Livingstone had told her on that occasion that he was sure she would make a good campaigner.

Alice's first child was born at Hankey on 28 October 1841, four days after her nineteenth birthday, and christened John Lethem Philip. Mrs Fullarton was not surprised by John, after William's father, but adds with more than a hint of disapproval, 'the other half of his name we were not quite prepared for'. Alice did not want William to be bothered by her 'first little pains', so she made him go and work at the end of the garden till sent for. Soon the 'little pains' became so intense that Minny, their devoted young Hottentot servant, was terrified. Native confinements were not like that. In a panic she rushed to fetch William, but all was going normally and soon a fine child was born.

Less than a week later, William received an urgent summons to a sick neighbour. His first duty, he felt, was to Alice and the baby. Alice overruled him, but could not help shedding a few tears once he had gone. She promised not to get up until after the ninth day. Soon after William's departure, Dr Philip arrived with a friend, and Alice heard his voice downstairs booming cheerfully: 'What, not up to see me yet?' Mrs Philip was likewise unperturbed by the makeshift arrangements for Alice's welfare. Not so, the anxious Mrs Fullarton. 'It will be through the mercy of God if your health has not been injured for life,' she declared indignantly.

William's visit was successful, the smallpox epidemic subsided, and he was able to devote his full attention to the future of the Mission. Recruitment was not the problem. 'There is never any lack of applicants for Church membership among the people, Religion being honourable and fashionable among them.' All their difficulties were economic in origin. Because of lack of water, the Mission land could not support more than about sixty families, and then only for four months in the year; at other times the labourers had to seek work far away. 'I have, since my arrival on the Missionary field,' William wrote to his mother, 'turned my attention to the agriculture and breeding of cattle amongst the People, deeming this the natural employment of a people in such a country and such a stage of civilization.' Durant thought that this was demeaning himself, but William had always been averse to any kind of artificial pose on the part of ministers of religion; and surely, he argued, 'the people will think more and not less of me if I show them how to improve their crops'.

Better agriculture was impossible without improved irrigation. Making use of his knowledge of surveying and engineering, he devised a bold plan: to drive a 260-yard tunnel through a nearby hillside and so divert the waters of the Gamtoos River onto the Mission lands. It was the first such irrigation scheme ever undertaken in South Africa.

William himself was not only surveyor and engineer, but also foreman, often working day and night in the tunnel. Alice ingeniously constructed candles out of mutton fat and cotton to be used by the workers. For most of the distance they had to hack their way through solid rock, using picks and hammers. It took them sixteen months, and 'what is the greatest wonder of all to the colonies,' William wrote, '*all* but a mere trifle of this work was accomplished by the Hottentots – a people who had never seen such a thing before, nor been engaged in any mining operation, and who had thus to accustom themselves to the forced position, the confinement, and the night's work, not to speak of the natural dread of being buried alive.' Perhaps they would have been more reluctant, had they not had such confidence in the man in charge.

The final blow was struck by William's most trusted workman from the tunnel on the far side of Hankey. Instead of scrambling through the hole, in his excitement he ran all the way back along the tunnel and round to the village. William describes what happened next:

About one or two o'clock in the morning I was startled out of a restless sleep, by a shot fired off at my bedroom window. I knew the signal and started up, while a voice shouted, 'The tunnel is through!' I looked out, and saw the messenger from the rock still running with a flaming brand towards the village and our house, and screaming as he ran. It is impossible to describe the state of the village a few moments after. In every direction was heard shouting, hallooing, yelling, screaming, while these serenades were constantly broken by shots fired off from the different houses. Lighted brands seemed as if they had got legs and were traversing the place in every direction; bands of children had, in the meantime, collected all the old iron pots and tin scuttles out of their houses, and were accompanying this novel concert with rough music and their shrill screams. I wisely went to bed again, thinking to snatch a little sleep before the morning, but in vain. The noises continued, or redoubled; our house was surrounded, and the kitchen filled, principally with women, who were all sobbing. One (our old washerwoman) burst into my bedroom and coming to my bedside caught hold of my hand – 'O! what a great work; and the Lord hath spared us to see it through.' She could not say any more, but went sobbing out of the room. All this enthusiasm was quite unexpected by me. I had no conception of the extent of feeling on the subject.

William derived particular satisfaction from the knowledge that his measurements had proved accurate and the two tunnels had met beautifully in the middle. 'The Governor' was highly delighted when the news reached Cape Town. 'The advantages of the work,' William concluded, 'are briefly that it is maintenance, food, and the gospel to at least as many thousands as there are hundreds on the place at present.'

In that same year, 1844, Durant Philip completed his studies and was ordained. He had been disappointed in his hopes of Ann Eliza, by this time Mrs John Smith, and was intending to enter the missionary field in India. On reaching Cape Town, however, he was advised on medical grounds to remain in South Africa, and in January 1845 began working as William's assistant at Hankey.

Towards the end of June Durant and his father left Hankey on a long tour of inspection. William's nephew, ten-year-old John Philip Fairbairn, had been sent to Hankey from Cape Town to recuperate after an illness. On the afternoon of 1 July William and Johnnie went down to have a look at the tunnel. Returning home, they had to cross the Klein River. It was a sunny day and William would normally have waded across, but the river was rather deep at that time and the boy might have caught a chill. They got into the leaky old boat that was moored permanently among the clinging weeds on the river bank.

A Mission labourer who spotted William's hat floating near the boat was the first to raise the alarm. Alice was among those who rushed down to the river, but there was nothing to be seen. When they finally recovered the bodies, William still had one arm clasped protectively round the boy's waist, as if, in failing to save the boy's life, he had scorned to save his own.

9

'Married & Went To Russia'

William Philip's life had been so varied, and his achievement so remarkable, that it is hard to realize that at the time of his death he was still only thirty. Had he lived, he might have become as celebrated as Livingstone. Durant took his place at Hankey, remaining there for the next twenty-one years, and became a Life Governor of Mill Hill School. William's death was a blow from which his mother never recovered. She died at Hankey in 1847 at the age of fifty-five; his father followed four years later, at the age of seventy-six. The Gamtoos Tunnel is now a National Monument.

News of the catastrophe took many weeks to reach Edinburgh, where Mrs Fullarton was then living. It came in a letter from her half-sister, Mary Jane Archibald, who was staying at Hankey. On Sunday 28 September Mrs Fullarton wrote to her daughter that she had not felt able to go up with the children to the house of the Lord from the overwhelming sorrow of her heart.

We got the sad, sad intelligence of our beloved William's death (oh how strange these words appear to me! My William – my William!) yesterday afternoon about 4 o'clock. From painful experience I especially am able to enter into all your feelings – and nature quickly prompts the wish, oh that I had been with my beloved in her affliction. But recollection of the past abundantly convinces me of the utter impotence of all human aid to heal the wounds that God has made. No! no hand but His can touch it. Mary Jane tells me that He has already been exceedingly gracious to you, in imparting to you a spirit of Christian meekness & resignation...

There are moments of agonizing, distress and anxiety and a continual sickening sorrow of the heart. These things must needs be borne by both you, and me, my beloved daughter. We should belie & disgrace our nature could we be found destitute of such feelings. Our tears become us, and our grief is just – he was well worthy of our love, for whom our tears so freely, and so sincerely flow...

Flora also sends her respectful regards & heartfelt sympathy – she was a great admirer of the dear departed.

On this letter Alice later wrote: 'Dear Mother's first letter after my terrible trial'. No doubt Alice did endure this trial in a spirit of Christian meekness and resignation, but one is also reminded of her in childhood, learning to keep her arms tight by her side while her little sister casually swept all her toys and treasures off the table.

Mrs Fullarton had further cause to be anxious, for Alice was expecting her third baby in December. A second son had been born in 1844 and named William Paterson Philip. His second name was a tribute to John Paterson: not the old friend of the Muir and Mirrielees families, but a young Scot from Aberdeen who had gone out to South Africa very soon after William and Alice to take up an appointment as schoolmaster at Port Elizabeth, and become a great friend of theirs. Alice acquired two lifelong enthusiasms in Africa: for homeopathy and for marmalade-making. From Port Elizabeth John Paterson wrote to William, asking him to remind Alice that the season for marmalade-making was approaching. He had long since finished his last pot. 'I took it to my bed with me under my pillow, and dreaming that there was more at Hankey, I thought it was of no use keeping mine, so I sat up in bed and finished it.'

On 12 December 1845 Walter Daniel Ralph Philip, who would later be identified with Muir & Mirrielees more closely than anyone, was safely delivered at Port Elizabeth, Alice having moved to the house of William's uncle for her confinement. Mrs Fullarton tried to persuade Alice to return to Scotland with her children at the earliest opportunity; if necessary, she would most cheerfully work for them with her own hands. But it was felt by Dr John Paterson in Edinburgh that the London Missionary Society would be more inclined to deal generously with Alice's case if she continued to make herself useful for a time on the Mission Station. Meanwhile, she received every possible assistance from the other John Paterson in Port Elizabeth. Eventually, he asked her to marry him and let him make a permanent home for her and the children. Alice replied that it was too soon after William's death for her to take such a decision. Had she accepted, she would have found herself married to a man destined to become, in the words of his biography, *One Titan At A Time*, 'a powerful personality not only in his profession but also in journalism, commerce, banking, municipal affairs and politics', and who, but for his untimely death in 1880, 'might well have forestalled Rhodes and become Prime Minister of the Cape Parliament'.

Alice finally reached London with her three small boys in June 1848. The kind Lethems invited them to make their home at Manor Villas before going on to Edinburgh.

Mother and daughter now found themselves in parallel situations: Alice a widow of twenty-five with three boys under seven, her mother a widow of forty-three with four teenage children. They decided to pool their resources. Money was very tight, but both were efficient organizers. From 1850-3, presumably for reasons of economy, they all lived in Europe, the town of Halle in east Germany being for some time their base. Alice had four beds in her room – her own and the three boys' – while Flora had a tiny room of her own. Soon they were baking almost all their own bread. Although she could not afford to buy music, Alice took up the piano with such characteristic absorption that her teacher asked if she was planning to start a school. She also devoted two hours a day to translating a little German book. As for Mrs Fullarton, she writes in January 1852 that helping her talented younger son Ralph to forward his education was her principal object and in this she was being zealously aided by his two sisters. 'If we can afford it, Ralph thinks that a year in Paris would be of great advantage.' Off to Paris they soon went, taking Flora, while Alice, equally enterprising and adaptable, placed her sons at a German boarding-school and went off to visit Munich.

Shortly before this, a family drama had occurred. Maggie Fullarton, the elder sister, was then twenty-two. There had always been a vague question-mark against her ability to cope with life. Now it turned out that she had formed an attachment to a young man. Mrs Fullarton had been asked to agree to an engagement, and had said no. Alice then intervened, pointing out to her mother that this was no ordinary attachment, but a matter of life and death.

It is this strong feeling which compels me to write and implore you to consider *well* the very great responsibility which you take upon yourself in deciding as you have done, for to my mind it appears *now* far greater than the responsibility of *consenting* which you feared so much. You feel strongly that M. is not of a constitution of mind or body to struggle with poverty. Are you sure that she will not sink under the efforts to crush a deep rooted affection? A high sense of duty to a beloved parent, will help to sustain her, but a severe struggle she will and must have.

And surely it is a serious matter to separate those whom the Lord hath so evidently joined together, for by such, I understand those, who being brought together in the providence of God, have discovered such mutual sympathies, and affinities, that a union of heart and mind is the *necessary* consequence, – aye, so necessary, and so impossible to prevent as the union of two affinitive gases, when brought into contact with each other – and this to my mind is the band with which the Lord binds, and which man dare not violently tear asunder, and compared to which the mere ceremony at the altar is as nothing.

M.'s peculiar character of mind and body does not arise from any constitutional weakness, but from a languor and listlessness of disposition... all that she requires is the influence of a strong passion to rouse her to activity. I would most certainly *in the circumstances*, recommend an engagement, as a means to a very high end i.e. the life and activity of M.'s heart and mind.

This eloquent appeal fell on deaf ears. Maggie was thwarted, as Durant Philip had been, and 'a high sense of duty to a beloved parent' ruled her life for the next forty years. The difference between anxious mother and sanguine daughter was not, however, one of temperament alone. Alice's talk of the union of affinitive gases, of marriages made in heaven, 'compared to which the mere ceremony at the altar is as nothing', would probably have seemed fanciful, even sacrilegious, to her mother. Her own marriages, one suspects, had been grounded on more practical considerations, and she would have shared Jane Mirrielees' view that esteem is the best foundation for love. Perhaps what the letter reveals most of all is how deeply Alice had been in love with William Philip.

Many years later, Alice compiled a tantalizingly brief synopsis of events in her life between 1853 and 1861. In October 1853 her three sons began attending a boarding-school at Blackheath for the sons of missionaries (still in existence as Eltham College). She herself lived in Scotland until 1856. On 12 January 1857 she wrote to her mother from Manor Villas that she had had 'a most busy day mending and packing. The poor boys went back to school this evening and Mrs Lethem kindly invited me to return here, so that I gave up my lodging today.' She had been asked to take four young ladies to Paris for several months. 'They are to pay their own expenses for *everything*. I am requested to teach them German & Music, for which I am to have £15 from each – not much certainly, but as much as they can afford and it will *help* to paying expenses.' Few possibilities were open to the genteel widow or spinster who needed to be self-supporting and did not want to lose caste – ladies did not work, only women did – and it sounds as if Alice had been supporting herself precariously for some time in this way by giving lessons and by chaperoning.

Unlike the courtship of Jane Muir by Archibald Mirrielees, described so methodically and with such a careful account of her own reactions by Jane herself, the relations between Andrew Muir and Alice Philip before their marriage are undocumented. Alice's synopsis is quite uninformative, until we come to its final laconic entry: '1861, April 16th. Married & went to Russia.'

Andrew Muir must have known William Philip in the late 1830's, when William was a frequent visitor at 'Rosebank' and read poems aloud with Jane, but it is unlikely that he did more than make Alice's acquaintance before she left for Africa. When in London, they would both have stayed with the Lethems, and even if their paths did not often cross in the 1850's, Andrew's solicitous sisters would have urged him to pay his attentions to the charming Mrs Philip – that eligible Scottish widow who was struggling so gallantly to make ends meet, and who was so well suited to him in age and tastes.

According to Maida Mirrielees, 'Uncle Andrew, who was a shy man, though he admired Mrs Philip, returned to Russia in 1859 without proposing to her, but happily was stimulated by the exhortations of his sisters in time to write her an offer which prevented her returning to the Cape of Good Hope to live with her eldest son.' He had probably proposed earlier, however, for in August 1858 Jane wrote: 'How well I can enter into your feelings of loneliness dear Andrew, it was anticipating that which made me so anxious about your providing against it, but it was God's Will it should be so for a time at least & He can turn it to your good account. Still there is room to *hope*, & try again.'

If that sounds like a qualified refusal on Alice's part, her hesitation would be understandable. Marriage to Andrew Muir meant going to Russia, and until her three boys were settled, that was out of the question. South Africa, where other members of the Philip family were prospering, seemed to offer the boys the most promising future. Jack, her eldest son, left for Cape Town in December 1858, and Willie in November 1860. It seems possible that about this time Alice had to decide between an uncertain future near her sons in South Africa, and a long-standing offer of marriage and security in Russia from Andrew Muir. What may have tipped the balance was the future of Alice's youngest (and most talented?) son, Walter – supposing that Andrew had already declared his willingness to take on Walter as his assistant at Muir & Mirrielees.

So Andrew Muir and Alice Philip were married on 16 April 1861 from the Lethems' home (by this time the more spacious, nostalgically named, 'Clyde Villa'), just as Archibald Mirrielees and Jane Muir had been seventeen years earlier. Andrew was forty-two and Alice thirty-eight.

This was not a marriage that had been made in heaven, but in the Lethems' drawing-room by Andrew's solicitous sisters. Practical economic considerations had played an obvious part in Alice's decision. Yet it worked, and worked remarkably well. There was not the imbalance of the marriage between Jane and Archibald. Here it was the wife, Alice, who had been married before, who had surmounted great sorrow, and who had already brought up children of her own. Unlike Jane, whose life before marriage had been sheltered and privileged, Alice had learned from childhood to be resourceful and independent; after Africa, Russia would hold no problems for her, and there was never any risk that she would sink into a state of apathy or resignation, as did poor Jane. All this made for a much greater sense of equality between the partners. Nor did Andrew have Archibald's inflexible religious convictions, which so inhibited the natural vivacity of his wife.

In character and temperament they were also well suited. They were both quiet people, with a dry sense of humour. Alice's sister, describing one of her own daughters, says: 'She is decidedly clever and in many respects reminds us of you... she is unlike you however in one respect – she is an inveterate *talker!*' Both were self-contained, with the capacity to become totally absorbed in anything that captured their interest – often, according to Maida Mirrielees, to the point of absent-mindedness. Andrew in particular, like his uncle before him who was always losing his umbrella, made many strange mistakes from this cause. 'He was once,' Maida writes, 'found gazing in mild amazement at a samovar from which he thought he had just poured out boiling water into a teapot. Clouds of steam were issuing from the central funnel in which the glowing charcoal was contained, for he had poured the contents of the teapot down it instead of into cups.'

On 17 April 1873 Andrew wrote to 'Dearest Alice' from a hotel in Florence. 'About eleven on Monday night,' he tells her,

just as I was dozing off, an alarming knock was heard at my bedroom door, and on enquiring the cause a telegram was handed to me which I opened with some trepidation fearing bad news, but I was soon relieved by its amusing contents. I should have been quite oblivious of the anniversary [their twelfth wedding anniversary on 16 April], and am therefore very glad that you telegraphed. My ineptitude for recollecting dates seems incurable, and is no doubt the result of my long, unsettled and wandering bachelor life. I felt almost unusually quiet all day yesterday and my thoughts took rather a serious turn. In fact the retrospect of my past life always pains me, and although I feel strongly that 'goodness & mercy have followed me all the days of my life', I am more disposed to reproach myself with my unworthiness of these gifts than to look forward confidently to their continuance in some form or other. Assuredly I look on our marriage day as the one that is by far the brightest in the calendar, and I cannot even venture to estimate the extent of the blessings that have followed on it. But I need not enlarge on the subject as all that is most worth saying is beyond the power of expression, at least by the pen.

Alice valued this letter, one of very few that she kept; in a family that hoarded letters, she was the exception. But it is doubtful whether she could have responded to it in quite the same terms, for Alice could never forget William Philip. In February 1886, when she was sixty-three, she and her daughter Molly attended a party at which a young actor, Norman Forbes Robertson, was introduced to her, who, in Molly's words,

devoted himself entirely to us and won Mother's heart wholly – he sat and talked to her for ever so long and Mother's eye brightened and she smiled and looked younger than I have seen for many a day. She told me softly last night when we were sitting alone by the fire in the drawing-room that he had reminded her so much of Mr Philip and then she went on and talked about her heart's treasure and told me all about him and described him with a far away look in her eyes as though she saw him before her till we could not see each other clearly.

After the poetry of marriage to William Philip, Alice's marriage to Andrew Muir was prose: very good prose, as we shall see, but prose all the same.

10

Turning the Corner

Once settled in St Petersburg, Andrew and Alice Muir lost no time in raising a family. With the calm resourcefulness that was characteristic of all her behaviour, Alice gave birth to five healthy children, including twins, in less than five years, the last child being born in her forty-fifth year. This remarkable feat of childbearing was achieved without any adverse effects on the health or good spirits of the mother.

The first child, born on 4 October 1862, was christened Margaret Alice, but always known as Meta. Then came the twins, Martin and Eva, born at the Muirs' Peterhof datcha on 14 July 1864. Mary Hilda, known in adult life as Molly, arrived on 15 December 1865, and last of all, on 28 May 1867, came Kenneth. Why Kenneth, Mrs Fullarton demanded indignantly: if the good old Scottish custom of calling the second son after his maternal grandfather was not to be adhered to, why could they not have chosen one of the beautiful family names, such as Hugh, Donald or Dougall? But Andrew and Alice, far from treating the subject with due seriousness, only laughed on receiving her letter. Mrs Fullarton would have been even more scandalized, had she known of the arbitrary way in which Kenneth was chosen. Meta remembered sitting on the ottoman by her mother's bedside. Her father was leaning over from the other side, discussing the new baby's name with Mamma. They could not make up their minds, so Papa said, 'Meta shall decide,' and ran through a string of names. 'I caught at Kenneth as a pretty name, and Kenneth it was.'

In the summer of 1867, when she was not yet five, Meta had an intriguing encounter.

Her father, who had been visiting London and Paris on business, found himself on the return journey sharing a railway compartment from Königsberg to St Petersburg (a run of 28½ hours) with two Oxford men about to start a tour of Russia: Henry Liddon, a well-known preacher and theologian, and Charles Dodgson, a mathematician. The latter noted in his diary that their companion, 'an Englishman, who had lived in Petersburg for 15 years', proved most pleasant and helpful, giving them a great many hints about what to see in Petersburg, and how to pronounce the language. Since Dodgson had brought his travelling chess-set with him, on the second day 'he & I had 3 games, which it is perhaps as well that I did not record, as they all ended in my defeat'. Liddon, though he identifies Andrew correctly as a Scottish merchant, was not, however, so enthusiastic, complaining that their new friend, who had 'great sympathy with Rationalism', woke them early 'and insisted upon talking about Jowett and matters of that kind. I don't doubt that he was a Free Kirk man.'

A few days later, Andrew invited the two of them to spend a day at Peterhof, and then dine with him at his datcha; his partner, William Mirrielees, would act as their escort. Accordingly, as Dodgson recorded, 'Mr Merrilies' called for them next morning and took them by steamer down the Gulf of Finland to Peterhof, where Mr Muir's carriage was waiting, and with its assistance they went all over the grounds of the two palaces. On their way for lunch, they looked in briefly at the house and 'saw Mrs Muir & some charming little children', and returned about 5, when they met Mr Muir. 'Other friends came in for dinner, & we finally returned to Petersburg with the indefatigable Mr Merrilies, who crowned the many services he had done us during the day by procuring a droshky & making the indispensable bargain with the driver, a feat we might well have despaired of by ourselves, in the dark, hustled about in a mob of drivers and a perfect Babel of uncouth noises.'

Next morning Andrew received the following note from the Hotel de Russie:

Dear Mr Muir,

Will you allow me, as a sort of suggestion, rather than expression of my sense of the kindness of Mrs Muir and yourself in so hospitably receiving two strangers, to present your dear little Meta with this book? It is one that has proved tolerably popular with children, as it was only published Xmas year, and is in its 9th thousand.

With repeated thanks,

I remain,

Very truly yours,

Charles L. Dodgson

P.S. Would you kindly give the enclosed to your coachman. We omitted it in the hurry of our departure.

Charles L. Dodgson is better known, of course, as Lewis Carroll, and the book that was proving no more than tolerably popular with children was *Alice's Adventures in Wonderland*, published in 1865.

Dodgson refused to acknowledge that he was the author of any books not published under his own name, and is careful not to do so on this occasion; but surely the Muirs must have seen through his little pretence? After much handling by several generations, the Muir family copy of *Alice* finally fell to pieces.

From Petersburg the two travellers moved on to Moscow (where Liddon preached at the English Chapel and was pleased to find the Chaplain, Mr Penny, 'a very good Churchman') and thence to Nizhni Novgorod. Returning to Moscow, they set off on an expedition to the 'New Jerusalem' monastery, and acting on Mr Muir's suggestion, applied at a cottage for bread and milk as a pretext for seeing the interior and the peasants' mode of life. Dodgson was favourably impressed and tried his hand at two sketches, but had to admit that though 'it would have been a capital scene for photography', it was rather beyond his powers of drawing.

In St Petersburg again, the first call he made was on Mr Muir at No.61 Galernaya. The droshky-driver asked for 40 copecks, but eventually they settled for 30, which Dodgson quietly handed over on arrival. The driver, however, rejected them with scorn and indignation, and again demanded 40, whereupon Dodgson held out his hand for the 30, returned them to his purse, and counted out 25 instead.

In doing this I felt something like a man pulling the string of a shower-bath – & the effect was like it – his fury boiled over directly, & quite eclipsed all the former row.

I told him in very bad Russian that I had offered 30 once, but wouldn't again: but this, oddly enough, did not pacify him. Mr Muir's servant told him the same thing at length & finally Mr Muir himself came out & gave him the substance of it sharply & shortly – but he failed to see it in a proper light. Some people are very hard to please.

Sadly, this episode with the driver is all that Dodgson records of his visit.

On the ground floor of No.61 Galernaya there were business offices. The Muirs' apartment consisted of the two spacious floors above. The children and their parents lived on the first floor, while upstairs were the 'young men's' rooms (the young men being Walter Philip and later, Archy and Fred Mirrielees), the kitchen and servants' quarters. Most of the children's time was spent in the nurseries or the sunny dining-room at the back of the house, which overlooked a rather dull yard containing the coach-house and a huge stack of logs.

The Petersburg seasons were unequally divided between a long winter and a brief summer. Meta recalled that when the first snowfalls began, 'against the glistening snow on the coach-house roof the sky looked dark grey and the snowflakes came on and on as if they would never stop'. But soon the ground froze hard, bright windless days arrived, and the snow underfoot became dry and powdery. They were all wrapped in layer upon layer of warm clothes and taken out for walks looking like little Eskimos; if they fell over, they could do nothing but wave their arms about helplessly like beetles until they were righted. Their favourite walk was along the English Quay. For several months the river was frozen solid, and a rectangular area was railed off with pine boughs to form the English skating-ground. Sometimes Papa came home to lunch and then the horses, which had been driven from the office at top speed, had to be cooled off by driving them slowly round a few times by the English Quay and back again. The arrival of the sledge was hailed with delight, for the good-natured coachman always stopped and took them in two by two for the drive round.

Christmas was a glorious time. Meta could not understand for many years how there could be *two* Christmasses, twelve days apart, but it spread out the festival very pleasantly. The English Christmas was heralded by the arrival of cards from England and Scotland. With their robins and holly, plum puddings and sweets, and churches with pointed towers that looked quite unlike Russian churches, these cards were a source of great interest, building up a picture in their minds of the different far-away country to which they all really belonged. Then there was Christmas service at the nearby English Church. They liked going there because it was such a change from the bald service at the Chapel, which they usually attended. The rumble of the responses made them feel puzzled and rather awed. It was an incomprehensible noise, a holy noise. There was also the thrill of seeing Mr Alfred Cattley, whom they knew, wearing a white surplice.

For the Russian Christmas the first mile of the Nevsky Prospect was lined with tall Christmas trees. The toy shops of the huge bazaar, the *Gostinnyi dvor*, were full of enchanting things, and as a special treat Meta was taken there by Mamma and consulted as to what toys the other children would like. At home their Christmas trees seemed to touch the ceiling. Mamma had all sorts of clever notions for decorating them and was helped on the day by the young men. For weeks she had been busy at her sewing-machine dressing dolls for the girls. In Meta's mind 'the story of the birth of Christ was deliciously mixed up with the resinous smell of pine trees, bright lights, sweets and exciting new toys'.

After the long winter came a period when the ice began to break, the wind was cold and raw from melting snow, and the pavements were very slushy. This was not a good time of year and they were kept much indoors. But mild days followed and walks again on the Embankment. There were new things to notice on the river now, boats and barges of all sorts and little excursion steamers. Every so often there were gaps in the granite wall with steps leading down to the gaily-coloured barges moored at the side, which served as stations for the steamers.

Then one day, after Mamma and Nurse had been extremely busy, they all walked out of the house carrying small bags and baskets, and actually went down to one of these stations and sailed off in a little paddle steamer. They passed the shipyards with their clanging noises and floated on over the silvery water, the river widening and widening until there was only a low fringe of trees on either side. This was the Gulf of Finland. At the Peterhof pier they got out and there was the calash waiting, with their own coachman smiling down at them. How had he got there? It was the same mystery every year. Then things began to happen, and they laughed with delight at the thudding of the horses' hoofs over the wooden pier, followed by a different noise when land was reached. They drove along the high road that ran westwards, separated from the Gulf by a strip of woodland. After a time they turned left and the horses dragged the carriage laboriously up a steep sandy hill. At the top they turned right, passing several datchas set along the crest of the hill, and then pulled up at their own. It was a long low wooden house. As they recognized all the landmarks, they had been getting more and more excited, and now they jumped down and rushed round the garden shouting. For the next two or three months all their woollen clothes were put away and they lived in cottons and muslins. When summer came it was real summer, they were in the country, and the long winter months in St Petersburg were quite forgotten.

In the summer of 1868, however, this familiar pattern was interrupted.

The previous winter had been an anxious time for Mamma. Meta had had rather a serious illness which meant six weeks in bed and a long convalescence. No sooner had she recovered than Eva began to peak and pine. There seemed nothing definite wrong with her, she was just fading away. In desperation Mamma tackled the doctor.

'Is there *nothing* we can do for this child?' she asked.

'Well my dear,' he replied, humming and hawing, 'what she really needs is sunshine and fresh air. If it were possible to change the seasons round, that might do the trick.' Then he sat back comfortably and took a pinch of snuff.

'We can't change the seasons round,' Mamma replied earnestly, 'but we can go to *meet* them.'

'If you could manage to do that, my dear, that would be capital.'

Mamma had what she wanted: the doctor's orders to take the family abroad.

Papa was not at all pleased by the news. His business hung heavily on his shoulders at that time, but after reflection, he said:

'Well, if it must be, let it be at once. The Easter holiday comes next week. That will give us five or six days. If you can be ready to start in three days from now, I can manage it.'

Mamma loved telling the story of that journey and all the preparations it entailed: the washing to be hastily rough dried and packed, the children's summer things wrested from the depths of cupboards and presses, exactly the right amount of linen and silver left out for Papa and the young men, careful lists to be made, elaborate orders given to the servants, and food prepared for the journey. But by the third day all was ready. Nurse and the under-nurse, fat Anna, were to go with them, but not baby Kenneth's enormous Russian nannie, who bade them goodbye at the station with tears streaming down her face. So they began the three days' journey across Europe. Meta, the eldest of the five children, was only five-and-a-half, Kenneth a very heavy baby in arms still being breast-fed, while Eva, ailing and plaintive, wanted her mother's knee all the time. But as David Livingstone had detected many years before, Alice with her calm temperament was a good campaigner.

Meta was very disappointed by her first impression of England. It was not at all like what the Christmas cards and 'Little Folks' had led her to expect. London after St Petersburg was like looking at an uncoloured picture after a coloured one.

*   *   *

Having deposited his family safely with the Lethems at 'Clyde Villa', Andrew hurried back to St Petersburg. It was the first time that he had been separated from his wife and children, and the experience did not agree with him. In his letter to Alice of May 17/29 he writes of 'suffering from depression of spirits arising from being out of sorts through biliousness or indigestion'. Alice had been moving about, taking her party up to Falkirk to stay with her sister and then on to the Isle of Arran, and had not been a very diligent correspondent. 'I had been fluctuating between anxiety and vexation,' Andrew writes, 'sometimes thinking that either you or some of the children must be ill, sometimes adopting the other alternative and setting down your silence to neglect. My own letters are to you comparatively unimportant, as you are always surrounded with interesting associations and are much less dependent than I am on our correspondence.' Did his depression arise from the thought that Arran was bound to be associated in Alice's mind with memories of her first husband?

Andrew interrupted his letter to take half an hour's walk on the quay. 'After a day of thunder showers,' he resumes, 'it is a bright calm evening and at half past ten quite light with the half moon shining softly on the Admiralty buildings. The lights in the water are beautiful, and the river looks quite picturesque being full of shipping. I am writing in the drawing room at the oval table which is moved up to the centre window, and the middle of the room is fully occupied by a large and handsome billiard table which I have hired for four months.' He himself played frequently after dinner, finding it a very good thing for health and amusement. 'The only plague is I play so badly that I feel a constant dissatisfaction with my performances.'

Throughout the 1860's Andrew Muir must have been an extremely busy man. After years of having only himself to consider, he now had a large family and an expanding business on his hands, yet he still found time to be active on behalf of the Bible Society. His main contribution was to supervise the re-translation of the Old Testament into modern Russian. In 1870 the Society invited him to become an Honorary Life Governor: an honour that Archibald Mirrielees had accepted in 1857 on leaving Russia. But whereas Archibald's work for the Society had required courage and diplomacy, and been undertaken in a spirit of missionary zeal, by the 1860's the situation had eased, and Andrew's interest in the Old Testament project seems more that of the scholar than the zealot. He declined the Society's invitation, explaining that 'men in this position are invested with a representative character, and I do not feel myself qualified to appear in that character. There are other more private reasons, which have decided me.'

These 'private reasons' are intriguing. Andrew had never shared the same narrow religious outlook as his sisters or brother-in-law. He and

Jane had exchanged views on the subject when the latter was anxious about her sons' religious welfare in Russia. She fully agreed with him that religion involved 'a high sense of moral obligation', but surely, she argued, one must also accept 'what ever else in the way of rites or ceremonies, or of *devotion*,' that could fairly be deduced from Christ's teaching. 'Variety of opinions there will be – but if He is our guide, we shall surely find more than mere morality in His teaching.'

But Andrew's unorthodoxy may well have gone further than putting the emphasis on 'mere morality'. His views had obviously been too unorthodox for Henry Liddon. Maida Mirrielees recalled that it was 'Uncle Andrew, a great reader of philosophy,' who in the early 1870's gave her a copy of Herbert Spencer's *First Principles*, published in 1862. It was Spencer who in 1852 coined that unfortunate term, 'survival of the fittest', and in the 1860's he was already building up an immense reputation in Britain and America. His optimistic view of evolutionary progress had a special appeal for the successful businessman or entrepreneur, who was enabled to see himself as a key figure in the process of social evolution. Andrew Carnegie, prototype of the self-made American, repeatedly described Spencer as the man to whom he owed most. One can easily imagine Andrew Muir, as the tide of success began to turn his way around 1870, seeing himself in this same evolutionary role, especially bearing in mind his description of the successful businessman as one who must 'prepare by arduous effort to enter the great world of competition as a trained athlete'. But Spencer was in no sense religious, relishing the idea of setting off for a Sunday morning walk in the opposite direction to the respectable Victorian church-goers, and even if Andrew did not accept all his views, it would have been incongruous, to say the least, for an enthusiastic reader of Spencer to accept the position of 'Honorary Life Governor of the British & Foreign Bible Society'.

Alice, too, seems relaxed in her attitude to religion, and can have had no qualms, as Archibald Mirrielees would have done, about attending Christmas service at the English Church. The Muirs' friends among the British and American community were not limited to that 'select circle' of Christian, i.e. non-conformist, friends, in which Jane and Archibald had moved; there were no sewing parties, religious meetings in the house, or offers of hospitality to passing missionaries.

Among Russians, however, they do not appear to have made many friends. When he was trying to find someone to undertake the transference of some Russian references for the Bible Society, Andrew

had to admit that his own circle of Russian acquaintance was so
limited that he could not suggest anyone from personal knowledge. It
was the Mirrielees family who seem to have become more fully
integrated into Russian life. William Mirrielees in particular, whose
bargaining with the cabby so impressed Charles Dodgson, appears to
have been bi-lingual, and it was to him that both his father and Andrew
Muir turned when an expert opinion was needed for the Bible Society
on the quality of a translation into Russian. He responded with
enthusiasm and consulted the leading Russian authorities, but several
months later the Society's proofs were liable to be still lying in his
desk drawer. It was the same with all his undertakings. Maida recalled
how on William's frequent visits to London in the mid-1860's, while
she sat enthralled as he recited his own poems or played his own
compositions on the piano, her parents were shaking their heads sadly
over his inability to stick to business. Today he might have come into
his own, putting his obvious social skills at the disposal of the firm and
'winning friends'; but not by any stretch of the imagination could
Henry Liddon and Charles Dodgson be thought of as useful business
contacts. Then in 1867 William married Pauline King. Pauline's family
struck Maida as far more worldly and fashionable than their usual
friends; they may also have been very wealthy, as William never seems
to have worked again.

William's withdrawal from the business life to which he was so
unsuited cannot have been a great loss to Andrew Muir, especially in
view of the young men coming along to take his place: Walter Philip
the heir apparent, and Archy and Fred Mirrielees. With the memory of
how he had been trained and disciplined by Archibald Mirrielees still
fresh in his mind, Andrew would probably not have given Archibald's
sons an easy ride, even had he not been warned of Archy's tendency to
procrastinate. The latter, as we have seen, found him a hard taskmaster.
In September 1868 he wrote to Maida that he had been down for a few
days with his 'old enemy' – he was prone to colds and chills – and
could not go to the warehouse for fear of catching fresh cold; when he
did return, he was a good deal behind hand with his work and resumed
long hours at once. In the following June he had what he took to be a
slight strain in his leg; it seemed to ease and he tried putting on a boot,
but paid dearly for it next day, when his ankle became swollen.

I saw it was more serious than at first thought, yet I went to the warehouse as
usual not wishing to *shirk* work when Uncle A. thought there was no

occasion; shortly after, the aforesaid personage left for Moscow and I felt more obliged than before to go as he was away and we were otherwise short of hands & very busy. Every evening I came home with my foot hot & uncomfortable & every morning I went with the resolution not to move a step from my stool in the office; but this was impossible to carry out and every day found me hopping about as best I could, like a stork, on one leg. At last I determined to lie up altogether... It is not very lively, however, for the whole household moved on Monday down to Peterhof, and I am alone most of the day in this large house... As yet I have been fully supplied with very *charming* work from the office to amuse me but there is not much more I can do, and now I think the best thing is to go down to Peterhof till my leg is all right again. This is my plan but I do not know how it may suit the authorities who seem to think that if I am well enough to go down to Peterhof I certainly should be in a state to go & work at the warehouse.

Such letters succeeded, as they seem calculated to do, in arousing young Maida's sympathies, and her replies apparently contained many mischievous allusions and inveighings against 'Andrew'. One day Archy was put on the spot when his uncle asked what kind of letters Maida wrote, and suggested that he might be allowed to read one sometimes. Archy told Maida that when she felt in a particularly good humour, she must write him a very clever and proper letter without any unfortunate allusions.

While I am on this subject I wish to say, that sometimes you have really spoken as if you imagined Uncle – well, to say the least of it, not a very kind Uncle or agreeable man in general, in fact a kind of *bear*. Now though sometimes he has a gruffness of *manner* that would certainly do honour to the king of bears, usually he is very agreeable and even affable in manner; and always I am sure perfectly kind in heart. I am sorry if anything I have ever said has given the opposite opinion to any one; and I feel, dear, that your spicy remarks are thrust against an imaginary being quite different from what you would find in Uncle A., if you knew him well.

The warehouse where Archy worked had been referred to by Jane in May 1867, when she apologized for not mentioning 'what Mr M particularly tried to impress upon me, that I must tell you how very much he & all of us had admired the drawing of the front of your new warehouse. What a vast improvement it promises to be to you & the young men.' Here, too, was the office where all the paper work was done, while in addition the firm had three booths (*lavki*) in the *Gostinnyi dvor*.

This characteristic institution was to be found occupying a central position in every sizeable Russian city. Kohl writes of the agreeable Russian custom of offering for sale within the same building almost everything, other than provisions, that could be bought.

They are mostly large buildings, consisting of a ground floor and an upper floor. The upper floor is generally reserved for wholesale dealings; the ground floor consists of a multitude of booths or shops in which the various descriptions of merchandise are sold by retail. The dwellings of the merchants are away from these markets; and when the business hours are at an end, each merchant locks up his own stall, and commits the whole building for the night to the guardianship of watchmen and dogs.

In St Petersburg the *Gostinnyi dvor* occupied a huge central site with a long frontage on the Nevsky Prospect. Kohl, writing in the 1830's, estimated that the number of merchants and dealers assembled in the *Gostinnyi dvor* and its dependent buildings was probably not much less than 10,000. For a stranger desiring to study the character of the people it was 'one of the most amusing and instructive lounges'. The typical merchant was a flaxen-haired, brown-bearded, shrewd fellow in a blue caftan and blue cloth cap. You seldom saw him engaged in writing or calculations.

If not occupied by a customer, or busy in his endeavours to attract one, you will mostly find him romping, playing or jesting with his brother traders. In fine weather, draughts is their favourite game; and for greater convenience, the chequered field is often painted on the tables or benches that stand before their booths. They eagerly thrust their heads together, examine the position of the pieces with the air of connoisseurs, bet on one player or the other, and seem completely absorbed in the game, until a purchaser makes his appearance, when the group is broken up in a moment, and each endeavours, with an infinity of bowings and assurances, to gain for his own shop the honour of the stranger's custom. In winter, they often warm themselves in the roomy passages of the bazaar, with a game at football, or crowd together round the steaming *samovar*, and sip down cans full of hot tea.

When Alice took Meta to the *Gostinnyi dvor* in search of Christmas presents for the younger children, they would have visited the ground floor, whereas the Muir & Mirrielees booths were on the upper floor reserved for wholesale dealings. Business there must have been conducted on a more formal basis: it is hard to imagine Andrew Muir romping, playing or jesting with his brother traders. These booths are likely to have served as showrooms where Muir & Mirrielees, Import Merchants, displayed their wares, of which sewing cottons, laces and related goods probably still formed the major part.

So far as the future of M & M's is concerned, the most interesting development of the 'Andrew Muir' years (1857-74) is that during this period the firm began trading in Moscow. Moscow had played second fiddle to St Petersburg ever since the time of Peter the Great, but its industries were expanding rapidly and as a distribution centre it was far superior. Andrew Muir is recorded as a merchant of the First Guild in Moscow in 1867, and a 'Trustee of the Commercial Court' from 23 May of that year. Walter Philip seems to have been given special responsibility for the firm's new Moscow branch: Andrew may have reckoned that Walter, then twenty-one, needed experience in acting independently. The spring of 1867 was also the time when Andrew summoned Archy Mirrielees to St Petersburg so urgently, suggesting that Archy was to take over some of Walter's work. If this supposition about Walter is correct, more than half a century elapsed between his first and last business contacts with Moscow.

One reason why Andrew Muir needed to have reliable people working for him was that he himself spent so much time travelling, visiting all the major European cities in search of suitable goods to import into Russia. It must have been on such a visit that he did not meet Maida's great schoolfriend, Emily Jowitt. Archy had met her for the first time in England early in 1870, and been so impressed by her appearance that his natural reserve was turned to 'absolute muleness'. That summer he wrote to Maida:

By the bye what a curious circumstance it was – our venerated Uncle and Emily Jowitt being at exactly the same time inmates of the Cavour Hotel and as Mamma suggests with her usual romantic freedom of thought perhaps sitting at the table d'hote cheek and jowl (would it have been my cheek!) without knowing or thinking twice of one another. If there was a thought on each side on their meeting we may put them down safely thus. Miss J. 'Funny old customer, rather crusty.' U.A. 'Spritely [!] young filly, not bad, ho! ho!'

This more cheerful vision of Uncle Andrew coincides with the period when he seems to have turned the corner at last in his business affairs. It was not only that he found himself able to delegate more and more responsibility to younger members of the family, especially Walter, but that M & M's itself had become established and highly profitable. In 1868, according to Meta, his business still 'hung heavily on his shoulders', he was reluctant to absent himself from St Petersburg for a day longer than was necessary, and Archy was feeling grossly overworked; whereas in the spring of 1870 there was a long family trip to Venice, and Archy was granted his first home leave for three years. The harassed businessman, uncertain of success or failure, is beginning to relax. A winter journey through Italy in 1871-2 proved rather laborious, so Andrew decided that they should spend the following winter in one place, and on 1 October 1872 they moved into a large house on the western hillside overlooking Nice.

It was summer before the Muirs again reached St Petersburg, and on 24 July 1873 Andrew made the following entry in his diary:

For a long interval of nearly seven years this book has unfortunately been laid aside. Frequent changes of abode, anxieties about business and family, and the fatigue of daily work, have left me too little leisure to think of such matters. I am now relieved from the details of business and more inclined for meditation than for action, and I resume, or rather recommence, my entries.

Today went with Alice and Meta to Makovsky's. First sitting of Meta and myself for a portrait of both together. We all helped to arrange the grouping and the artist was much pleased with it. I am sitting comfortably in the corner of the sofa and Meta is perched on the back or rail close to me, a rather uncomfortable position, but producing a good effect. A very full sketch in crayon was completed today.

To commission a portrait from a fashionable young artist of the day set the seal on Andrew's recently-acquired affluence.

There was more European travel in the following winter, and then in the spring of 1874 the Muirs left Russia for good. Andrew could feel that he was leaving M & M's in a highly satisfactory state. Thanks to his 'sanguine disposition and love of improvement', the business had grown considerably, and in expanding its activities to include Moscow, he had taken a risk that had paid off. Walter Philip, though still under thirty, was quite capable of running the whole concern, assisted by Archy and Fred Mirrielees. Fred was a great asset to the firm.

Interested in all kinds of social and sporting activities, and himself a good athlete, he was far better suited to business life than the introverted Archy. Yet however competent the three young men might be, Andrew still intended to direct the overall policy of M & M's, remaining a partner with a financial interest and paying frequent visits to Russia.

Andrew was fifty-seven, three years younger than Archibald Mirrielees at the time of his retirement, and had been in Russia for twenty-two years compared to Archibald's thirty-five. Taking his life as a whole, he might conclude that for all its difficulties – his unsettled, wandering bachelor life of which the retrospect still pained him, the five years of drudgery and rigid business discipline under Archibald Mirrielees, the anxieties about business and family, and the fatigue of daily work – everything had turned out right in the end. In Alice he had a wife who satisfied all Jane's criteria when she had written to him as long ago as 1846: 'Assuredly there is nothing in this world that would add so much to your happiness, and the improvement of your character in every respect, as the possession of such a wife as I would desire for you – a good, prudent, amiable and clever woman.' He had five strikingly attractive children of whom he was very fond and proud, including two sons who might be expected – if not for a few years yet, then at least within his lifetime – to take their places in the family business. He was also a very wealthy man, and not short of ideas on how this wealth might be used for the pleasure and satisfaction of himself and his family.

11

London and Cambridge

Holland Park is still a pleasant oasis of green within the densely-populated London borough of Kensington. Criss-crossed by paths, it is a favourite meeting-place for dogs, some of which are accompanied by their owners. On the south side it is bounded by the busy Kensington High Street, but to the north there is less traffic and one enters what might still be regarded by London standards as a quiet residential area. These tall elegant houses – originally designed for large well-to-do middle-class families with half a dozen servants, and now often divided into flats – have not lost their style and self-confidence.

The Muirs moved into 42 Holland Park in October 1874 as its first owners. Unlike Archibald Mirrielees, who lived in rented houses, Andrew Muir bought the property. He could afford to do so, and no doubt expected it to remain in the family for many years to come. In this comfortable well-appointed home, leading comfortable secure lives, the Muir children grew up, and for the girls especially 42 would always be associated with their happiest memories.

The energetic Andrew was not content to restrict his business activities to the supervision of M & M's, but embarked on various new ventures. He started the London Portland Cement Company, purchased orange groves in Florida, and invested heavily in South African mines. But he had no intention of letting his retirement be ruled by business. He began collecting pictures, purchasing a landscape by Corot in December 1875 for the considerable sum of £130. To make up for time lost in Russia, he joined the London Library and became a voracious reader. Philosophy he found too inconclusive to be entirely satisfying as a field of study: free will and determinism, he commented, would always have their partisans. He preferred history, chiefly because of its human interest, its concern with man and his doings.

Alice's activities were centred more on the house and her children, but as her daughter Molly once commented: 'I don't think she could become a slave to anything, though she has such an extraordinary power of absorbing herself in anything that she does.' One such absorbing activity was marmalade-making, while each December she became absorbed in preparing the 'Cape box': buying, making and packing Christmas presents to be sent out to her Philip relations in

South Africa. For this purpose, as for many others, she relied heavily on Whiteley's, the rapidly expanding department store at nearby Westbourne Grove. The piano was her chief diversion, and she still played well enough to give informal concerts or to act as an accompanist. But she was in even greater demand among family and friends as a medical adviser. It was from William Philip that she had received her first training in homeopathic medicine, and she regularly diagnosed, prescribed treatment, and often administered it herself.

Visits to art galleries and Private Views, to lectures on English literature, to the theatre and to concerts (including Saturday Pop concerts at the St James's Hall), figured prominently in the Muirs' life, and once they were old enough, the Muir children accompanied their parents to all these events. Alice and Andrew also 'discovered' Stopford Brooke (1832-1916), an Irishman who made many reputations: as a charismatic preacher, an unorthodox religious thinker, a connoisseur of art, and the prolific author of books of literary criticism. In 1876 his friends presented him with the lease of Bedford Chapel, Bloomsbury, and in 1880 he seceded from the Church of England. The Muirs were members of his fashionable, sophisticated congregation for many years and had their own pew. Brooke's mixture of religion, art and literature was an intoxicating one. 'Mr Brooke never more eloquent,' Andrew wrote of his sermon on judgment. 'Glorious!' was Alice's description of his sermon on the death of Moses, and such was the force of his sermon on the force of prayer that she recorded in her diary: 'I now pray again' – suggesting that she had previously ceased praying and left her evangelical past far behind.

On their return from Russia the Muir children found themselves surrounded by sympathetic relations, adding to the atmosphere of unusual warmth and harmony in which they grew up, but it was from within 42 itself that this atmosphere originated. The girls' great friend, Helena (Nellie) Sickert, younger sister of Walter Sickert the painter, had had an unhappy childhood and recalls in her autobiography how the Scottish hospitality of the Muir family 'warmed and irradiated' her life as an adolescent. 'I never knew more generous parents. They kept open house for as many young people as their children would bring. We danced and sang and played games all over the big house and talked interminably and made a little circle all our own, known as "the girls".' Maida Mirrielees, however, comments that the Muir children, when little, used to take advantage of their parents' absent-mindedness to indulge in the wildest pranks almost under their noses. Maida must have been struck by the contrast between this free-and-easy upbringing and her own childhood. Wild pranks were unthinkable under the nose of Archibald Mirrielees.

A reserved man, Andrew Muir is unlikely to have been as demonstratively affectionate as Archibald, but he cared deeply about his children and took a particular interest in their education. Martin and Kenneth were sent to Uppingham, where the rigours of public school life were partly offset by support from home. The girls' education was not, however, of less account. In 1873 the Notting Hill & Bayswater High School opened at nearby Norland Place. Meta was enrolled in 1875, her sisters and Nellie Sickert following later. According to Nellie, the girls were of all social conditions, but it was the prosperous middle classes who most welcomed the establishment of this pioneering school for girls and ensured its immediate success; and it was with the daughters of such families that the Muir trio made their own little circle and formed their most lasting friendships. West London was the home of a large number of artists. Nellie's father, Oswald Sickert, a naturalized Dane, was a painter. William Morris's younger daughter, May, was enrolled at Notting Hill in September 1874 and his elder daughter, Jenny, in the spring of 1875, but found to be suffering from epilepsy. The Morris family had long been friendly with that of Edward Burne-Jones, whose daughter, Margaret, was also enrolled at Notting Hill in September 1874, when she was only eight. Nellie admits that they were very cliquish, but, she asks herself – expressing a sentiment that the Muirs would have echoed – what is so wrong with cliques? 'Life is not long enough to enjoy the company of those one loves and with whom one has points of contact.' Boys, she vaguely felt, 'spoilt things'. Exceptions were made in the case of brothers. In spite of having to darn their socks, Nellie was quite fond of hers – all five of them – as were the Muirs of Martin and Kenneth. Philip Burne-Jones, elder brother of Margaret, was also acceptable. The volatile Phil and his more equable younger sister were the trio's closest friends of all, and for many years there was much coming and going of young people between 'The Grange' at Fulham and No.42.

The Muir girls, Nellie writes, were delightfully pretty and wore 'Liberty clothes'. All three sisters are wearing identical full-length dresses of Liberty material in the photograph taken by Hollyer in 1882, although Meta has added an amber necklace – distinguishing mark of a young lady of culture – and Molly a flamboyant sash and bangle. Meta gazes impassively ahead; Eva is looking inwards, preoccupied with her own secret thoughts or contemplating some mysterious distant world; while Molly, too eager perhaps to look grown-up, succeeds only in looking rather bad-tempered. It was the wistful Eva, the favourite of Burne-Jones, who could best be described as beautiful; Molly, likewise much painted and photographed in her time, was the most handsome and striking; whereas Meta's face is pleasing, because one can read in it the pleasing features of her character.

For Meta was the most calm, dependable and even-tempered of the trio. 'Knows her own place as eldest,' Archy Mirrielees had written of her when she was seven, and a feeling of responsibility for her brothers and sisters seems to have persisted. Meta was her father's daughter. She was reserved ('already promises to be a *coquette*,' Archy wrote, 'won't kiss young men'), had a quiet sense of humour, loved books, and even inherited his occasional absent-mindedness: once, having missed her train, she returned home, but forgot to leave in time to catch the next one.

'Little Eva as lovely and sweet as ever,' Phil Burne-Jones wrote in 1890. That Eva was charming and delightful no one could deny, but there was also in her personality what Austin Birrell called 'a gentle vein of invalidism'. Did it all go back to that prolonged illness in infancy, when she seemed to be just fading away and wanted her mother's knee all the time? 'How is Eva?' Birrell writes in 1886. 'I still fancy her pale and recumbent, sitting by an open window and wistfully gazing out thereof.'

There was nothing pale or wistful about Molly, the most vital member of the trio. 'Has will of her own,' Archy noted when she was four, 'considers herself quite on a par with her elders.' As the sash and bangle in the photograph suggest, Molly did not meekly follow her elder sisters' example; on the contrary, it was they who seem to have looked up to this dashing young sister of theirs. For Molly was wilful, forthright and outspoken, with a lively and wicked sense of humour. 'Molly the Mutinous,' Birrell called her. 'It never seems quite the old 42 without you,' Meta wrote in 1889, 'wonderful peace and harmony no doubt, but 'tis dearly bought by your absence oh Molly mine, bad angel, beloved villain!'

All three girls were equally devoted to their mother, worrying constantly lest 'the little Mother' overdo things. With their father relations were not so straightforward. Though indulgent, Andrew could be difficult. Meta knew best how to handle him, but with Molly

there was liable to be friction. As for the girls themselves, although –
or because – they were so unlike each other, the bond of mutual
devotion was extremely strong, so that they seem to be not so much a
trio, as a clique of three.

In 1873, the same year that Notting Hill High School was opened,
Emily Davies moved her tiny band of students to the small village of
Girton outside Cambridge. Each year one or two girls went up from
the High School, including Meta Muir in 1881 and Nellie Sickert in
1882. With two others in her year Meta was reading for the History
Tripos. Andrew followed his daughter's studies with close attention, as
if relishing the opportunity to enjoy at second-hand the kind of
education that he had never had. 'You need not be afraid of tiring me
with either Italian Republics or constitutional history, in fact that is the
kind of news that interests me most.' When Meta began studying
Italian history, he borrowed six volumes of Sismondi from the London
Library and sent them to her, and a few days later bought the set itself:
'It will be helpful, since there are three of you studying.' He is
surprised that Meta has to attend only six lectures a week – 'I should
say twelve would be a moderate amount' – and deplores the bad
example set to students by dons not turning up for lectures: what
would businessmen say about such failure to keep appointments? Meta
had complained that the standard of lectures in History was inferior to
that of other Triposes, to which Andrew replied: 'The fault of history
as a Cambridge course is not in the subject but in the manner in which
it is treated. Judging from your experience I should say the treatment
is arbitrary, unmethodical and fragmentary.' He then spells out his
ideas on how history *should* be treated at Cambridge, but fears that his
system 'is too Scotch (i.e. methodising) or too German (that is
encyclopaedic) for the English mind, which seems not to take readily
to generalising.'

Andrew wrote this letter in May 1883, soon after his daughter had
returned to 'happy Girton', and in view of his close involvement with
her studies, it is all the more surprising that Meta did not complete the
three-year Tripos course, but left Girton at Christmas after two years and
a term. The decision must have been taken in the summer, and to all
outward appearances Meta accepted it with perfect equanimity. Regret,
though, there certainly was, as later references to 'my beloved room at
Girton' and 'the dear dear College days' make clear.

The reasons behind this decision are not obvious, but some light may
be thrown on the problem by comparing Meta with her contemporaries.

She was not at all a typical Girton student – indeed, her presence there was something of an anomaly. Girls who went up to Girton at that time did so, often in the teeth of fierce family opposition, because they wanted to make themselves independent and hated the idea of living as dependants at home while they waited for a husband. Of the twelve students in Meta's year, nine completed their Triposes. All went on to pursue careers: seven took up schoolteaching, three becoming headmistresses; Janet Case taught privately and numbered Virginia Stephen (Woolf) among her pupils, while Ethel Sargant became the first woman member of council of the Linnaean Society. According to the Girton Register, none of these women married; they put their careers first. The other two students who did not complete their Triposes were Margaret Llewelyn Davies, who left a term before Meta, and Rosalind Shore Smith, who left a term after: Meta's two fellow-historians and her very great friends. Margaret's father, the Revd John Llewelyn Davies, was Principal from 1878 to 1886 of Queen's College, London, founded for the advancement of higher education for women; her aunt, Emily Davies, was the founder of Girton. Margaret and Rosie saw eye to eye on women's questions and were to be very active later in supporting women's causes. For them Girton had probably served its purpose, and they were eager to go out into the world and set it to rights.

In various ways, then, all the women at Girton were rebels; all, that is, except Meta Muir. There had been nothing for her to rebel against, no difficulties to overcome. In sending her to Notting Hill and Girton, her parents had probably been moved by a very Scottish belief in the value of education for its own sake. Yet although they were very indulgent to their daughters, Andrew and Alice still held conventional views on the role of women. On 17 March 1883 Meta wrote to her father abroad, seeking permission to attend the Women's Suffrage Ball at the Kensington Town Hall. She worded her request with obvious care: 'Almost everyone I know is going. It is what is called a *private* subscription ball. Would you ask Mother and let me know as soon as possible? Mrs Alt or Mrs Sickert would take me. I think it would be such fun, but I wish Mother could be here to chaperone me herself. All the educated world are to be seen there I believe.' But Andrew was not deceived into thinking that the Ball was no more than a cultural gathering. 'Your mother says that if Mrs Alt will be kind enough to chaperone you, you may go to the subscription ball on the 6th but we both of us strongly *disapprove* of the women's suffrage business, you will of course not let it be thought that you approve of women's suffrage in anything but *dress and balls*. Perhaps education and the guardianship of the poor might be added. But as for governmental affairs it is all wrong.'

From this one might infer that Andrew and Alice were not thinking of Meta's studies at Girton as the stepping-stone to a career, but took the conventional view, to which Archibald Mirrielees had subscribed a decade earlier, that until she married, a daughter's place was in the home. By 1883 Andrew and Alice were both in their sixties, considerably 'older' then than now. It was time for Alice to hand over the running of the household to one of her daughters. Neither Eva nor Molly was so suited to this task as Meta. But what if Meta took it into her head to become a teacher or to dedicate her life to improving the lot of women? Suddenly alarmed by this prospect, did Andrew and Alice decide that it was time for Meta to assume her 'rightful' place as the unpaid housekeeper of 42? There would be ample opportunity, after all, to continue her studies in London – for instance, by attending the lectures given by her old favourite, Stopford Brooke.

Nellie Sickert would have resisted any such attempt to curtail her studies tooth and nail. But Meta was not Nellie. She did not have the rebel's temperament. She was more of a middle-of-the-roader, always able to see both points of view. Nor could she with honesty regard family life as some kind of prison from which it was essential to escape without delay by achieving economic independence. Her loyalties were far more evenly divided than those of her contemporaries. Girton she adored and for the rest of her life she would be proud to think of herself as a 'Girtonian'; but she was also a loving and dutiful daughter, devoted to her two sisters and fond of her own home. Though Girton might exert its pull, so did 42. Once, during term-time, she went back there for a weekend and enjoyed 'tea in the quite "home" style, such as it never is elsewhere – to me, fresh from this academic home, quite peculiar and delicious. Lazy afternoon tea in the boudoir with Dundee cake and macaroons!'

So Miss Muir exchanged the academic life of Cambridge for the social and domestic life of London, where she was to be in charge of running the Muir household for the next six years.

10. Mrs Anne Fullarton, wearing her 'Mary Stuart' cap

11 & 12. Alison Bell and William Philip before their marriage in 1840: from watercolour portraits

13. Alice and Andrew Muir with Meta, 1863. Alice's golden hair looks darker in this early photograph.

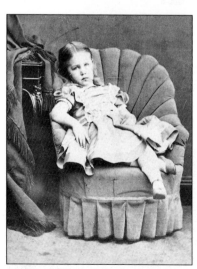

14. Meta Muir at about the time she met Lewis Carroll in 1867: photograph by the Scottish photographer, William Carrick, who had an atelier in St Petersburg from 1859 until his death in 1878

Phot. H. STEINBERG   Was. Ost. 11 L. 26.

15. A young Scot in Russia: Martin Muir in 1872, aged 8

16. L to r: Kenneth, Alice Muir, Eva, Molly and Meta, with Maggie Fullarton standing behind

17. 42 Holland Park, as it is today

18. Sitting-room at 42 Holland Park, looking into conservatory, 1890

19. L to r: Molly, Meta and Eva Muir, 1882. Photograph by F.W.Hollyer.

12

A Gathering of the Clans

In 1877 the Muirs visited their datcha near Peterhof for the last time. It was a long way to go for a summer holiday. From 1878 until 1886 they spent much of the summer on Arran, re-creating on this unspoilt Scottish island something of the free-and-easy atmosphere of Russian datcha life. More than seven years passed without any member of the family visiting Russia apart from Andrew, but in January 1885 Alice, then sixty-two, and her nineteen-year-old daughter, Molly, went out to St Petersburg to stay with Walter Philip and his wife Laura, who was expecting her first baby. 'During the past week or two,' Austin Birrell wrote to Molly, 'I have caught myself wondering what foundation was being laid for that novel of the future which is to be entitled "Molly in Russia", or if you fall in with the foolish fashion of alliteration, "Molly in Muscovy".'

A telegram announcing the baby's safe arrival caused great excitement in London, although Granny Fullarton, now a great-grandmother, was predictably outraged by the parents' choice of Guy as the name of their first offspring. Molly as usual did not mince words: 'The babe displays a good deal of temper – Walter is amusing on the subject of his son & heir.' Instead of baby-worshipping, Molly concentrated on having a good time. Walter was a very expert skater and agreed to instruct her. At the Yusupov Gardens, while the band was vigorously playing 'Carmen', she skated about for the first time on her own. 'You should see me doing outside edge. Walter insists on my putting my head on one side and it really does help one, though it seems ridiculous.' One Sunday he took her to St Isaac's Cathedral, where the congregation impressed her more than any service could have done. 'I never saw such a mass of people so entirely earnest & devout – it seemed to equalize them all, for people of every degree were all mixed together, all intensely serious & infinitely melancholy, & the singing added to it was a cry that rent one's heartstrings so strange & sad & beautiful it was.' After that they went to the Peter & Paul Fortress. Molly describes it in terms that would have been worthy of 'Molly in Muscovy', with its 'wretched & hopeless gratings so low & close to the water where brave men are kept like thieves & murderers, devoured by the damp & maddened by the incessant discordant chimes of the gaudy Fortress church.' Having been 'driven into her boots completely', she was then taken by Walter to the Balagans or show-booths:

We went into one of the theatres & saw a romantic play which we shrieked over – it was all on such a rustic scale – the beautiful princess had a large powdered nose & brilliant cheeks & big coarse hands & a most ungainly figure & the prince was a caution – the limelights were fixed somewhere above the heads of the audience & took a long time to fix on the right person, it reminded one forcibly of trying to catch sunbeams on a looking glass – the curtain didn't work either & once came down on the heads of the actors – the whole thing was most comic – one heard the prompter shouting & the band master lost his temper with his band & they had a regular row.

Molly must have regretted those uncomplimentary remarks about the babe when the news reached London in May that Guy Philip had died after a short illness, caused by his inability to digest the rich milk produced by Russian cows in the spring; confined all winter, the animals often became so weak that after the thaw they had to be carried out to the fields, where they devoured the fresh grass voraciously.

In November 1886 Andrew Muir left for Moscow with Eva and Kenneth. The latter had spent a year at Oxford, but since his elder brother Martin was in London reading for the Bar, Andrew must have decided that the sooner Kenneth began his business career and re-established a Muir presence in Muir & Mirrielees, the better. Having settled him in to his satisfaction, Andrew returned to London, but Eva stayed on for a couple of months, informing her friends that Christmas cards and letters would arrive sooner and be less likely to go astray if they were addressed to the Office. Its address was very simple: Muir & Mirrielees, Moscow, Russia.

In the summer of 1887 there was an even bigger Muir invasion. Andrew, Alice, Meta and Molly spent July and August at Walter and Laura's datcha outside Moscow. It was, indeed, a great gathering of the clans. No less than sixteen individuals, all related in some way to the Muir or Mirrielees families, were gathered together in one place. Not, however, in one datcha. Living in 'the other house' nearby were Archy and Annie Mirrielees, Harry and Maida Bernard (née Mirrielees) with their infant daughter, and the Willie Cazalets with their infant son. Had Fred Mirrielees arrived with his wife and son a little earlier, the total would have risen to nineteen.

What had been happening to the members of the Mirrielees family in the ten years since Archibald's death?

Fred's connection with M & M's had ceased some years before. In the summer of 1875, while the dying Jane Mirrielees sat in the garden at Ealing under a favourite weeping ash oblivious of what was going on around her, a romance had begun between Fred and Maggie Currie, whose mother was Jane's old friend from Liverpool days, Margaret Miller. Maggie's father would agree to the marriage only on condition that Fred join his business, the Donald Currie line of steamers to the Cape of Good Hope. Uncle Andrew was most reluctant to part with the energetic Fred, who had been very successfully expanding the Moscow branch of M & M's, nor did Fred himself have the slightest wish to give up a business in which he would soon have been a junior partner for one that he knew nothing about. There was a stormy interview between Uncle Andrew and Mr Currie. But the latter had true love on his side. It was agreed that Fred should give up working for M & M's in the spring of 1879, prior to his marriage in September. He invited Maida to join him in Moscow for his last winter.

On her return to England, the first people Maida went to see were her sister Maggie and Austin Birrell, who had been married the previous summer. Maggie seemed particularly well, with no trace of the low spirits that had dogged her in the past, and was expecting a baby in October. From London Maida went up to Arran to stay with the Muirs, and it was there, one Saturday afternoon early in September 1879, that Uncle Andrew broke the news to her that Maggie had died giving birth to a stillborn child. Since there were no boats in Scotland on Sundays, she and her uncle had to wait until Monday before they could leave. 'The house was full of merry young people,' Maida recalled, 'and I felt sadly out of place. Kind Aunt Alice did her best for me and talked to me for hours about her African experiences to distract my mind.' As a result, Maida was unable to attend Fred's grand Scottish wedding on 30 September.

After Fred's departure, Archy took over control of M & M's in Moscow. He was not sorry to leave St Petersburg. On an earlier visit he had been much impressed by 'the general character of the Englishman in Moscow – a more hospitable set I never met with'. On the other hand, the increased responsibilities brought extra pressure. To Maida he wrote in August:

This brings me to a confession I wish I had not to make. The truth is that I have been out of sorts for some time, and have now been nearly a week at the datcha, nursing myself with only an occasional short visit to town. It is a return of my old feeling of nervous weakness & prostration which without any actual pain makes me unfit for any prolonged exertion, bodily or mental. I am of course greatly disappointed to break down in this way when I thought myself so much stronger, but I think I can trace it clearly to overexertion and I hope with rest and quiet to get all right before long. I expect Walter down for a few days to help in business and when that anxiety is off my mind I shall get better more quickly I think. In the mean time you better keep this as quiet as possible as I don't wish any unnecessary alarms about my health to be spread in certain quarters.

This was an allusion to Uncle Andrew, who must have been wondering whether Archy would be able to cope on his own in Moscow. Like William Mirrielees before him, Archy was not cut out for a business life, but unlike William, he was anxious and conscientious, and could find no way out of the situation in which circumstances had placed him other than by periodical escapes into ill health.

Maida was to spend her next four winters in Moscow as Archy's housekeeper and general emotional support. They were joined in 1881 by the Cazalets' nineteen-year-old son, Willie, who began working for M & M's. The big event in the spring of 1882 was the production by the British community of *Our Boys*, in which Maida took the part of Violet, and it was at the dance afterwards that she first made the acquaintance of the new British chaplain in Moscow, Harry Bernard. She warmed at once to his high-minded socialism and unorthodox religious views, and also felt sorry for him: 'His childhood had been such an unhappy one and his youth, troubled by religious scruples, had left a tinge of melancholy.' When Harry proposed in the following summer, she accepted without hesitation, her heart 'full of pity for him and desire to make him happy'. Determined to have a quiet wedding, they were married on 3 November 1883 by the British Chaplain in Vienna. Una, their first child, was born on 11 April 1886. Maida's preparations for the new arrival were characteristic. Convinced that it would be a boy, she began brushing up her Latin, feeling it to be inadequate, diligently read several works on 'the child', such as Preyer's *Die Seele des Kindes*, and studied the notes on their children taken by such eminent men as Charles Darwin. Quite unprepared for the reality, she was a very anxious mother and Una a very nervous child. To the upbringing of their children – Una was followed by two more daughters – Harry and Maida brought the same kind of moral earnestness that characterized all their activities. By the time of the family gathering in 1887, however, Harry had become disillusioned by religion and far more interested in biology, and a year later he resigned the chaplaincy and left with his family for Jena to study under the famous proponent of evolutionary theory, Ernst Haeckel.

In November 1886 Archy Mirrielees married Annie Kirkwood. When the Muirs arrived in Moscow in the following July, the delicate Annie – who lived for another forty years and survived her husband, as delicate ladies so often did – was still in Paris, not well enough to travel, but Archy was able to fetch her later.

The journey across Europe, Meta wrote home to Eva, had been inexpressibly tedious, without enough books to read. At the station they were met by Walter and Kenneth. The datcha was at Zhukovka, some way beyond the Sparrow Hills. 'We had a terrible drive right across Moscow over cobble stones under a scorching sun & clouds of dust which fairly finished us. After an hour and a half we turned into a delicious shady avenue, most cool & green with rays of sunshine glimmering through. You can't think what a paradise it seemed like after all the dust & discomforts.' It took them a week to recover from the journey. All that time it was bitterly cold and wet, but at last the real Russian summer set in, and they were thankful for the shady trees and creepers and tall plants reaching to the roof. They took all their meals on the large balcony. 'Our rooms are rather small but the house is so delightfully roomy & large that one is sure of always getting some place to oneself among all the different balconies & sitting rooms. This morning I discovered the coolest part of the house, the empty room beyond the drawing room, and here I am sitting looking out on the balcony with its cool white curtains and the grass & trees basking in the sun beyond. It would be a splendid place for a large "At Home" or a garden party.'

Meta was in the garden one evening with her mother when they saw a thunderstorm approaching and hurried in. The others stayed to watch but were surprised by a second storm which came up behind them. Without the faintest warning there was a great flash of lightning and a crash of thunder at the same moment. Maida confirms that it was one of the worst and most sudden thunderstorms she ever experienced. On rushing home, she found a curious scene. All the servants were assembled in the hall, most of them on their knees before the ikon. When she told them to go round the house at once closing all the windows, no one would budge, they were so terrified.

Kenneth seemed to be thoroughly enjoying his new way of life. 'He is as cheery as ever, and rattles on all meal times, telling story after story,' Meta writes, 'but is still rather given to spots and has nettle rash.'

On their first evening Archy called, looking careworn and anxious, as he had had worse news of his wife. Maida and her husband also dropped in on their way to tennis; for Archy (one of the founders of Moscow's first tennis club on the Petrovka) no datcha was complete without making a tennis court. Next afternoon Meta went to tea at the other house. 'Naughty Molly was invited but wouldn't go.' She may have anticipated that the talk would be all of housekeeping and babies, not subjects dear to Molly's heart. Mr Bernard was starting on an eleven hour journey to bury someone. The moral earnestness of the Bernards clearly caused some amusement among the more worldly Muirs: 'I don't think they are keeping entirely to Spencerian principles with Una but Mr Bernard still firmly refuses to let her have dolls.'

In spite of his seventy years, Andrew still had plenty of stamina, but his idea of a pleasurable outing did not always coincide with other people's. 'Yesterday Father took us a long drive in what he called the cool hours of the morning – between 10.30 & 1.30. We drove all along the top of the Sparrow Hills & back through Moscow. Poor Mother was dreadfully knocked up afterwards by the heat & rattling over the stones.' Andrew had always been a great sightseer and indefatigable visitor of art galleries, and since Meta had not been to Moscow before, she was his most frequent companion. The Tretyakov Gallery she found interesting, since the pictures were all Russian, but there were only two that she wanted to linger in front of: portraits of Tolstoy and Dostoyevsky. Meta visited the Tretyakov a second time with Molly and two other young guests at the datcha, Vic Paton and a Mr Smith. They were met by Kenneth at the M & M Warehouse, taken out to lunch, then on to the Gallery – 'swishing off gaily in three droschkis'– and finally to tea at the famous hotel-restaurant, the Slavyansky Bazaar. Here Kenneth 'again did the honours of the place and discoursed much on his favourite topic, the pleasures of the table'. The day on which Vic and his friend were due to leave was a very hot Sunday. They attended morning service at the Church of the Redeemer, and after drinking plenty of apple juice and iced water, felt strong enough to go on to the Sunday Market in Sukharev Square.

We elbowed our way through the crowd and had great fun bargaining for all sorts of things, but there was no chance of getting anything at a reasonable price, they looked at our respectable clothes and instantly stuck on high prices, and Kenneth's expert bargaining was of no avail. Mr Smith & Vic were supremely happy, they went flying round with beaming faces bargaining by means of fingers & bits of paper and really got some very nice old icons & things. At four o'clock we saw them off with much sorrow. A newly married couple were starting at the same time, the whole wedding party seeing them off, and we watched the embraces with great interest. In the waiting room they called for champagne & all stood up & kissed all round & this ceremony was gone through a second time on the platform, it was all I could do to prevent Molly from going into shouts of laughter.

At the datcha Meta and Molly went about in Russian costume, finding it delightfully cool and just the thing for tennis, which they liked to play between tea and dinner, when the courts were shaded. Sundays were the grand tennis days. Among Russian visitors for tennis were the Khvoshchinsky sisters. Laura Philip had become friendly with this old Russian family three summers before. 'They are the first really nice girls Kenneth has yet got to know in Moscow. He amuses them very much by the way in which he imitates Russian ways of saying various words and by his hopeless struggles to pronounce the letter *kh*. He made himself very agreeable to the youngest, a nice "backfisch", and promised to come home by an early train on Thursday when he heard they were coming to play tennis.'
Other visitors to the datcha were two English officers. Meta found them very nice,

but it's so difficult to get on with army people, there seems to be nothing to talk to them about. One of them, Mr Mardale, brought his bride, the funniest little person in the piquante style. Maida was going about in Russian costume. 'Don't care for Russian dress,' says Mrs Mardale, 'prefer Parisian.' She is small, wears unusually high heels, and treats her husband in a coquettish & truculent manner. She is very amusing for a time, but palled on us rather by twelve o'clock. 'That train goes an hour too late,' says Archy, putting his foot in it rather, and indeed it makes one think twice about asking people from Moscow when there is no means of getting rid of them before midnight.

Kenneth had an Oxford friend, Charles Eliot, who had recently been appointed Third Secretary at the St Petersburg Embassy. He and another attaché, F.D.Harford, had been given the task of entertaining the Marquis of Ailsa on a visit to Russia. Meta describes Mr Eliot as 'the regular Balliol man, very refined, precise in his language, not much given to joking and hardly ever laughing at other people's jokes' – clearly a born diplomat, as his later career would confirm; whereas Mr Harford 'had a rapid and stammering way of talking that made his comical remarks all the more comical'. Kenneth acted as their guide to the Kremlin and asked them out to the datcha one evening.

So on Friday they appeared, having done the Sparrow Hills on the way. To our surprise & amusement old Ivan Ivanitch [a family friend?] turned up before them. He had been told by the Governor-General to look after the Lord and had shown them about and even tried to squeeze himself into the troika making a pretty large fifth but had been gently but firmly ejected by Kenneth. He arrived here in a peasant tarantass clad in evening dress and bearing in each arm a huge sieve of strawberries! Lovely picture, oh how we laughed. At dinner Lord Ailsa sat between Laura & me and we had the greatest difficulty in keeping the conversation going. He didn't seem to be interested in Russian things at all, regarded all his sightseeing as so much 'knocked off'. One could see that he had the real British scorn of foreigners. When I said something about Russian novels he merely turned his eyeglass upon me and said 'Oh, are they really civilised enough to have novelists'. What ignorance. Fortunately Father who was sitting opposite got him over yachts and as he is a great yachting man that topic served for a good while.

What ignorance, indeed! It was, after all, eight years since Turgenev had received an honorary doctorate at Oxford. The Muirs went to the other extreme, discussing the Russian novelists all dinner time; Walter and Laura thought them 'quite mad'. This enthusiasm was not a result of their Russian connection, for few of the British residents were similarly affected, but of the great surge of interest at that time in the Russian novelists, especially Tolstoy and Dostoyevsky, in the educated English-speaking world. Andrew Muir must have been particularly attracted to the religious, moral and philosophical elements in the two great Russian writers. None of them read the novels in Russian, but in French or English translations. Nor do they seem to have known much *about* the Russian novelists; otherwise, they would not have been so eager to quiz every new set of people that came to dinner about the novelists' lives and the opinions held of them in Russia. One German guest seemed rather a nice little man, but he sank almost as low as the Marquis of Ailsa in Meta's estimation when he made the commonplace remark that Tolstoy was mad: 'I should have thought better of him, but of course he speaks from hearsay and there are all sorts of absurd stories afloat about the old Count.' They were all very struck by the similarity in appearance between Dostoyevsky and Mr Burne-Jones: a likeness of Dostoyevsky, taken after his death and included in a volume that Father picked up in a second-hand bookshop, brought out the resemblance even more strongly than the portrait in the Tretyakov Gallery. Meta also enjoyed discussing literature with the elder Khvoshchinsky girl. They compared notes as to what books were considered fit *pour les jeunes filles* in Russia and England. Meta was amused to find that Russian girls were allowed to read Ouida's highly-coloured fiction, but not the novels of Dostoyevsky. 'It seems that all English books are considered harmless. They were very much surprised to find that *we* read Dostoyevsky and shouldn't think of reading Ouida.'

In August the Muirs visited St Petersburg, all except Alice, who preferred to remain at the datcha. 'Dear little Mother is very well and enjoys immensely the peace & quiet of this place, she declares that she hasn't had such a restful time since we were in Russia ten years ago! She looks so young & fresh in her pretty new dresses.' They spent only three days in St Petersburg, on two of which it rained. Meta and Molly walked along the Galernaya and Meta succeeded in picking out their old house. 'The pavement, the waterspouts, all looked familiar and reminded me of all sorts of forgotten things. So did the English Quay with its low granite wall.' Their day at Peterhof was fearfully wet, but Meta found the drive there intensely interesting – 'for I remembered every corner of the old Datcha & the road through the wood to the Gulf, & even the place where we used to play with the white sand round the roots of an old tree.' They were staying at the Hotel de France, 'the place where all the English come to lunch'. Mr Harford was in town and got them a pass into the Winter Palace, Kenneth discovered two or three Oxford men, on their third day the weather was fine and friends were gathering round, but Father was inexorable – 'the sumptuous rooms in the best part of the hotel made the expenses pretty heavy and off we had to go'.

The Muirs spent September touring in Germany, and on 10 October Meta wrote to her friend Mr Hogg in America, describing their delightful summer.

We were staying with my married brother & his wife in their pretty country house some miles out of Moscow, surrounded by a thick wood of silver birches which made a most delicious shade. I read a great many Russian novels and got very much interested in the people. The government is unspeakably bad, the nobility try to be as French as possible, the bourgeoisie are as vulgar as elsewhere, but the people who come between these, & also the peasants, are intensely interesting: people who have fallen into poverty or moujiks who have had a little education & have been seized with new ideas. They are fanatical & wild in their ideas, some of them quite mad but all very sad & hopeless. It is from this class that the novelists get their most tragic subjects – and a black picture they draw. The moujiks or peasants who live in the country are quite different. They ask no questions & are quite content. They are a very friendly good natured set full of fun & ready to love you if you make a joke. We were very much amused to see my youngest brother Kenneth bargaining hotly with the cab men calling them all sorts of names, while they stood around grinning at his very English Russian.

But I am forgetting that you are probably not much interested in things Russian & if so I must be boring you horribly.

Meta was being too modest as usual. Stuart Hogg was a young Englishman whom she had met with her father and Eva in 1886 on the crossing to New York. He had a cattle ranch in Kansas and also worked for the British Land and Mortgage Company of America, of which his father, Sir Stuart Hogg, was president. Meta and Eva corresponded with him irregularly, in the summer of 1890 he came over on a visit, and after a whirlwind romance he and Meta were married on 9 September at St George's, Campden Hill. Three weeks later they sailed for America.

20. Molly Muir in her Liberty cap: Christmas card from Phil Burne-Jones

21. L to r: Kenneth, Eva and Martin Muir, probably 1891

22. 'The girls', 1883. L to r: Madge Alt, Eva Muir, Nellie Sickert, Meta Muir, Bessie McLeod, Mabel Alt, Molly Muir, Margaret Burne-Jones. Photograph by F.W.Hollyer.

23. Zhukovka, the Mirrielees datcha, 1887

24. 'Miss Muir's Wedding' (from Phil Burne-Jones' sketch-book)

25. Village of Hambledon, showing 'Bryony' on hill in background: early 20th century postcard

26. Alice Muir

27. Andrew Muir: photograph by
F.W.Hollyer

13

Andrew's Final Speculations

The village of Hambledon, some five miles south of Godalming in Surrey, is not to be confused with that other famous Hambledon in Hampshire, where cricket was first played. Ever since 1868, when Tennyson started to build his new home near Haslemere, this wooded, hilly, and very rural corner of Surrey had attracted writers and painters. It was also to be the final setting in the story of the Muirs. Andrew first took a lease on a house there for holidays called 'Furze Hill', known to the younger generation of Muirs as 'Fuzz'. Here, on 28 September 1890 he received among other callers 'the great Oscar Wilde and Graham Robertson' (a young painter friend of the Burne-Jones family). In 1890 Oscar's greatness was still only self-proclaimed; the great stage successes lay a few years ahead. His first play, *Vera*, subtitled *The Nihilists*, was set in Russia, but its London première had been cancelled when the assassination of Alexander II in 1881 made its theme uncomfortably topical, and in New York it had been taken off after a week, so it would not have provided an ideal subject of conversation between Wilde and Andrew Muir. The latter would have appreciated Wilde's epigrammatic wit, but what did Wilde make of the taciturn old Scot? Quiet listeners, however, never bothered Oscar.

By now Andrew was little more than a Scot in name. Meta describes how he had taken up gardening 'as he would a new business' and was mastering the minutest detail. 'He is becoming more of the Tory as he grows older, and is a great supporter of the Church and goes regularly, though there is only an old fossil in the pulpit and the singing is the most discordant I have ever heard! Who would have expected the radical Scottish philosopher to turn into "such a good old English gentleman"!'

Fifteen years of comfortable English living had taken their toll. He is still able to comment that 'we tie millstones round our necks by the complications of our daily lives and its incessant demands for money', and often feels ashamed at leading such a luxurious life, whereas the ladies, 'fortunately for themselves, seem to have no such qualms'; but, he supposes, he must submit to it. Submission to the status quo is his watchword. He deplores the insane hostility to capital being whipped up 'by a set of socialist scribblers who never conducted any business', and applauds Herbert Spencer's collection of essays, *A Plea for Liberty*, in which his old mentor 'points out the danger we are in from similar Socialistic notions spreading among the lower classes'. To Meta and Stuart in America he writes that when summer comes, they will be tempted to spend much time on the farm, but he does not think that as a result they will wish to adopt Tolstoy's ideal of life there and the renunciation of all attempts to make money. 'Habits and tastes we have acquired are too much for us and we cannot separate ourselves from our social attachments.' To live simply, to be one's own cook and scullery-maid, waiter and groom, might be fine in America, but in London, to which Meta and Stuart were planning to return, 'it won't do, at least for people above the working class'.

At the time of Meta's marriage in 1890, Andrew was seventy-three. Looking back at his past life, he could derive greatest satisfaction from the success of M & M's, of which he was still a partner. His policy of expanding the Moscow side of the business had been continued by his fellow-partners, Walter Philip and Archy Mirrielees. On 8 June 1878 Alice recorded in her diary: 'Andrew is off this morning to Russia to determine the matter of purchasing or leasing new premises in Moscow etc.' It may have been at this time that they took the far-sighted decision to purchase a three-storey building in the very heart of Moscow, situated on a corner site, its longer frontage on the Petrovka facing the side of the Bolshoi Theatre, and its shorter frontage looking out into Theatre Square. They had certainly purchased the building by 1885, when an advertisement in the Moscow press announced that as from 10 September, alongside the wholesale departments housed in their own building on the Petrovka, 'a retail millinery and haberdashery shop' was to be opened next to the Arcades. This is the first indication that we have of M & M's entering the retail trade. In that same year, 1885, Walter Philip and his family moved permanently from St Petersburg to Moscow. By 1888 M & M's had decided to rent further premises in the Gagarin Building on nearby *Kuznetsky most* – literally, 'Blacksmith's Bridge', though bridge and smithy had long since disappeared – where they opened a second retail shop, selling carpets, oilcloth, furnishing fabrics, lamps and household equipment.

A year later the firm's St Petersburg operations were reconstituted with the setting up of the independent Oborot Company (*oborot* is the Russian word for 'turnover'), a wholesale business working in conjunction with M & M's. It was a joint-stock company, with its own board of directors; Willie Cazalet later joined the board, and Andrew Muir purchased a large number of shares. It operated very successfully until the Revolution, and in 1916 had branches in both Petrograd and Moscow, with a managing director in each. The Moscow branch had sixteen departments, selling a wide variety of materials and fashionable items of clothing.

In the summer of 1888 a five-year contract of partnership was signed by Walter Philip, Archy Mirrielees and Andrew Muir, renewing a contract made in 1883. All three were full partners. The firm's fixed capital was 300,000 silver roubles (£30,000), each partner contributing 100,000. The conducting of business was committed to Walter Philip and Archibald Mirrielees, who were under obligation to reside in Russia and to be present daily in the offices and warehouses; absence was permissible only if one of them remained in actual management. The clear profit was to be divided as follows: Andrew Muir 10%, Walter Philip 50% and Archibald Mirrielees 40%. Andrew might withdraw his profits in full, but the other two not more than 20,000 roubles (£2000) a year. The adoption of new partners or the transfer of partnership rights would require a new legal contract; should one partner die, his place was to be taken by the person designated by each partner in a sealed packet. Andrew was empowered at any time that he wished to retire from the company on such conditions as might be accepted by the other partners. Any possible disputes should be decided by the Moscow Commercial Court.

In April 1891 Meta had a letter from Austin Birrell, who by this time had remarried (his wife Eleanor was the widow of Tennyson's son Lionel), become well known as a witty man of letters, and been elected Liberal M.P. for Fifeshire West; from 1907-16 he was to be Chief Secretary for Ireland. 'I think your Father,' Birrell wrote, 'is settling down into a very happy and noble old age.' To the casual observer that might seem so, but life at 42 after the removal of Meta's harmonizing influence was less serene than Birrell's words suggest. For a start, the future of 42 itself was uncertain, since Andrew had started to build a new house at Hambledon, designed for him by young Bob Macdonald, son of George Macdonald the Scottish novelist. The position chosen was on a steep slope commanding a fine view, and the excavations, Andrew told Meta, aroused enormous interest: bent old men from the Hambledon almshouses repaired to the site as if to their club and looked on for hours at a time. 'When the new house is ready I think we must really give up HP and draw in our horns.'

Andrew had lost none of his youthful spirit of enterprise, but this latest venture received a very cool reception from the other residents of 42. 'My place will cost £4500,' he wrote to Meta, 'but I think it will be good value, *to me at least.*' Alice took only a passive interest, while the girls never went near Hambledon. 'I miss you every day,' he keeps telling Meta. 'There is no one who has the same sympathy in my pursuits. I hope Stuart and you will by & by make it your home.'

In June 1891 Meta and Stuart came over on a visit. Eva and Molly met them at Euston Station. 'We had a happy drive in a fourwheeler,' Meta wrote in her diary, 'our two pretty girls opposite – a feast for the eyes. Then old 42 and dear Mother looking fresher and prettier than ever, and Father and Kenneth just lately arrived from Russia. It felt so queer being in the old house again, everything just the same only that now I inhabited the spare room.' Father could not wait to take her down to Hambledon to see the progress that had been made. Even the girls began to show more interest: each room was to have a William Morris wallpaper, and after going through the big pattern books, Molly finally chose 'Lily' and Eva 'Daisy' on a light ground. Their father was more excited by the thought of hot baths at short notice and by his new greenhouse. Then in November, while Molly was staying with Meta and Stuart in America, dear old Grannie Fullarton died. She was eighty-seven, but still full of life and intelligence, and Andrew was convinced that had she been living in the country, she could have gone on much longer.

The year 1891 was a very bad one for Russia. 'Trade there is fearfully depressed,' Andrew wrote in April, 'owing to the low price of grain and the occurrence of two indifferent harvests. At present all manufacturing and wholesale business is bad. M & M are winding up their wholesale trade and going in entirely for retail which, if it can be established, is much less risky.' From this time onwards the firm was to be a purely retail concern. In February 1892 they had a fire at their main shop in which two Russian firemen lost their lives. This misfortune added to the despondency that Andrew was already feeling over the falling rate of exchange and the famine, about which he had been reading a very interesting article in the *Telegraph* by Count Tolstoy.

In Britain, too, business was very bad, even in the usually reliable cement trade, and Andrew's income was diminishing rapidly. This strengthened his resolve to give up 42, but houses in Holland Park, he found, were very unsaleable. They were not of red brick in the Queen Anne style – 'as if architecture mattered anything in London'. His dormant Puritan conscience was reawakened by necessity, and he determined to reduce expenses. Molly returned from America to find Father suffering from a bad attack of 'economizing fidgets'. Having to account for every penny was getting on Eva's nerves. When Molly ordered a Spanish grammar, price half a crown, Father made a great fuss, and told her and Eva that they would have to pay for any lessons out of their own allowances. Eva took this bitterly to heart, nasty things were said, and Molly had to leave the room abruptly. But as the time of Meta and Stuart's final return drew nearer, so the family tensions began to ease. Andrew decided that there was no immediate necessity to sell 42. The new house had been given a name, 'Bryony Hill', usually shortened to 'Bryony', and Molly was busy making muslin curtains for the top of the stair, fancying that the villagers, Andrew told Meta, would assemble on the tennis lawn and spend their evenings looking in on them. When Meta arrived from America, she was expecting a baby, and it must have given Andrew particular satisfaction when his first grandchild, Alison Mary, was born at 'Bryony' on 31 August 1892.

In the mean time, he had been exercising his right to withdraw his capital from M & M's – hence his despondency over the falling exchange rate – and on 30 June 1892 his connection with the firm finally came to an end, a year before the contract was due to expire. But he was not, of course, severing his ties completely, for his two sons would very shortly be taking over where he had left off. To Meta and Stuart, who was trying to decide on his future career, Andrew explained in December 1890 that for all kinds of business training was required, and an apprenticeship had to be served. 'For instance, in our Russian business a man of Stuart's age would require five years' training to fit him for a responsible post in the management. During this period his time would be given to repulsive details and he would be confined to the office and warehouse the whole day. Besides this his ultimate fitness would still be in question, as it is to this day in the case of Martin and Kenneth.' A year later he wrote that the boys were taking 'a stronger hold on the business, Martin is head cashier, a very difficult and laborious office, and I hope he will be able'. In the same way that Andrew Muir had served his apprenticeship under old Archibald Mirrielees, and Walter Philip and young Archy had served theirs under Andrew, so now Martin and Kenneth were about to complete their apprenticeships under Walter and Archy and to become junior partners. The stage was set for the next phase in the M & M story.

But that phase was never reached. Instead, early in 1893, Martin and Kenneth were dismissed.

For half a century, if one stretches a point and goes back to 1843 when Archibald Mirrielees first began courting Jane Muir, the fates of the two families had been finely interwoven on the personal as well as on the business level – never more demonstrably than in the summer of 1887, when so many of their representatives, from the elderly to the very young, were gathered in one place near Moscow. All that complicated fabric was now destroyed. Where harmony and friendship had once reigned, bitterness and hostility took over.

At the centre of this crisis was the Muirs' elder son, Martin. From Uppingham he had gone up to Pembroke College, Cambridge, where he read Law and was awarded a B.A. degree in 1886. He does not appear to have been placed in any class, perhaps because his first year at the Inner Temple in London ran concurrently with his final year at Cambridge. He was admitted to the Bar in July 1889, having left for Moscow the previous autumn.

Archy Mirrielees described him at five as 'apparently full of strange fancies; always saying queer things and then screwing face afterwards to counteract as it were, very good-natured'; and predicted that he would be the cleverest of the children. Certainly, Martin shared the family's cultivated tastes and interest in all the arts, and at the age of eighteen wrote a letter to Eva 'in the Victor Hugo style', which so impressed her that she sent it on to her parents behind Martin's back. When his father took on the task of coaching him for Cambridge, he found, however, that the great plague was his apathy. Martin seems also to have been chronically short of money; Molly did not at first recognize a letter from him in Cambridge as a very delicate request for a loan. It is Meta, always inclined to see – or bring out? – the best in others, who gives the most attractive glimpses of him: 'Dear old Martin shone in upon us yesterday with his beaming face...'; 'Martin goes into the Temple every day... the foolish boy says he would rather go to Florida or out west, he feels the want of out-of-door exercise'; 'Martin has been in one of his sweetest moods... What shall we do without his merry face and his views on life!'; and, writing from Paris: 'Martin is an unspeakable comfort and refreshment to me. We went to the Salon yesterday and enlivened by Martin's comments I managed to get through it. I was pleased to remark that he was the only well-dressed man in the city.'

But all these cheerful glimpses are strangely at odds with the picture he gives of himself in the letter he wrote from Moscow to congratulate Meta on her forthcoming marriage: 'Dear kind patient Meta, your brother has been a trying person to you, as to everybody else he has come across, but he does love his old Meta very much and he knows that she loves him, and so he is happy in her happiness, and more than ever down in the mouth about his own bad helpless self.'

Kenneth seems less complex. From Uppingham he went up to Trinity College, Oxford, to read for a Pass degree, but left after only a year. He did, however, distinguish himself in the College Boat Club (Martin, too, was a rower) and is included in the photograph of the successful 1886 College VIII. It was a year later that Meta described him in Moscow, cheery as ever, rattling on all meal times telling story after story, discoursing much on his favourite topic, the pleasures of the table, causing amusement by his attempts to imitate Russian words, and socializing with friends from Oxford.

Writing to Kenneth in 1912, Walter Philip stated that not once since the unfortunate misunderstanding between them of 1893 had he spoken a word against him, for he had no reason whatsoever to do so. 'Unfortunately people are totally ignorant of the real circumstances; how the whole trouble arose through Martin, whom your father wished to insist upon our taking into partnership when we considered him unfit. Your misfortune was that you – and who can blame you for it – sided with your father and brother.' By 'we' Walter means himself and Archy, although Walter almost certainly took the final decision. Whether there were other, more specific, reasons for the dismissals than Martin's general unfitness, is something we are unlikely ever to know.

A pattern had indeed repeated itself, but it was not the one that Andrew Muir had in mind. Martin's fate reminds one of William Mirrielees and Archy, and of all those sons expected by their fathers to take on roles for which they are not suited. Writing many years later, Austin Birrell claimed that even in the old Arran days, he could not help feeling that Martin was not getting his fair chance. 'His father, so proud of him as he was, always seemed to me to praise him for the wrong things and to encourage him in the dangerous directions.' Martin was not a strong character, and his letter to Meta hints at a lack of self-confidence, and a strain of self-pity (describing himself as 'more than ever down in the mouth about his own bad hopeless self'), like that to be found in his twin sister Eva. He could probably have found an undemanding job in London that would have suited his particular talents, and led a contented life. As it was, his life was wasted.

The early stages of the dispute are unclear. Mindful, perhaps, of his advancing years, Andrew seems to have been over-eager to force the issue: Martin, after all, had served only four years of his apprenticeship. Walter resisted the paternal pressure, the dispute escalated, sides were taken and positions became entrenched. On 24 February 1893 Meta wrote to Eva that Father had been cheered by a reassuring letter from Epstein, his lawyer in St Petersburg.

He advises that the boys should not demand arbitration but send in a declaration of their claim to the firm carefully made out by a lawyer showing the strength of their legal position, and if the firm still hold out, then the matter must be brought before the commercial court. So there is one chance more for compromise, but I fear there is little hope of the other side making use of it. In the meantime I have said no more to Mother and she does not yet know about the dismissal of the boys. [In his letter of 1912 Walter suggests that Kenneth left of his own accord, out of family loyalty, but he may have been rewriting the record to save Kenneth's face.] I keep putting off in the vain hope that something may happen to make it unnecessary.

Nothing did happen, however, and ten days later Meta wrote:

We have had rather a gloomy time of it with the parents both in bed, not seriously ill but ailing. I told Mother about the dismissal of the boys and the whole thing shook her a good deal. I heard that they had put off sending in the declaration and I thought it was only right to give Mother a chance of writing to Walter before it was too late. She did this at once but I doubt if it will have any effect in averting the lawsuit. Poor darling, it is terrible that she should suffer like this. I try to be with her most of the time because as soon as I go away Father begins talking about the Russian affair and he cannot keep within bounds and must needs pour vinegar on the wound. Mother is up again today, but she looks sad and aged.

Alice's position was the most painful of all. Her loyalties were impossibly divided. Placed between her son Walter, and her sons Martin and Kenneth, she must have felt as if she were being asked to choose between her first and second husbands, between William Philip and Andrew Muir.

Andrew, too, felt deeply wounded, but was in no doubt where his loyalties lay. Much emotional capital had been invested in the boys: both parents grieved constantly at their failure to write more often from Russia. But Andrew also wanted to have the satisfaction of knowing that after his death something of himself would be perpetuated in his children. The boys, he hoped, would make the same kind of mark in the business world as he had done, while Meta pursued his other absorbing interest, discovered late in life: that of creative home-building. In his response to the boys' dismissal, Andrew Muir, philosopher and advocate of common sense, emerges as a very passionate man. Having written two years earlier that 'you have to guard against being led away by feelings when it comes to business', he himself was led away completely. Unable to obtain satisfaction from the Moscow Commercial Court on his sons' behalf, he pursued his lawsuit with tragic obstinacy and disregard of expense to the very highest level over a period of six years, thereby prolonging Alice's agony and ruling out the possibility of any family reconciliation. Even more tragically, he encouraged his sons to embark on a new and very ambitious business venture.

A more dispassionate man might have stopped to ask himself whether Martin and Kenneth were the right people to be in charge of any large business undertaking, but Andrew was blind to his sons' shortcomings. The man who had begrudged Molly her half-a-crown Spanish dictionary now threw financial caution to the winds. In the years remaining to him he parted with huge sums of money to enable his sons to set up and run Muir Brothers & Company: a Chemical Works on a 40-acre site at Degunino, eight miles from the centre of Moscow and close to the railway. The Muirs bought it at auction in 1895, the previous owner having exhausted his resources by building it on far too lavish a scale; its offices, in particular, were palatial. Later in the year the Works went into operation producing sulphuric acid, oil of vitriol, hydrochloric acid, nitric acid, acetic acid and borax. It was all a gambler's throw on Andrew's part, reminding one of how Jane at the very outset of his career, in the old Clyde Pottery days, had warned her brother against allowing his sanguine disposition to tempt him into taking unnecessary risks.

Andrew at this time must have been thinking constantly about money. In May 1897 he revised his will, pointing out in a Memorandum that he was having to do so because the value of his estate had been reduced from over £100,000 to less than £90,000, largely owing to the fall in South African shares. 'The first thing my Executors have to do is sell 42 Holland Park and dispose of furniture. As Bryony Hill is so much a family house and a creation of my own and as it possesses many advantages it is to be supposed that Mrs Muir will continue to occupy it if income permits' (these last three words were added later). The biggest question-mark was against his investment as a deposit partner in Muir Bros. & Co., 'the success of whose chemical works still remains uncertain, the business being little more than half way towards a satisfactory development'.

A year later, he had become so anxious that he decided to go out to Moscow to see for himself. He was eighty-one and took the precaution of inviting his nephew, Claud Muir, a London G.P., to go out with him for a holiday. One letter only, to 'dearest Alice', survives from this visit. Considering how little he had slept on the train, Andrew writes, he was feeling wonderfully well. At St Petersburg, after a hot bath and lunch, they drove to the *Gostinnyi dvor*, where they found Faleyev, manager of the Oborot Co., at his post of duty.

I was glad to meet him again. There was also one old clerk of my time who gave me a pleasant greeting. It was rather sad to see how the charm of youth had vanished from Faleyev, and there was instead the plodding, middle-aged business man. The business is thriving thanks to its old good organization and Faleyev's steady management.

After showing Claud some of the principal rooms of the Hermitage, Andrew felt very limp and went back to the hotel to rest before they caught the night train.

We reached Moscow at 10.10 a.m., catching a sight of the works as we passed them about 10 minutes before Moscow. Martin and Kenneth were on the Station and it was a very joyful meeting for us. You may be sure the sight of them did my heart good. Martin was looking thin but Kenneth quite hearty.

At last I have the great pleasure of being with our dear boys, of finding them quite their old selves, and of having a long and pleasant chat. I shall probably go to the works tomorrow if it is fair.

In August Austin Birrell told Meta how delighted he was that her father's courageous visit to Moscow had been successful and that he had come back satisfied. 'It would have been tragic otherwise.'

Courageous it undoubtedly was, but it was tragic, also. Andrew must have convinced himself, with some help from the boys, that the firm was still experiencing teething troubles and its heavy annual losses would soon be reversed. So eager was he to believe that his boys would make a go of things that he heard and saw only what he wanted to.

The saddest aspect of this visit, however, does not concern Muir Bros., but M & M's. Intrigued though Andrew must have been to see the two thriving retail shops that carried his name, it seems unlikely that he went near them. For M & M's was still the enemy, and the protracted series of appeals to ever higher legal authorities was still pursuing its course.

Then, on the evening of 1 March 1899, as Meta wrote to Stuart from 'Bryony', an astonishing thing happened.

I was sitting sewing and Father reading on either side of the little table when a telegram was brought in at which Father gazed at first in a bewildered sort of way and then studied for about 5 minutes finally handing it to me to read. 'Glorious victory' it ran 'decree of the Senate annulled Epstein.' Here was a bombshell indeed. 'Well it rather bothers me' says Father 'I thought the whole thing was buried.' However he could not entirely conceal his triumph & satisfaction, and had to take another cigarette to calm himself. He does not know what will happen next and whether the whole thing won't have to be gone through from the beginning. I feel vexed and don't see what good can come of it and it will be too annoying to have all the old bitterness & ill-feeling revived.

She dreaded the effect on Mother, but felt that Father was aware of the necessity of avoiding the subject with her.

Maida in her Family Record states that this final appeal was to the Emperor himself. She had naturally sided with Walter and her brother Archy in the family quarrel; Martin and Kenneth, she writes, 'did not fit into the business and would not submit to the rigid discipline which had made Walter and Fred good businessmen'. But such was the strength of feeling aroused by the affair that this otherwise reliable informant remained under the impression that the final appeal, too, had been unsuccessful. Indeed, bearing in mind the terms of the original partnership agreement, it is hard to see what kind of case the Muirs were able to present. Nicholas II must have been swayed by the emotional appeal of a father striving so persistently to vindicate his sons' honour.

Meta's fears of renewed bitterness were not to be realized, for on 11 June 1899 Andrew Muir died at 'Bryony'. His younger granddaughter, three-year-old Margaret, who had amused him greatly on his eighty-second birthday by presenting him with a little gilt doll's saucer and two chocolate drops, was sorry not to find Granpa in his room any more, but felt he had not been very clever. '*I* shall never die,' she announced to her mother with complete conviction.

Other considerations than M & M's now filled the Muirs' minds. They awoke to the realization that they were no longer wealthy. There was very little ready cash in the estate. *Both* houses would have to be sold. Alice must have been relieved that she was under no obligation to go on living at 'Bryony'. Reduced circumstances probably meant little to one who had known so many vicissitudes in the earlier part of her life. She and Eva moved into a flat in London at 11 Campden Hill Court, while Molly took a set of rooms on her own in Tachbrook Street.

What primarily concerned the major beneficiaries of Andrew's will, however, was the future of Muir Bros., since so much of the estate was tied up in the firm. In the month after their father's death Martin and Kenneth took out a second mortgage to raise capital, while Molly in the course of a long winter visit agreed to lend them £6000, her legacy from the estate. It was Kenneth who now saw himself as the hero of the hour and stepped forward to replace Martin as the man in charge. In May 1900 he wrote to Meta complaining that the executors of the will, one of whom was his brother-in-law, Stuart Hogg, did not have any confidence in the managers. 'I don't care a rap or a snuff what people think of me personally if only I can save the family's fortunes.' But only a few weeks later Molly received a 'horribly disturbing' letter from him. She consulted Meta, but found her 'vague and helpless'. Stuart, however, agreed to go out to Moscow with a proposal that Kenneth should stand down, but the latter was uncooperative.

The executors also arranged for auditors to go out to assess the firm's finances and prospects, and on 1 October 1900 they presented their report. They found that no books had been written up since the end of 1897, with the result that for a considerable time certain goods had been produced at a heavy loss without anyone noticing. Andrew Muir's capital, amounting to some £50,000 if unpaid interest were included, had vanished completely. The main cause of the unsatisfactory results had been mismanagement, combined latterly with shortness of working capital. This lack of capital – and here the auditors made what must have seemed to the rest of the family their most damning judgment – had been due, to no small extent, 'to the heavy drain on the business by reason of the large drawings of the partners. These were much in excess of the amounts stipulated in the partnership agreement.' It was a wrong that was never to be righted.

Under good management, the report concluded, the business could still be turned into a profitable one, but 'we are strongly of opinion that no further amounts should be invested in the business by the family unless someone could be found possessing their confidence who would have entire control of the management.' Kenneth did eventually offer to step down, and the Works limped along under outside management until the Revolution, never becoming profitable enough to enable the Muirs to sell it.

It was a sad postscript to the career of Andrew Muir, the man who had returned in such triumph from Moscow. Seen in retrospect, his life is full of ironies. Far from perpetuating him, his sons let him down badly; even during his lifetime they must have fallen far short of his expectations. For the last six years of his life he was completely alienated from the business that owed its success to his inspiration. As he had half-anticipated, 'Bryony', the house on which he had lavished so much care, passed out of the family with his death. Even his paintings fetched very poor prices at Christie's when they, too, had to be auctioned.

Andrew Muir's fate was more complex than that of Archibald Mirrielees, but then he was a more complex man. He recognized the extent to which his whole life had been shaped by his Muir merchant background when he wrote to Meta in 1892: 'I wish I had kept more clear from business troubles,' (his London Portland Cement Co. was involved in two lawsuits) 'but I have a hereditary tendency to enterprises of all kinds, and this is an expensive taste.' Unlike his cautious brother-in-law, he saw himself as a born speculator and was fully prepared to run the risks which that entailed. Before leaving Russia he had written that he felt 'more inclined for meditation than for action', but in the event he could not resist becoming involved in all kinds of new business enterprises, until he embarked on his last – and most costly – speculation in the Chemical Works. That 'expensive taste' seems more like an addiction.

But Andrew also possessed a restlessly active, enquiring, independent mind, in contrast again to Archibald, who from the time of his conversion was untroubled by doubt or introspection. This, too, went back a long way: to the period in his youth when he realized that he could not share the same religious faith as his family and struck out on his own. Andrew Muir the thinker, the critical observer, was constantly striving to impose some meaningful pattern on what the businessman was doing. Lacking the simple religious framework that enabled Archibald to reconcile Profit with Piety, Andrew found in the ideas of Herbert Spencer an evolutionary justification for his moneymaking business activities. In the 1880's he studied a very different thinker, Tolstoy, who asked searching questions about the moral justification for individual wealth and luxurious living. There were those like Aylmer Maude, the head of M & M's carpet department from 1883 to 1890, and later Tolstoy's biographer, who were persuaded that no such justification could be found and who felt obliged to renounce the world of buying and selling completely. Andrew Muir the businessman was too firmly entrenched for that to happen, but even when the businessman is assuring Meta and Stuart that Tolstoy's ideal of a self-sufficient life 'won't do, at least for people above the working class', one suspects that the thinker has still not abandoned this controversial field. Those were the years, of course, when 'the good old English gentleman' was still riding high, complacently making sense of his own life in terms of what he had achieved and what he would pass on to his children.

These two aspects of Andrew Muir are neatly captured by the two senses of the verb 'to speculate': on the one hand, to reflect or theorize or conjecture, and on the other, to buy and sell with a view to making a profit. What makes him unusual is that he was a speculator in both senses. The two activities, as his case makes clear, are not so far apart as they might seem. Common to both is the element of uncertainty and guesswork – of setting out on a voyage of discovery with nothing but your own wits and resources to rely upon.

Throughout his life Andrew Muir engaged in metaphysical as well as commercial speculation. In those final years the businessman might be thinking constantly of money, but the thinker was preoccupied with the mysteriousness of life. 'Naturally at my advanced age,' he wrote to Meta in 1892, 'the riddle of life comes constantly into the mind. I seek a solution, but I seek in vain, and I envy those old believers who never doubted.' On learning of Andrew's death, Austin Birrell wrote to Meta: 'One feels he has escaped as out of a cage into the blue heavens, the mystery of which he so long pondered. I am sure I never knew a more thoughtful man or one who so gravely considered the problem of existence.'

A month later, Meta wrote from Hambledon to Stuart in London:

It has been another lovely evening, and I have been wondering & wondering about Father – where he is now and if he knows anything about our doings.

But what use is it knocking one's head against that mystery?

We keep coming across markings in books of his & even little poems copied out, touching things showing how his mind was latterly always working on this problem.

Perhaps this was the deepest continuity in his life, after all.

Identifying with the Firm

Walter Philip (1845 – 1919)

14

An Uncompromising Nature

Walter Philip, the third and last head of M & M's, was born at Port Elizabeth in South Africa on 12 December 1845. He never knew his father, the missionary William Philip, who had been drowned five months earlier, nor can he have remembered his celebrated grandfather, the Revd Dr John Philip, since Alice left South Africa with her three boys in 1848. Later, he was to turn his back completely on his religious forebears, not attending the British Church in St Petersburg or Moscow, nor even, in spite of being one of the community's wealthiest members, making a token annual contribution to church funds.

Walter also grew up without ever knowing a settled home. South Africa was followed by three years in Europe. He was still under six when he began attending a boarding-school in Germany with his elder brothers and learned to 'gabble away' in German; still under eight when they were sent in October 1853 to the school at Blackheath for the sons of missionaries. Alice was not an uncaring mother, but she had few options open to her. At boarding-school the boys would receive a sound, inexpensive education, while she herself would be free to earn a modest income from teaching and chaperoning. The boys spent Christmas Day 1854 with the Lethems, returning that same evening to the school, and two days later Johnnie, the eldest boy, loyally informed his mother that they were all quite well and enjoying the holidays very much.

For the young Philips it was an improvised, makeshift sort of life, and probably not a very happy one. Alice herself in January 1857 referred to 'the poor boys' having just returned to school. Writing to her on 28 October 1858, Willie, the second brother, apologizes for missing her birthday, but he had 'been so stupid as not to ask Mrs Flower [the headmaster's wife?] for a penny': in other words, he had no stamps. Alice had sent him and Walter second-hand greatcoats, which they like, 'but Mrs Flower wishes you had got some new ones'. Did the indignity of having to wear someone else's cast-off coat as a teenager lodge in Walter's memory in the same way that Archibald Mirrielees never forgot the porridge from breakfast that had to be finished before he was allowed to start his dinner?

Nor was Johnnie much help to his younger brothers. 'Do you remember how you neglected us two when we were young 'uns,' Walter wrote to him later, 'you never could be bothered with us.' Walter emerged from these early experiences well able to stand on his own feet, but also, it seems, with a somewhat cool, withdrawn attitude towards other people. Archy Mirrielees offers an interesting comparison, for he strikes one as both warmer and more vulnerable. Andrew and Alice could not understand why Archy felt miserable and homesick on his arrival in St Petersburg in 1867: was he not over seventeen and 'decidedly past boyhood'? But Archy, with his settled home and loving family environment, had not learned the same lessons of stoical endurance as Walter.

Maida Mirrielees, a seven-year-old bridesmaid, remembered the fifteen-year-old Walter at Andrew and Alice's wedding in April 1861 as 'a very good-looking youth with a rosy complexion as beautiful as a girl's'. In 1862, when he was sixteen, he went out to St Petersburg to start working for his stepfather. One of his very few letters to survive was written to his brother Johnnie in Cape Town and dated 'St Petersburg, 17/29 January 1863'. Christmas and New Year, Walter writes, 'went off awfully slow, some keeping old style and others the new; had there not been mincepies & plum pudding I think I could almost have forgotten it'. He finds the office rules rather strict: 'we may not read if we have nothing to do & must always sit till the hour of departure strikes' – a legacy, no doubt, of Archibald Mirrielees. The business being import, they work as hard in winter as in summer. He is receiving £27 a year, but hopes it will soon be increased. 'You will laugh at this salary compared with yours, but I think keeping oneself is dearer with you than with us. Mr Muir has given me a room, which however is rather empty of furniture & is rather dark & cold.' Skating is his daily outdoor exercise. He had recently joined a party and skated to Strelna and back. 'Being the first time I have skated any long distance, you may believe that I was tired.' He is also looking forward to ice-boating. 'The boat goes almost as fast as the wind which blows it & could easily outrun a train.'

The greatest drawback to his new way of life, however, is the want of companions of his own age.

You know that I am never in a hurry to make friends & that I cannot bear a friend to be too intimate. I don't know how it is. You always liked your companions to be older than yourself, but I don't. I will finish this letter by a few questions which you are to answer by return mail. Who are your best friends? What jollifications do you have? Do you ever see Punch? And do you intend to marry in England?

With the arrival of Archy in 1867 and Fred a year later Walter could no longer complain of lack of companions. He and Archy became lifelong friends. To Walter, who could not bear a friend to be too intimate and did not like his companions to be older than himself, it must have been an advantage that Archy was four years his junior.

Matrimonial prospects were a constant preoccupation of the British young men in Russia. 'Unluckily there are few girls of a very *eligible* kind here,' Archy wrote to Maida in 1869, 'too Petersburgy for my taste; rather measly on the whole: not to say there are no nice girls, but I am not at present over head & ears in love with any of them.' Three years later he spells out the difficulties:

I begin to think that we stand a very poor chance in the matrimonial way, exiled out here as we are, and have every probability of remaining bachelors to the end of our days. How for instance is a man to fall in love, well perhaps he won't take so long about that, but to court and marry a girl according to modern notions of these things in a month's or even say two months' time? There is another alternative, perhaps we can find some delightful Russian damsel to suit us in every respect, but then those Russian parents and relations that won't be able to speak a word of English and with their queer foreign manners and ways, how will you like that, you dear English sisters?

Maida was always making helpful suggestions. 'Your proposals for Walter were not quite so unpromising,' Archy wrote to her in March 1872, 'though I think he is almost too cosmopolitan to suit a thoroughly English girl'; while in December, commenting on an outbreak of 'love-fever' in their circle, he wrote: 'I wish we could get Walter on the list of patients, and when he is in England next year it will be a shame if he still perseveres in his obstinacy.' Walter perseveres in his obstinacy for the next ten years. He himself always said that somewhere a tall graceful blonde was waiting for him, and at Christmas 1882, during the holidays that he spent as usual at 42, this fantasy materialized in the person of Laura Reid, who was staying with the Muirs. Laura was nineteen, half Walter's age. Her parents, of Scottish extraction living in South Africa, at first refused permission for an engagement. Meta thought that it was almost certainly the fault of Laura's interfering aunt in London 'for saying that Walter was not a Christian in Mr Reid's sense', but the Muirs, led by Alice, campaigned skilfully on Walter's behalf, the decision was reversed, and the marriage took place in September 1883.

At the time of Walter's engagement, Meta remarked on how much he loathed congratulations and 'inharmonious jesting', while Austin Birrell, discussing a proposed visit by Walter and Laura, comments: 'I think we might have squeezed them in, but Olive [Austin's unmarried sister] dreaded their well-known fastidiousness.' This fastidiousness offers a point of entry into Walter's character. Everything, it seems, had to be just right for him; second-best would never do. He was not content with being a good skater or a good businessman; he had to be first-class. As for his future wife, he had always had a clear picture in his mind of what she should look like, and would settle for nothing less. When the Philips threw a children's Christmas party, their tree was sure to be bigger than anyone else's; when they went to stay on Arran, they rented the best house on the island; and Terence, their only son (who followed five daughters), was sent to Eton. All these demonstrations of superiority might be seen as a reaction to earlier circumstances: the spectre of genteel poverty that had hovered constantly over his formative years needed to be comprehensively exorcized. But they also suggest something more fundamental: a wilful, uncompromising element in his nature that was to be very much in evidence at the time of the boys' dismissal in 1893. To Meta it was obvious then that once Walter's mind was made up, not even his mother's intervention would have any effect.

It takes two sides, of course, to make a family quarrel: so what of Walter's side of the affair?

From Maida's comments in the Family Record it seems likely that Walter tried hard to stop Martin joining the firm in the first place, but was overruled by his stepfather. In later pronouncing him unfit, he was exercising a right that Andrew himself had fully acknowledged earlier, when he wrote to Stuart that at the end of an apprenticeship his ultimate fitness would still be in question, 'as it is to this day in the case of

Martin and Kenneth'. Moreover, there is good reason for thinking that Martin *was* unfit: that he was lazy, irresponsible – to make time to write his letter of congratulation to Meta, he simply took a day off work – and incompetent (his father does not sound very confident when he wonders how Martin will cope as head cashier). Yet many a family business must have carried a family passenger or two, and Walter was happy enough later on to find a comfortable niche in the firm for William Mirrielees' not very competent son, Guy. Nor can he possibly have failed to foresee the painful consequences that the dismissals would have in the family circle. He had known Martin and Kenneth all their lives, for years before his marriage 42 had been his second home, and the Muirs had all rallied round to make sure that his marriage went ahead in spite of difficulties from Laura's 'obdurate papa', as Andrew called him. So why did he dig his heels in so firmly?

Was there some deep-seated resentment of Mr Muir, the usurping stepfather? This seems unlikely. Walter had never known his own father, he had every reason to feel grateful towards Andrew, and relations between them before 1893 appear to have been perfectly cordial. Or did he feel resentful of Martin and Kenneth? Unlike him, they had grown up in complete security. Their family background was very settled; everything had been made easy for them. Whereas Walter and his brothers had been educated on a shoestring at the mission school, Martin and Kenneth had been sent at considerable expense to public school and university, made many friends, and developed expensive tastes and interests. Like Eva and Molly, so taken aback at being told to pay for their own Spanish lessons, they had been brought up to expect to spend money freely. For them, joining the well-established family business in Moscow was no more than a means to an end: to perpetuate as soon as possible, and with minimal effort, the kind of comfortable life to which they were accustomed. Visiting the Moscow theatres, going on bear-shooting expeditions, and in Kenneth's case, training borzoi dogs to be shown on his visits to England: such activities were more to their liking than poring over the repulsive details of office ledgers. 'The firm has started having its own van horses,' Kenneth wrote, 'and has acquired some old racing stables with 32 loose boxes and a small manège where one could ride in winter at a pinch. Martin and I intend having small Military tournaments there all to ourselves.' One can understand how Walter, having devoted his whole life to the business, might resent these two privileged young men, who showed little interest in the business for its own sake and were now about to reap the benefits of what he had sown, walking into junior partnerships which they did not deserve. It must have riled him especially to think that Martin of all people was likely to become the next head of the firm. Andrew Muir's withdrawal from the partnership gave Walter the opportunity that he had long been awaiting.

Yet perhaps even this explanation makes Walter's behaviour seem too deliberate and rational. According to Archy, writing in 1872, Walter used to refer to Martin then as 'the born cad'. It is a strange phrase to use of a seven-year-old, and suggests someone whose own standards of integrity are very uncompromising. By 1893, with his stepfather no longer on the scene and the business expanding so rapidly, Walter's sense of personal identification with M & M's must have become complete. Its advances were his advances, its standards his standards. The whole enterprise was in danger of being compromised by Martin and Kenneth's laxity and lack of commitment. Although Walter may have abandoned the religious beliefs of his father and grandfather, he seems to have inherited from them the same kind of single-mindedness and strength of purpose that made Dr Philip champion the Hottentots in the face of violent hostility from the White settlers, or William Philip push through virtually single-handed his daring irrigation scheme. M & M's was Walter's 'missionary cause', and he was not going to let it be compromised by 'non-believers'.

Of the three men who ran M & M's over a period of seventy-five years – Archibald Mirrielees, Andrew Muir and Walter Philip – it is the one closest to us in time who remains the most enigmatic. Partly this is because relatively little biographical material about him has survived, but partly because he himself was not a very open person. Aloof and uncompromising, a perfectionist, formal and dignified – in a photograph taken in his sixties he looks every inch 'the company chairman' – yet with a certain discreet flamboyance, Walter was a more appropriate figure than his predecessors to preside over what ceased to be merely a business or a shop and became a famous Russian institution: the Muir & Mirrielees department store.

15

Moscow's 'Universal Provider'?

A department store has been defined as a large retail store with four or more separate departments under one roof, each selling different classes of goods of which one is women's and children's wear. The shopkeeper who had to put several assistants in charge of departments could not rely upon their individual bargaining skills, so fixed prices had to be introduced: an innovation that caused much resentment among those elderly female shoppers who had always prided themselves on their tact and management in obtaining goods at the lowest prices.

The Bon Marché of Paris is often referred to as the first department store. Dating back at least to the 1830's, by 1852 it had four departments and twelve employees. But as Alison Adburgham points out in *Shops and Shopping 1800-1914*, its innovations – fixed prices, no obligation to purchase, entitlement to exchange of goods or a refund, periodical bargain sales, daily deliveries to every part of the city, and the cutting of profit margins through quantity sales – had already been anticipated in England by such firms as Bainbridge's of Newcastle and Kendal Milne & Faulkner of Manchester.

London's stores were slower to diversify, but once they began doing so in the 1860's, there was no looking back. It was an era of retail adventurers, and the most successful soon became household names. The élite still patronized the expensive little shops, would never have dreamed of paying cash for goods, and settled their accounts once a year if the shopkeeper were lucky. The department stores were not for them, but for the new Victorian middle classes, who had earned their prosperity, expected good value for money, and attached great importance to such outward signs of prosperity as fine clothes for all the members of their large families, and fine furnishings for their correspondingly large houses. Especially did the stores appeal to the ladies. With improved railway services, they developed the habit of coming into London from the suburbs and beyond for a day's shopping, knowing that they could make all or most of their purchases under one roof and have the goods delivered promptly free of charge to their own homes. Even their less affluent sisters could enjoy the pleasurable diversion of window-shopping.

It was nearly always, Adburgham writes, from little drapery shops that the big stores grew. This applies to Jenners of Edinburgh, which opened its doors on 1 May 1838 and now describes itself as 'the world's oldest independent department store'. Of all the famous London stores the one most relevant to M & M's is that of William Whiteley, in view of Andrew Muir's comment about their Moscow fire in February 1892, that 'it may be a case of incendiarism originating with jealous rivals as with Whiteley, whose case is very much parallel with ours'.

William Whiteley was born near Leeds in 1831 and apprenticed in 1848 to the largest draper in Wakefield. A visit to London in 1851 to see the Great Exhibition may have fired his ambition. The day after completing his apprenticeship in 1855, he left Wakefield for London with £10 in his pocket. During the next eight years he devoted himself single-mindedly to gaining experience, saved £700, and was ready to start his own shop. He spent a long time choosing the best locality. Oxford Street and even more so, Regent Street, were the most brilliant and fashionable shopping areas, while in New and Old Bond Street many of the establishments were entitled to carry Royal Arms. He opted instead for Westbourne Grove in the Bayswater district. On 10 January 1863, London's first Underground Railway had opened with its terminus at Bishop's Road on the edge of Kensington and Bayswater. From 3 to 5 every afternoon Whiteley positioned himself on the pavement opposite the premises that he had in mind and counted the passers-by. Westbourne Grove, previously nicknamed 'Bankruptcy Avenue' because so many shops failed there, was, he decided, a street with a future. He leased No.31 and took on two girls as counter assistants – one of whom he married four years later – and an errand-boy.

Shopkeeping morality was at a very low ebb. Prices were high and profits exorbitant; customers were pestered and often cheated. Whiteley reversed all this, and his success was immediate. By 1867 he had seventeen departments, of which silks and dresses had the biggest turnover. He was regularly leasing additional premises, not only for new departments, but to house his growing army of employees. 'The spirit of the firm,' writes his biographer, Richard Lambert, 'was paternal, not to say patriarchal; and its enterprise partook of the fierce, barbarian energy of its patriarch.' In 1872 Whiteley the draper began to style himself Whiteley the 'Universal Provider', a title of breathtaking arrogance which he embodied in his trademark. From now on, God might stick to the heavens; William Whiteley would take care of you on earth from the cradle to the grave – always assuming that you could afford his prices.

By the time that the Muirs took up residence in Holland Park in 1874, the Universal Provider had moved from strength to strength. He had seen the importance of attracting male as well as female customers, and gentlemen's outfitting had become one of his most successful departments. From Holland Park to Westbourne Grove was no more than a short carriage drive. Alice Muir's diaries for the late 1870's show that she shopped at Whiteley's far more frequently than at any other store. Mostly, she ordered dresses and other items of clothing for herself and her daughters, though on one occasion she took Kenneth there for boots and shoes. When Eva was about to accompany her father and aunt on a visit to Spain, Alice was relieved to find that the store stocked everything her daughter might need. She also patronized Whiteley's provision shop, especially before Christmas when she was preparing her famous 'Cape Box'. Like other shopkeepers, Whiteley made a great fuss of his 'carriage trade'. Alice did not have to pay cash, but was probably one of those customers encouraged to deposit sums with him and draw on them as needed: a practice that enabled him to build up his own banking business and to finance his alterations and enlargements.

By this time the Universal Provider was offering all kinds of services as well as goods. He was infinitely anxious to oblige. 'Ladies,' he would announce, 'it shall be done.' During the 1870's he introduced a restaurant, serving ten different kinds of soup daily and numerous delicacies, all remarkably cheap; a house-agency, a cleaning and dyeing service, furniture repairing, building and house decoration, a hairdressing service, a shipping department, and an agency selling opera and theatre tickets. His most famous department of all, the 'Hire and Exhibition' department introduced in 1881, was prepared to take on anything, however outlandish the request, and its exploits made Whiteley's name legendary. The story was told of the clergyman who announced: 'Mr Whiteley, I want an elephant. Today!' Within four hours a tuskiana had appeared in the reverend gentleman's coach-house. Another joker asked to be supplied with a second-hand coffin.

In September 1878, however, Maggie Birrell found a chink in Whiteley's armour, when she and Austin were about to move house. To Maida she wrote: 'I hope we may be safely carried through this next week, but I have my doubts. Your friend Whiteley has at last succumbed! He has fallen. Whiteley the GREAT has fallen! has fallen! He does not undertake to remove Furniture. He is *not* a universal provider. Woe! Woe! WOE! You must hide your diminished head and no longer brag of your friend.'

Maggie's comments only confirm the extent to which Whiteley's claims had seized the imagination of the middle-class public.

*   *   *

As mentioned above, M & M's opened their millinery and haberdashery shop in September 1885, but the decision to go in for retail trading must have been taken much earlier. The acquisition, some time before 1885 and perhaps as early as 1878, of their Theatre Square building is likely to have been the first step in implementing this policy. Why bother to choose such an expensive central position unless they intended opening their doors to the public? Why else choose a corner site so reminiscent, for example, of those favoured in London by John Barker in 1870 or by Marshall & Snelgrove in 1876? One may suppose that the phenomenal success of the great department stores in London had a decisive influence on how M & M's saw their future role in Moscow, and that once they had decided to become retailers, it was to London stores like that of William Whiteley – 'whose case is very much parallel with ours' – that they looked for examples to follow.

They could not have chosen a better site for a large retail shop. There was no need for Walter Philip or Archy Mirrielees to station himself on the pavement every afternoon to count the passers-by; a glance at the map shows what a focal point in the life of Moscow Theatre Square was bound to be. Lying just north of the Kremlin and Red Square, it was dominated at its far end by the Bolshoi, or Great Imperial Theatre, which staged opera and ballet on the grand scale. This imposing classical edifice, rebuilt in 1856, was decorated inside in white and gold, contained five balconies and over a hundred boxes, and seated in all some 2500 spectators. M & M's three-storey building on the corner opposite barely reached to the height of the Bolshoi's eight Ionic entrance columns. On the right-hand side of the Square stood the Malyi, or Little Imperial Theatre, built in 1841, which staged dramas and could seat a thousand. This part of Moscow was not, however, frequented by theatre-goers only. For many years, right next to M & M's, there had been very popular shopping arcades, so that the habit of shopping in the area was well established. The Petrovka, the busy street leading out of the Square and on which M & M's had their longer frontage, contained some of the best shops in Moscow, but even better were those on *Kuznetsky most*, the street crossing the Petrovka, where M & M's rented their second shop in the Gagarin Building.

In choosing to start their retail life with a millinery and haberdashery shop, the firm was playing safe. These were the kind of goods in which they had long specialized as wholesalers, and which would remain an essential part of their retail trade. That their long-term strategy was daringly ambitious, however, is confirmed by the speed with which, like Whiteley, they then added new departments. 'There is absolutely nowhere in the whole of Russia,' a writer commented in 1888, 'where you will find such a vast shop, both as regards floor space, and the variety and abundance of goods being offered for sale.' He was particularly impressed by a refinement likely to have been copied from London: the provision of a special gaslit room to enable ladies to see how different-coloured materials for evening dresses would look by artificial light. By 1889 the Theatre Square building had twenty-five departments, with the emphasis on items to wear of every description and on dress materials, and the number of staff had grown to 400. At that time the top floor was still wholesale. When M & M's gave up wholesale trading in 1891, the number of retail departments must have increased still further. At the Gagarin Building, in addition to the bulkier furnishing goods, such as carpets, oilcloth, fabrics, lamps and household equipment, they also sold stationery. By 1898 the combined number of departments in the two shops was forty-four, a rate of expansion that is impressive even by Whiteley's standards. The staff numbered almost a thousand.

Success came quickly to the new shops, as it did to Whiteley's, and for the same basic reason: that the firm could be relied upon to give its customers an absolutely fair deal. Goods were of excellent quality and reasonably priced as a result of quantity purchasing, prices were fixed and clearly marked, the assistants were scrupulously polite, complaints were dealt with promptly and replacements or refunds given, and customers with accounts could be sure that the bills they received were accurate. For Moscow in the 1890's these were all novel features, just as they had been in London a generation earlier.

Like Whiteley's, M & M's appealed especially to the prosperous new middle classes – professional people, civil servants, 'white collar' workers, the owners and managers of small businesses or factories – who appreciated good value for money, whether they were buying a fashionable item of clothing or merely some routine piece of household equipment. They spoke at least one foreign language, usually French, had probably travelled in Europe, and liked the idea that at M & M's it was possible to buy under one roof the best goods imported from all over Europe. In their advertising the firm stressed that their goods could not be obtained elsewhere. Their catalogues carried a prominent 'Warning' to the public that they were not represented anywhere else in the Russian Empire, that they had not opened any branches and that they would not be doing so in the future. Shopping at M & M's therefore bestowed a certain social cachet.

No attempt appears to have been made to present the shop as a specifically British concern. To some extent, this may have reflected the cosmopolitan outlook of Walter Philip himself. In general, however, the British management appears to have pursued a policy of self-effacement. In London William Whiteley was a public figure, who made a point of stationing himself just inside the main doors of his shop and greeting his wealthier customers with what his detractors described as fawningly obsequious smiles, and who even at one stage offered portraits of himself for sale (they were a flop). In Moscow not many people outside the British community are likely to have been familiar with the name of Walter Philip. He remained a figure in the background, unknown to the public at large. The shop must stand or fall on its own merits – and stand it triumphantly did.

But M & M's were by no means universally popular, any more than the Universal Provider had been. The dislike and dismay that Whiteley inspired among the smaller shopkeepers in his neighbourhood swelled into rage in 1875 when he announced his intention of opening a provision shop, and on Guy Fawkes' night in the following year the local butchers paraded through the streets carrying Whiteley's effigy and then ceremonially burned it. For ten years the local council did everything in its power to thwart his plans. In Moscow, too, as M & M's opened more and more departments, the smaller shops specializing in particular lines must have felt that they were being priced out of business by unscrupulous competition from their powerful neighbour. These were the 'jealous rivals' to whom Andrew Muir referred in his letter of 1892, although Walter is unlikely to have attracted the same personal animosity as Whiteley.

*   *   *

Conditions of employment for shop assistants in 19th century Europe were generally appalling. In Britain the Shop Hours Act of 1886 stipulated only that persons under 18 must not work more than 74 hours a week; adult hours were not restricted until much later. The worst offenders, however, were the small shops, not the stores. In the 1880's Whiteley's was open from 8.30 to 7, and until 2 on Saturdays. A fortnight's holiday was allowed. Salesmen received £40-50 p.a. and saleswomen £20-25, but Whiteley also provided free board and lodging: large nearby properties were taken over as dormitories, while meals, including breakfast before work, were served in the shops' basements. (Marshall & Snelgrove were regarded as exceptional in allowing 40 minutes for lunch and 20 for tea.) Whiteley's employees had no cause to complain about food or living conditions, but what they did resent was the firm's rule-book. Infringement of any of its 176 rules resulted in fines, varying from sixpence to half a crown, which went straight into their employer's pocket. Probably in retaliation, employees engaged in a considerable amount of theft, fraud and pilfering. When detected, they were invariably prosecuted. As his biographer concludes, 'the amount of petty thieving for which Whiteley felt called upon to put his employees in the dock was more than was good for his reputation as a manager of men'.

The grandmother of A.Yu.Bazilyevich (co-translator of *Muir & Mirrielees* into Russian) grew up in a Moscow girls orphanage. In their final year the girls were offered free tuition in accounting by the mathematics teacher, and she was then taken on by M & M's, for whom she worked in a variety of capacities from 1906 to 1914. The regime was very strict, she recalled in old age. 'The Englishmen liked taking on girls from our orphanage because they were well-disciplined. The girls chosen were tall and thin from orphanage food, quiet and obedient.' They worked from 9 to 7, with 30 minutes for lunch and two 10-minute breaks. 'Sales assistants had to clock in well before the shop opened at 9, and clerks by 10 past. At the staff entrance stood the porter. There was a large control clock on the wall behind him, and hanging on a board were keys with the employees' numbers. The porter had to punch the clock if anyone was just one minute late.' (She does not mention fines or penalties.) 'The Englishmen loved uniforms. In winter the saleswomen had to wear black dresses, and in summer a white blouse with a skirt of any colour.' All the staff had to wear uniform, including the kitchen maids who served the staff's two-course midday meal. The saleswomen had young girls helping them, whose job was to fetch items to show customers; they, too, wore bright uniforms. 'However much the rich capricious *baryshni* ("ladies"), as women customers were called then, might wear her out going through the goods and choosing, the saleswoman always had to remain polite and smiling.'

In spite of the strict regime, jobs at M & M's were keenly sought after. Successful salesmen received an annual bonus in addition to their salaries. When Tolstoy in 1893 wanted to illustrate the point that it was not always the best educated people who received the highest salaries, he cited the case of salesmen at Muir & Mirrielees, saying that he knew they were paid 3000 roubles (£300) and more. The firm soon acquired a reputation as good employers, and in 1900 a Russian journalist wrote that the proprietors had always treated their employees with great consideration. 'There is no trading on Sundays and employees can relax, doors are closed at 7, and in addition to their wages, employees receive a free meal.' Unlike Whiteley's, they had not, however, introduced Saturday early closing, nor did they provide free lodging, although the wages they paid seem correspondingly higher.

M & M's treatment of their employees was not therefore remarkable by London standards, but, again, it was novel for Moscow. Their practices can be compared with those of 'Fyodor Laptev & Sons', the fictitious firm described by Chekhov in his story, *Three Years* (1895). These well-known Moscow wholesalers deal in haberdashery and employ about fifty people. The warehouse in which everyone has to work is dark, overcrowded and unbearably noisy; the boy apprentices are regularly flogged and given bloody noses. Like Whiteley's staff, the employees live in, but not in dormitories. All of them, including the two chief assistants, are housed in their employer's own home, three or four to a room. If a member of the Laptev family comes in while they are eating at the communal table, they all spring to their feet and answer questions timidly, without looking up, like convicts. They are allowed out in the evening, but the outside gate is locked at 9, and every morning old Laptev, a vigorous eighty-year-old, looks them over suspiciously and smells their breath for vodka. The assistants are also allowed to marry but seldom do so, for fear of displeasing the boss and losing their jobs. Like all Russian merchants, the old man is an ardent observer of religious ceremonial, and entirely convinced of his own righteousness as an employer and a father. His younger son, who had been flogged before he was five and put to work in the warehouse at the age of eight, later went on to university, and eventually has to take over the business. He does so with great reluctance, although at least he can stop the flogging. Their provincial customers, he discovers, are being hoodwinked: the assistants send out old goods, passing them off as the latest stock, and find this a great joke. When his father finally divulges his commercial secrets, he makes it sound as if it had not been trade that he was engaged in, but the black arts.

If this picture is typical – and Chekhov was not the kind of writer to invent or exaggerate – it is little wonder that M & M's so quickly acquired the reputation of being fair traders as well as good employers.

*   *   *

The busiest times of year in the shops' calendar were the weeks leading up to Christmas and Easter, when extra staff had to be taken on. Before Christmas they offered 'an elegant selection of all kinds of decorations for the Christmas tree', or, for their lazier customers, already prepared sets of decorations at prices ranging from 3 to 50 roubles; while for Easter they advertised 'the most varied and elegant selection of eggs with and without surprises'. June was the month in which prices were reduced in all departments to clear old stock before the start of the new season. Bargain sales were also held in individual departments at intervals throughout the year: of underwear in January, in March of gloves, and in April of perfume ('extremely convenient for those desiring to provide themselves with a small stock for the summer and the datcha'), while in August there was a large display of carpets at reduced prices. Clearance sales of carpet remnants were held in March and December.

These bargain and clearance sales attracted a wider range of customers than usual – not necessarily from the lower classes only. When Whiteley's held a salvage sale in December 1882 after a fire, the proletarian bargain-hunters from Notting Hill resented in rough language the intrusion of plutocrats from Prince's Square or Lancaster Gate, who operated under the pretence of buying to stock charity bazaars or aiding the district visitor. An unlikely devotee of such sales in Moscow was Countess Tolstoy, as her daughter Alexandra records:

She and I would drive to the arcade, to Muir & Mirrielees, and buy remnants of lace and other materials. On one occasion my father surprised us by remarking:

'*I* was at Muir & Mirrielees today! I spent more than two hours outside the Bolshoi Theatre, watching. Whenever a lady drove up in a carriage and pair, the commissionaire would dart forward, unfasten her rug and help her to climb out. If it was a one-horse carriage, he merely opened the door respectfully, and if she arrived by cab, he ignored her completely.'

A similar observation could have been made in London or Paris in that intensely rank-conscious age. Tolstoy, who reserved his deepest scorn for the bourgeoisie, would have had little time for such a thoroughly middle-class institution as M & M's, although it seems to have exercised a curious fascination over him.

William Whiteley was in the habit of sending out a free annual catalogue, but his customers must have been taken aback when they received his 'Illustrated Catalogue & General Price List for 1885'. This amazing volume was 1293 pages long, and began with a typically flamboyant Whiteley boast: 'In no other Establishment in the world can goods of every description be purchased with such great economy of money, time, trouble, & fatigue; to this it owes its unequalled success, which is believed to be without parallel in the history of commerce.' The books section alone occupied 40 pages. The list of patent medicines likewise went on and on. A Remington typewriter, very expensive at £18, was especially recommended for those clergymen who prepared their sermons in full. From the men's hairdressing department came the offer of a daily shave in return for an annual subscription of £1. Then there were the new Whiteley Lawn-tennis tables with revolving china tops and matching cups and saucers, and page upon page of hideous glass ornaments.

M & M's catalogues were modest by comparison, but they appeared more frequently and were sent out free of charge to all parts of the Russian Empire. Thus, in 1903 the Spring & Summer catalogue of 'Paris fashions and novelties' was published in February, a similar Autumn catalogue appeared in August, while the Winter catalogue came out in November and concentrated on 'Christmas presents and novelties'.

The catalogue for November 1900 includes a wide selection of toys suitable as Christmas presents. M & M's had a large toy department, which they cultivated with great care, as did Whiteley, since it was an effective way of bringing into the shop not only the children but their parents. Many of the toys illustrated were either mechanically operated or on wheels. The 'wooden horses with hair' were on wheels, and you could choose between two different qualities and a wide range of sizes; at 10 roubles 40 copecks, the biggest top-quality horse was the most expensive item listed. A clockwork bear or monkey turning somersaults cost 3 roubles 60, while for less affluent (or less generous) customers there was a clockwork seal that moved in a zigzag (95 copecks), a furry poodle that could be made to jump by pressing an attached rubber squeezer (70 copecks) or an appealingly humble wooden cart and donkey (55 or 65 copecks). There were toy soldiers in

six different uniforms ('please indicate which one you require');
buffoons with pointed caps and frilly collars, playing drums or bells,
all mounted on wheels; a chimney-sweep sitting on the front of his
three-wheeler, while his boy swathed in black perches on the back rail
holding up his brush; and an expensive fireman's set, including a metal
helmet and an axe that looks as if it might be dangerous in the wrong
child's hands. Very up-to-date was the 'Boer farmer, metal, clockwork,
on horseback – 1 rouble': the Boer War had started in 1899 and
Russian sympathies were with the Boers, not the British, so it is an
indication of M & M's national self-effacement that they should have
stocked such an item. Even more topical was the 'fight between a
Russian and a Boxer – 3 roubles 85'. The two figures face each other
in threatening postures, and by pressing rubber squeezers it must have
been possible to make their arms and bodies move, though whether
contact could be established is hard to say. The Boxer Rebellion in
China had been put down as recently as August 1900, when the
European allies, including the Russians, entered Pekin.

As for the catalogues of the latest Paris fashions – with what
eagerness they must have been awaited in the distant provinces! How
carefully Mamma and her daughters studied the different models and
mulled over prices! Here in the Spring & Summer catalogue for 1902
is jacket no.6457, available in black, dark-blue or beige, with satin
trimmings, mother-of-pearl buttons and a satin lining: price 28 roubles.
A little too expensive? Lined with taffeta, it cost only 23 roubles 75.
With what trepidation Papa was finally approached! Then came the
anxious period waiting for the new purchase to be delivered, and
wondering whether the right choice had been made. If only Chekhov's
Three Sisters had thought to put their names down on the mailing list
for M & M's seasonal catalogues! Then they would not have felt so cut
off from their beloved Moscow.

Moreover, knowing the sisters' refined tastes and generous natures,
they would have placed large orders, in which case the goods would
have been delivered free of charge, even though they were living 700
miles from Moscow. William Whiteley prided himself on his delivery
services, pointing out in the 1885 catalogue that his carts and vans
delivered free of charge three times a day anywhere in London and
several times a week in outlying areas, and undertaking to deliver free
of charge by rail goods which customers had ordered in person or by
post. Delivery vans bearing the name of Muir & Mirrielees, at first
horse-drawn and later also motorized, likewise soon became a familiar

sight in the streets of Moscow. But M & M's were also very conscious of the need to give their customers outside Moscow every encouragement, irrespective of the distances involved. An order for goods to the value of 50 roubles or more, accompanied by payment, would be delivered free of charge *anywhere* within the Russian Empire, i.e. from Poland to Vladivostok, the only exclusions being particularly heavy or bulky items, like the children's wooden horses. In 1901 a 'special offer' reduced the 50 roubles to 25 for customers within European Russia other than the Caucasus. Goods to any value could also be sent on a 'cash on delivery' basis, but this was not carriage free, and customers were reminded that with such an arrangement the postal and railway authorities imposed a surcharge. This service applied to European Russia, the Caucasus and Western Siberia; customers from further afield had to send a deposit in advance. Precise instructions were given in the catalogues on how to place an order. The firm also sent out free samples of materials, with an earnest request for the return of those no longer required. Customers were assured that there was absolutely no difference between the prices of goods sold in Moscow and of those sent to the provinces.

*   *   *

In the second half of the 1890's the firm took another important step forward. Like William Whiteley, they had decided not to confine their activities to retailing. They purchased a large site in the Presnya, Moscow's industrial suburb, where land was comparatively cheap; among the many manufacturing concerns located there was the Smith Boiler Works, founded in 1856. On this site they put up a number of buildings to house their workshops and technical departments, of which the most important were a furniture factory, a printing works (which among other things printed all M & M's catalogues), and a department specializing in all kinds of plumbing, drainage and sewerage.

In December 1902-January 1903 an exhibition of furniture 'in the new style' was held in Moscow and attracted considerable publicity. Among the exhibitors who helped to give the Exhibition an international character were Charles Rennie Mackintosh and his wife Margaret, although their reputations did not prevent one dyspeptic Russian critic from likening their white drawing-room with its horrible straight lines to a hospital operating theatre, or dismissing Mrs Mackintosh's drawings as case-studies in sexual psychopathology. One of the prime movers behind the Exhibition was a young architect of British birth practising in Russia, William Walcot, who had become famous in 1899 when his plans were adopted for the rebuilding of Moscow's Metropole Hotel. Two rooms at the Exhibition were devoted to a dining-room and study designed by Walcot and executed by M & M's, while another two rooms consisted of a mahogany bedroom and a study designed by L.I.Lishtvan, the artist in charge of M & M's furniture workshops and another member of the Exhibition committee. M & M's had clearly become established by this time among the two or three leading furniture manufacturers in Russia, producing a very wide range of furniture, from specialized commissions like those for the Exhibition to more run-of-the-mill items for sale in their own retail shop.

Can M & M's be described as Moscow's 'Universal Provider'? Certainly, they were stating no more than the truth in their 1898 advertisement when they described themselves as 'Russia's first and largest universal stores'. In Moscow itself they had become a household name, whether abbreviated to Muir, Muirka or Mirrielees. They would provide everything that you might possibly require for clothing your person; everything that you could possibly need to equip, furnish or decorate your home. Unlike Whiteley's, however, they dealt in dry goods only, not perishables: they did not provide for your stomach. Nor did they offer Whiteley's extraordinary range of customer services: you did not go to M & M's for elephants or second-hand coffins. One might also, however, take 'Universal Provider' to mean 'provider for every*one*', but in that sense neither M & M's nor Whiteley's was universal, since they catered only for the middle classes and above. Finally, 'universal' might be taken to imply not everything, nor everyone, but every*where*, and in this sense M & M's – regularly sending goods of every description north, south, east and west, to the furthermost corners of the Russian Empire – comes closest to deserving the title of 'Universal Provider'.

16

A Loyal Customer

During the Soviet period the idea was cultivated that Muir & Mirrielees had been no more than a very beautiful shop for rich people. This was deliberately misleading. In the previous chapter it was characterized as a thoroughly middle-class institution, but that does not mean that it was not also patronized by the upper classes. In London it was an open secret that all the members of the Royal Family were regular patrons of William Whiteley's: the Queen sent a courier, Princess Louise shopped there incognito as Mrs Thompson of Kensington Palace, while the Princess of Wales let her children wander about freely for a couple of hours. What it does mean is that the store appealed mainly to, and was mainly supported by, the middle classes. With its bulk buying, wide range of goods, competitive prices and rapid turnover, the department store was at the other extreme from the exclusive shop charging high prices; and even when it had become established and no longer felt the need to undercut its rivals, it could still not afford to turn its back on that broadly-based middle-class support. Tsarist Russia, it has often been said, lacked a middle class. The success of M & M's over a period of thirty years before the Revolution suggests that in Moscow at least, this was not the case.

A well-documented and by no means untypical customer of the shop around the turn of the century was Anton Chekhov (1860-1904). No one could call Chekhov a rich man; at best, he might be described as fairly well-off by the end of his life. The grandson of a serf and son of a failed shopkeeper, he had acquired middle-class status in 1884 by qualifying as a doctor at Moscow University, but it seems unlikely that he became a regular customer at M & M's until the late 1880's, when his short stories and vaudevilles had begun to bring him in a healthy income just when the firm was capturing the imagination of Moscow's shoppers by its rapid programme of expansion. It was around this time of reviving Chekhov family fortunes that the blue-and-white family dinner service was bought from M & M's. Many survivors of the original set are still on display in the Chekhov House museum at Yalta, but there were also many breakages, and from time to time a blue-and-white shard surfaces in the Yalta garden.

In 1892, with the help of two loans and a mortgage, Chekhov

purchased the small estate of Melikhovo, some two hours by train from Moscow, for use by himself, his parents and his sister Masha. Along with the estate, the family inherited a variety of farmyard dogs, including two mongrel puppies. It must have been Chekhov who decided to call them Muir and Mirrielees: the no-nonsense monosyllable for the dog and the skittish trisyllable for the bitch. In the following year he acquired two pedigree dachshunds, also a dog and a bitch, which Masha named Bromide and Quinine. The dachshunds enjoyed pride of place among the canine residents, and a well-known photograph of 1897 shows Chekhov sitting with one of them on the wooden steps of the terrace at Melikhovo. Here, according to Masha, he would conduct lengthy conversations with both dogs, and on one occasion was overheard by her having a 'serious talk' with Bromide, taking him to task for 'falling in love with Mademoiselle Mirrielees' and causing so much suffering to his wife Quinine.

Now Chekhov was no linguist, but he knew the difference between French 'Mademoiselle' and English 'Miss'; so was he under the impression that M & M's was French? Possible evidence to the contrary is contained in a letter of 6 December 1902 to his wife, Olga Knipper, in which he writes: 'Those envelopes of yours are useless, your letters are practically open by the time they arrive. Buy yourself some plain envelopes for five copecks and throw those aristocratic ones away. Or buy yourself some fine English notepaper and matching envelopes from Mirrielees. I'll write to you tomorrow on English paper.' But given that M & M's imported goods from all over Europe, this evidence is far from conclusive, and one must reluctantly suppose that Chekhov shared the widespread assumption that the firm's management was French.

This misconception arose partly because the names Muir and Mirrielees (simplified in Russian to *Meriliz*) sound more French than English to a Russian ear, and partly because French shops were far more numerous in Tsarist Russia than British ones. Another very fashionable British shop in Moscow, the outfitter's started by an Englishman, James Shanks, even went so far as to call itself *Le Magasin Anglais*! M & M's had no reason to conceal their origins, but neither did they have any reason to emphasize them, so that the knowledge that they were British-owned seems to have been confined to members of the British community and a small number of well-informed Russians. From 1918, when the name, Muir & Mirrielees, officially disappeared (though it continued to be used for many years by older Muscovites who were incapable of changing), that number became fewer and fewer. Some curious notions arose, like that of the elderly lady in Moscow, who asserted with disarming confidence that Muir was an acronym, made up of the initials of a wealthy Moscow merchant, and that Mirrielees was a combination of the names of his daughters, Maria and Liza! She may have been influenced by the children's counting-out rhyme that became popular after 1900: *Plachet Meri, plachet Liza, / Byl pozhar u Meriliza*, which might be rendered as 'Liza's crying, so's Maria, / Meriliz have had a fire.'

The house into which the Chekhovs moved at Melikhovo, a one-storey wooden building with a large number of rooms, had been badly neglected by its previous owner. Much needed to be done to furnish and re-equip it, and there can be little doubt that M & M's served them well at this time.

In 1897 Chekhov's T.B. was diagnosed. He was advised to live in a warmer climate and finally took up permanent residence in Yalta, a thousand miles south of Moscow. Did this mean that M & M's ceased to be part of his life? Far from it. Thanks to the efficiency of the firm's delivery services, he was to remain a very loyal customer. Unable to reconcile himself to his southern 'exile', Chekhov, like the three sisters of his play, began to hanker desperately after Moscow, and must have derived some consolation from the thought that through M & M's he was continuing to shop there. He received their catalogues regularly, ordered goods (using the cash on delivery service) through his ever-obliging sister in Moscow, or after 1901, his wife, and was quick to seize the opportunity, whenever members of the family or friends were due to visit him, of asking them to make some purchase on his behalf at M & M's and bring it down with them.

In addition, Chekhov had a personal contact at M & M's. A female cousin of his had married a salesman in the Materials department, Pyotr Vasilyevich Petrov. On 14 December 1898, when his new house in Yalta was still being built, Chekhov wrote asking Petrov to arrange for him to be sent 'a price-list of household equipment, beds and wash-basins'; while on 7 December 1899 he asked him to send by post a warm scarf and a pair of felt slippers (size 15) for their old cook, and a pair of felt slippers (size 16) for his mother. If these were intended as Christmas presents, he may have decided that the only way of ensuring that they reached Yalta in time was to write direct to Petrov at the shop.

What kind of person was this M & M salesman? His names could not be more ordinary. We do not know his age, but by 1899 he must have been fairly elderly: in 1892 he already had a grown-up son serving in the artillery. Towards Chekhov his tone is deferential. In his reply of 18 December 1898 he addresses him in terms that would have amused the writer as 'Deeply-respected and Dear Anton Pavlovich', and remarks that he received his letter 'with special pleasure and read it several times' (an honour that its contents scarcely deserve). It had arrived on the day after the first night of the Moscow Art Theatre production of *The Seagull*, and been passed on to him by the staff of M & M's Office. 'They were all asking how come you know Anton Pavlovich, I replied he's my cousin, they said to me you lucky chap, to have a relation like that whom everyone knows, *The Seagull* produced a huge success with the public...' Petrov clearly did not see *himself* patronizing the Art Theatre. He strikes one as a highly respectable member of Moscow's lower middle class, literate but not very well educated, a trusted employee who has been with the firm for some time, is popular with colleagues and obliging towards customers.

It is through Petrov that we see how the firm dealt with a customer complaint. On 17 September 1899 Chekhov wrote to him:

Dear Pyotr Vasilyevich, the 'cassowary' blanket I bought in your shop this summer [cassowary = a genus of birds, found especially in New Guinea, closely related to the emu] is moulting badly. I've brushed it frequently, but that didn't help. I can't leave it in my room, because the hairs get all over my clothes, which are then difficult to brush. I am taking the liberty of sending it and would ask you to be kind enough either to have it cleaned in Moscow and sent back to Yalta by cash on delivery, or to take whatever action you find necessary. You will receive the blanket from my friend, Prince S.I.Shakhovskoi...

Petrov decided that the firm should take responsibility and passed the blanket on to the appropriate department. How did M & M's respond to Chekhov's complaint? They certainly gave the matter prompt attention, returning the blanket a few days later with the following note:

Having received your blanket delivered to us by Prince Shakhovskoi, and your letter addressed to P.V.Petrov, we have the honour to inform you that it is a property of blankets of this kind that until they are worn in, they release fluff. Since the cleaning of your blanket by experts could not eliminate this property, we have brushed it in our shop and return it herewith.

There seems to be an element here of blinding the customer with science, but no more is heard in Chekhov's correspondence of the 'cassowary' blanket, so presumably he was pacified – if not exactly pleased – by this explanation.

*   *   *

What kind of purchases did Chekhov make from M & M's?

One point is immediately obvious: very few of them can be classed as luxury items. To counteract the image of M & M's as a shop catering exclusively for rich people, one need only refer to Chekhov's letter of 2 December 1899, in which he writes to Masha from Yalta: 'Don't you think we should instal two kerosene stoves... it would be a good idea to buy them from Muir, but I'm afraid he'll send something *very cheap*' (italics added).

Almost all Chekhov's purchases fall into one of three categories: furniture and household equipment, stationery, or clothing.

Of these the first was the most important. Although little information has survived about items bought for Melikhovo other than a rocking-chair, there is one intriguing purchase from that period which illustrates the variety of goods stocked by the firm. In April 1898 Chekhov wrote to Masha: 'When you're next on the Kuznetsky, buy a flag at Muir & Mirrielees for the cottage, the same size as before or a little bigger, and the cord to go with it.' The explanation of this purchase is to be found in Avdeyev's book, *In Chekhov's Melikhovo*, where the author describes how a flagpole was erected on the cottage balcony, with a small red flag which Chekhov hoisted to let the local inhabitants know that he was available to give advice or medical assistance.

In the autumn of 1898, before completion of the new house at Yalta, Chekhov bought a small seaside cottage further down the coast. In December he wrote suggesting that if Ivan, his younger brother, were coming for Christmas, he might bring with him two or three camp-beds for the cottage from M & M's and also ask them to send two beds (three if they were cheap), a small samovar, half-a-dozen knives and half-a-dozen forks. In Moscow the following summer Chekhov himself ordered furniture for the new house, including a green Viennese chair, a red Empire-style chair, and a Jacobean armchair. He moved in at the end of August, but found that when the winds of late autumn began to blow, his hillside house overlooking Yalta Bay was decidedly draughty. It was then that he asked Masha to enquire at Muir's about a heavy windproof curtain for the door leading from his bedroom to the balcony, and about kerosene stoves for the chilly area at the foot of the stairs. In the autumn of 1901 he and Masha placed another large order. 'They've sent our purchases via Novorossisk,' he wrote on his return to Yalta, 'so that means they won't arrive before April.' 'Would you believe it,' he writes a week later, 'by some miracle the things from Muir have already arrived. They're all in one piece, all the lamps, only Arseny [Chekhov's man-of-all-work] managed to give the white shade for my lamp a kick and smashed it.'

Chekhov the writer made particularly good use of the firm's stationery department in the shop on *Kuznetsky most*. In November 1899 we find him stocking up: Masha is asked to order a ream of foolscap, a ream of notepaper, a box of pens, and enough envelopes of different sizes to last him a year. To have his ink sent from Moscow was not so easy, and in February 1902 his wife was entrusted with the task of buying a bottle of Muir's 'medium-price' ink and bringing it down with her. The fourth and last of Chekhov's literary notebooks, into which he copied unused material for stories that were never to be written, is a simple little blue exercise-book bearing M & M's label.

There was another, no less indispensable, kind of paper that he continued to buy from M & M's, even in Yalta. Here, too, he made bulk purchases, convinced, as with the English envelopes, that the firm's product was bound to be entirely reliable. He refers to it coyly as 'the paper costing 18 copecks a packet at Muir's' and as 'non-writing paper'. Loyalty to Moscow and to M & M's could go no further.

Chekhov also depended heavily on M & M's for his wardrobe. In October 1898 he asked Masha to buy him a *bashlyk*, a Caucasian hood with long ends, as a protection against the cutting Yalta wind. Two months later she received further instructions:

Dear Masha, tell Mirrielees as soon as possible to send me by cash on delivery a black astrakhan cap, No.216 in his autumn catalogue; choose a soft one, size 59 centimetres. If Vanya [Ivan] is coming, he can bring it with him. Only be quick, or my old cap will have had it. The price is 7r. or thereabouts. If the American forage-caps (no.213) are warm, get Mirrielees to send one of them, too.

Both these items are preserved in the Chekhov House museum, but are completely upstaged by Chekhov's Homburg. This stylish piece of headgear was made in London and also bought from M & M's. He is wearing it in the famous photograph of 1901, which shows him sitting outside the house at Yalta on a wicker chair. He is smartly dressed for the occasion, showing off an inch or two of very white cuff, probably one of the half-dozen detachable ones ordered for him by Masha from M & M's in November 1899, and wearing a starched white collar from the same source – the whole topped off by the light-coloured Homburg, which looks slightly incongruous in this garden setting (though useful as a protection against the sun), but would have come into its own when Chekhov was strolling along the fashionable promenade.

At the beginning of December 1903, Chekhov left Yalta for Moscow to attend rehearsals of *The Cherry Orchard*, which had its first night on 17 January, his forty-fourth birthday. During this visit he and his wife chose a large writing desk from M & M's to replace one that had come from Melikhovo. It must have been the most expensive and luxurious item that Chekhov ever bought from them. When he returned to Yalta alone in mid-February, the desk had already been delivered, and he spent his first day transferring things from the old desk to the new, carefully arranging all the familiar objects on its baize top. He found the drawers stiff, but in general was pleased with his acquisition. There is a poignancy about this final purchase, embodying, as it does, the assumption that Chekhov still had many more fruitful years of writing ahead of him. In the event, it was scarcely used at all and today, covered by a glass case, still looks as it did when Chekhov left Yalta for the last time on 1 May 1904.

Thus did Chekhov – householder, writer, and dandy – assisted by family and friends, add to the comforts and conveniences of life through M & M's, but there was one occasion on which he proposed making use of the shop in an entirely novel way. To a young female friend he wrote in October 1898: 'Yes, you are right, the number of women with plays is increasing not by the day, but the hour, and I think there is only one way of dealing with this affliction: to invite all the women to Muir & Mirrielees, and burn the shop down.'

A few years later and this joke might have seemed in bad taste as well as sexist.

17

Setback

When Andrew Muir wrote of the fire at M & M's in February 1892 that 'it may be a case of incendiarism originating with jealous rivals as with Whiteley', he still had fresh in his mind a series of events that had been the talk of London in the 1880's. For five years William Whiteley was haunted by the spectre of fire. He may have had misgivings on Guy Fawkes' night, 1876, when the local butchers burned his effigy, but he was not a man to be easily intimidated. His anti-fire precautions were thorough. He had iron doors installed at each partition wall, employed two firemen to act as patrols, and took out large insurance policies.

On the night of 16 November 1882 Whiteley did not leave his office until a quarter to eleven; this was quite usual for him. Twenty minutes later the fireman Duke discovered a fire and raised the alarm. Six shops were involved and the damage amounted to £42,000, but buildings and stock were fully insured. Whiteley ordered all other departments to open next morning for business as usual. The cause of the fire was thought to be a gas leak, but there was one curious circumstance. At 11.15 a stranger called out as he ran past in a nearby street: 'Whiteley's is in flames, if you want to see a blaze!' – but there was no blaze at that time, only the beginnings of one. Six weeks later, in the early hours of Boxing Day, fire struck again, this time in a workshop area that had been empty for more than 48 hours, and spread with great rapidity. Whiteley's menagerie narrowly escaped. For the next day or so wild rumours circulated: the two fires were more than a coincidence, Whiteley himself was involved and his arrest imminent. The cause of this fire remained even more of a mystery. Fire No.3 on the afternoon of Saturday 26 April 1884 was the worst yet. Again, there was no holding the blaze once started. It caused £123,000 worth of damage, of which only half was recovered from insurance. Though badly hit financially, Whiteley was undeterred – 'I am no sooner down than up again' – and at the end of 1884 sent out his defiant 1293-page catalogue. After the fourth fire a year later, he commented to the press: 'One hardly likes to think that there may be motives of business jealousy at the bottom of it.' He asked Scotland Yard to investigate, and offered a reward of £1000. His buyers suspected a particular individual, but no proof was ever forthcoming. Of the total loss of

£74,000 very little was recovered, but Whiteley wasted no time in rebuilding, even though he was running up huge debts. At least, however, no one could still suspect him of starting the fires deliberately. Messages of sympathy poured in, from royalty *and* from the local traders. Spurred on, Whiteley in the year ending 28 February 1887 made a record profit of £75,000.

The biggest conflagration, however, was yet to come. In 1887 Queen Victoria celebrated her Golden Jubilee. Whiteley's illuminations were suitably lavish, but he dared not keep them on at night for fear of fire. The July sales passed off satisfactorily, and on Saturday 7 August Whiteley left with his two sons on a visit to the Continent. That same evening, soon after 7, as if at a pre-arranged signal, fire broke out, and all Whiteley's elaborate precautions – the hydrants on every floor, iron doors, firemen patrolling day and night, and hoses ready for immediate use – were powerless to stop the blaze. Great walls fell out without warning, crushing people in the street; floors fell in with a roar resembling the discharge of artillery. At ten o'clock the central tower and flagstaff of the Queen's Road block – the symbolic heart of Whiteley's empire – were engulfed. The situation was complicated by calls to fires in other parts of London that kept coming in with extraordinary frequency. Nevertheless, Whiteley's fire monopolized 34 of London's 45 steam fire-engines, 96 out of 131 horses, and 171 of the 589 firemen. Three people were killed, crushed by the falling walls, and sixteen injured. It was London's biggest fire since 1861. By Sunday evening Whiteley was back in London and giving an interview to the press. He was convinced that treachery or foul play was responsible, since his fires always appeared to break out in twenty places at once, and this outbreak had been simultaneously observed on three different floors. 'Someone,' he said with unfortunate alliteration, 'is animated by an animus against me.'

The *Pall Mall Gazette* posed the question that all London was asking: 'Why is Whiteley's so often Burnt Down?' Was it the work of 'some rival tradesman whom he has crushed under the juggernaut car of low prices and unlimited competition'? This was Whiteley's own explanation, though he would not have used such colourful language, and was the one accepted by his Moscow counterpart, Andrew Muir. But the theory had a flaw. Whoever was responsible for starting the fires had brushed aside Whiteley's precautions and security measures with such impunity that he or she must surely have intimate knowledge of all Whiteley's premises. Or was the incendiary 'some injured lady who seeks to assuage the fire that consumes her own heart by the spectacle of Whiteley's goods and chattels ascending to heaven in a flaming, fiery furnace'? This was not so far-fetched as it might sound, since it was well known that the Universal Provider had left Mrs Whiteley, his original shop assistant, and set up house with another of his assistants in Kilburn; and if there was one mistress, might there not have been others? Most widely held, however, was the theory, which Whiteley himself preferred not to entertain, that the fire was due to 'some discontented employee who has some grudge against his master'. Although Scotland Yard interviewed more than a hundred people, not a scrap of real evidence was ever found. The mystery of Whiteley's fires – five major outbreaks in less than five years – can be compared only with that other great unsolved London mystery of the 1880's: the series of murders committed by Jack the Ripper. Like the Ripper's murders, Whiteley's fires stopped and were never resumed, and in the words of the press, the 'Bayswater Phoenix' rose again from the ashes.

M & M's fire in February 1892 began on a Sunday, when the building was unoccupied. 'The place was fully provided with self-acting extinguishers,' Andrew wrote, 'and I fancy the damage to goods proceeded more from them and from water thrown by fire engines than from fire.' First estimates put the damage at £20,000, but in the event the damage to goods was £9500 and to the building about £4500. The insurance company paid up promptly. Unlike Whiteley, who made it a rule that unaffected departments should open the next morning, M & M's did not reopen until Tuesday; even then, Andrew commented, the exertions demanded from all their staff, especially the head men, would be enormous.

The business is not much inconvenienced by the fire, and the repairs will be done in six weeks time. The worst of the affair is that two of the firemen lost their lives. Willie Cazalet had a very narrow escape but got off with a cut on the head and the loss of his fur cap. A whole flight of stairs fell down as they were going up, on account of the heat, and those not protected by the platform above were hurled down by the debris. We may be glad it is no worse, as a general conflagration would have been a fearful loss to us.

By the time that such a general conflagration occurred, Andrew Muir was no longer alive. It began early in the evening of Friday 24 November 1900, when Theatre Square was still full of people. At the Bolshoi they were giving the fifth performance of *The House of Ice*, in which

Shalyapin was singing the leading role. The play at the Malyi was a now-forgotten comedy with the intriguing title of *Scum*. At M & M's the last customers had been shepherded out by seven o'clock and the doors locked. On the top floor of the building three people were still working. Willie Cazalet was in his office, while next door the head cashier and chief salesman were balancing the day's takings. This usually took them about half-an-hour, but Willie expected to carry on working until about 10. Finding that he needed a particular ledger, he asked the chief salesman to fetch it from the ground floor. After waiting for five minutes, he concluded that the salesman had been unable to find it and sent the head cashier down to help. More time passed and still neither of them had returned. Sensing that something must be wrong, Willie hurried downstairs himself. He eventually discovered the two of them in the basement, where they had been engaged, apparently successfully, in helping the man in charge of the electric dynamo and gas motor to put out a small fire. The firm's own firemen did not begin patrolling until two hours after the shop closed.

In the mean time, however, flames had been spotted at a window on the second floor, and the alarm raised. First on the scene was the local fire-brigade from the Tverskaya district. This had its headquarters on Tverskaya Street, in an elegant building of Empire design with a Doric colonnade stretching the length of its facade. Alexander Pasternak (1893-1982), younger brother of Boris, never forgot the impression made upon him as a boy by the speed and skill of the fire brigade's turn out. In his memoirs, *A Vanished Present*, he writes: 'They were a terrific sight – driving full tilt down the middle of a street suddenly drained of traffic and noise, the carters and drays drawn up dead, crammed out of the way against the pavement. This headlong gallop was an undisputed privilege unique to the fire-brigade; in normal circumstances, of course, the city would never have put up with such speeds, when the cobbles sprayed sheaves of sparks and the clatter seemed to set the houses swaying.'

By the time that the local fire-brigade had reached M & M's, the flames were already leaping from the second-floor windows over-looking Theatre Square. No sooner had the firemen succeeded in erecting a ladder than flames appeared at the first-floor windows and spread rapidly through both floors. Five more district fire-brigades were summoned, but within about half an hour the whole building was alight. It was usual in the case of serious fires for the chief city fire-officer to take charge, mounted on his black stallion and wearing full regimental regalia, but on this occasion no less a personage than Moscow's chief of police, Major-General D.F.Trepov, himself turned out to take command of the situation. Before long all Moscow's fourteen district fire-brigades were in action, using seven steam fire-engines, compared to the thirty-four that had attended Whiteley's in 1887. Their efforts were soon directed into trying to limit the damage and prevent the blaze from spreading to nearby buildings. One newspaper reported that there had been an explosion in a basement where fireworks were kept, but next day changed its story: it was *rumoured* that firemen had prevented the flames from reaching a store of gunpowder. The blaze spread so rapidly because of all the wooden window-frames, staircases and partitions, shelves and cupboards, and the huge quantity of goods stored inside the building. Soon the roof caved in, and girders began to collapse. Pieces of burning material, sucked high into the air by the colossal draught, spun round and round, and landed at a considerable distance. But as Alexander Pasternak writes, how can words, 'lying so silent on the page, convey the din of cracking beams, bursting glass, the clang of metal girder jarring against girder, the scattered burst of explosions'? He was only seven at the time of M & M's fire, but later, as a schoolboy on his way home, he twice lingered with the crowd in Theatre Square to watch the Malyi and the Nezlobin Theatres burn to the ground. He recalled how 'huge cross-beams like lit matches leapt from the fire', and the gutted building 'turned into the bars of a giant grate, its prodigious blaze laid by titanic hands'.

By midnight the first and second floors had burned out completely, and the ground floor was well ablaze. In Moscow, as in London in 1887, the brilliant red glow lit up the city for miles around and crowds flocked in from the suburbs to enjoy the spectacle. The pickpockets were out in force and seven were arrested, including one who had the misfortune to try to pick the pocket of a plain-clothes police detective. At the Bolshoi all the doors opening onto M & M's were locked, but news of the fire spread quickly, and many of the audience at the Bolshoi and the Malyi left at the end of the first act. By the end of the performance both theatres were practically deserted, yet in spite of this, according to the Theatre & Music critic of *Russian News*, Mr Shalyapin received his usual 'noisy' ovation. Had the critic written his notice in advance and taken the evening off?

Reporters speculated on possible causes: a faulty electric wire in a lift, a steam heating pipe, a dropped cigarette. What soon became clear, however, was that although the fire had been successfully put out in the basement, the flames must already have found their way up the shaft of the goods lift and invaded the second floor.

All through the following day the building continued to smoke, and Theatre Square was filled with spectators. Fragments of silk, lace and women's dresses hung down like fringes from the charred window-frames and on nearby lamp-posts. Smouldering goods were still being thrown out of the windows, and the exhausted firemen were allowed white bread as a special dispensation. When it was all over, only the walls of the building were still intact, but adjoining premises were unaffected, and at least on this occasion there had been no loss of life.

According to the correspondent of *Russia*, the building had been insured with the first Russian Insurance Company for 450,000 roubles (£45,000) and goods for one million roubles (£100,000). 'Thus, the store's owners,' he wrote, 'are unlikely to be much out of pocket, but the people who have been really badly hit are the employees. What are they going to do? Where will they find work? At least six months will be needed to restore the building to its former condition. The owners of the unfortunate store have always treated their employees with great consideration... so there is every reason to suppose that Messrs Muir & Mirrielees will pay out a month's wages. But that, after all, is no more than the most insignificant palliative.'

Walter Philip was not a man, however, to avoid his responsibilities. On the Saturday morning after the fire all M & M's employees turned up at the smouldering ruins of their building, and in the words of the *Courier*, anxiously awaited news of their fate. The directors' decision, announced straight away, could not have been more reassuring. 'They have promised to continue paying all their employees, 988 in all, on the same basis as before, until new premises can be arranged. That could take up to six months, and in that case the humane directors would have to pay out as much as 300,000 roubles [£30,000] to keep their employees for that period.' In the event, M & M's moved far more swiftly. They rented the top three floors of the newly-erected Khomyakov Building, on a corner site at the intersection of the Petrovka and *Kuznetsky most*, and close to their other premises.

On Wednesday 29 November a large advertisement appeared in the press:

Muir & Mirrielees. *Kuznetsky most*, Gagarin Building. Announcement. We respectfully inform our customers that we have taken every measure to re-establish at the earliest opportunity those departments that were destroyed by fire. We shall be making a special announcement of the day on which they will be opening. All orders taken by our stationery department will be fulfilled and executed on time, as our workshops are unaffected. All enquiries relating to them should be made to our picture department, Gagarin Building, *Kuznetsky most*, where orders will also be taken. Our *Kuznetsky most* departments are functioning as usual.

Andrew Muir had predicted that a general conflagration would be 'a fearful loss to us'. The *Courier* of 26 November claimed that the figure had already risen above 1½ million roubles (£150,000). In contrast to Whiteley's, this was largely offset by insurance payments, but in spite of the confident assertions of 'business as usual', the fire must still have been a considerable setback, bearing in mind the loss of Christmas trade and the amount of time needed to build up depleted stocks. This is indirectly confirmed by the fact that although the first plans for a new and bigger store on the Theatre Square site were drawn up as early as 1901, work did not start until 1906. More cautious perhaps than Whiteley, who started rebuilding as soon as the embers were cold, M & M's waited until they were confident of their financial situation before embarking on a major new venture.

28. Walter Philip in his thirties

29. Muir & Mirrielees shop in 1898

30. Fire of 1892, from Illustrated Supplement to the 'Moscow News-sheet' (the artist has wrongly assumed that the firm's name appeared in English as well as Russian, and has misspelt Mirrielees!)

31. The hat department

18

Symbol of the Twentieth Century

If the old building had to burn down, it was as well that it burned down completely, for it meant that a fresh start had to be made, and the new building could be designed specifically for use as a department store. London's stores had expanded by the piecemeal acquisition of different shops in a street until eventually a block was formed. Not until 1900 did the first purpose-built department store open to the public. This was John Barnes, planned as an ultra-modern store with fifty departments and Axminster carpeting throughout, and intended to appeal to the prosperous residents of Hampstead and London's other northern suburbs.

M & M's site measured approximately sixty yards by forty, but its overall area was slightly reduced by the need for a long narrow yard to let in light at the back of the shop. Being hemmed in by other buildings, they had no choice but to expand vertically, thereby more than doubling the size of the original premises: from three floors and a basement to seven floors and two basements.

A further reason why Walter Philip delayed rebuilding until 1906 may have been that he was determined not to have to do things by halves. This building would be a monument to his enterprise, and nothing but the best would do. As their architect, M & M's employed Roman Ivanovich Klein (1858-1924). The son of a Moscow businessman, Klein grew up in a household frequented by artists, writers and musicians, and belongs to that gifted generation which reached its maturity around 1900 and made the early years of this century such an extraordinarily rich period for all the arts in Russia. 'If one were to assemble in one's mind all the buildings in Moscow for which Klein was responsible,' writes L.M.Smirnova, 'one would end up with a whole small town (or *Klein-stadt*).' The building for which he is best remembered is the Museum of the Decorative Arts (1898-1912), the brainchild of Professor Tsvetaev, father of the poet Marina Tsvetaeva; but Klein was a versatile architect, equally at home with the Museum's neo-classicism, and with M & M's, in which, as Catherine Cooke writes, 'a thoroughly progressive concrete framed structure is clad in a belated essay in European Gothic that has features of the *Moderne*'.

The new M & M's was the very first building in Russia to use walls of reinforced concrete, a technique that had become well established in America as a means of facilitating the construction of multi-storey buildings. Although its seven storeys made it tall by Moscow standards, M & M's was no skyscraper, and the main reason for adopting the new technique was that it enabled the building's walls and columns to be thinner, thereby producing a dramatic increase in the amount of available floor space. Another important design requirement was to obtain as much daylight as possible, since the site was so enclosed. The new technique enabled them to dispense with the usual wide stone columns along the facades, and to use instead an iron and steel frame, which maximized the amount of window-area. This had the further advantage that the shop's window display did not have to be divided into sections, but could run continuously right along the ground and first floors on both frontages: another completely novel feature for Russia.

Moscow had never seen a building quite like this before. As Anastasia Tsvetaeva, younger sister of Marina, wrote in her memoirs: 'Long before the shop opened, Muscovites kept going to see the building as it rose higher and higher into the sky, to be crowned eventually by its little pointed towers, and as its windows began to sparkle.' Like all the big department stores, M & M's was designed in the grand manner to confer a sense of self-importance on its customers. The eye is drawn at once to the impressive corner tower with its arched windows and triangular gables, which sets the tone for both facades. The Gothic style – all lines and curves and angles – is thrown into sharp relief by the four-square classical style of the buildings round about. Today it still strikes one as a building of considerable character.

Inside there were many innovations. The London stores, Adburgham argues in *Shops and Shopping*, played an important part in the emancipation of women by making a day's shopping in town a pleasurable and socially acceptable form of independent activity. Cloakrooms were particularly appreciated. The Ladies Lavatory Co. had opened its first establishment at Oxford Circus in 1884, but ladies did not like to be seen entering a public convenience. In Moscow the new M & M's provided two ladies' lavatories. Moreover, as Adburgham points out, stores that had restaurants gained tremendous pulling power. Here a lady might have a meal by herself or with friends, and be seduced by dainty teas and luncheons into spending more on her purchases than she had intended. M & M's new restaurant was to prove extremely popular, even without the pianist or ladies' string quartet engaged by some of the London stores. Other innovations included an enquiry-desk, a waiting-room, a Moscow information service, and two customer lifts. In London the first lifts had been installed by the Junior Army & Navy Stores in 1879, while in 1898 Harrod's introduced the first escalator, but in Moscow the novelty of M & M's lifts caused a sensation. No other feature of the new building provoked such excitement and anticipation.

Work began on 15 March 1906 with the boring of an Artesian well. After the fire, the derelict site had become overgrown with willow trees, which had to be cleared before work could begin on the new foundations. The management of the properties adjoining M & M's on the Theatre Square side agreed to deepen their foundations to the same level as the new building, but the owner of the shopping arcade next to M & M's on the Petrovka refused. On 5 June he informed the firm by registered letter that cracks caused by their operations had appeared in the wall of the arcade adjoining M & M's, and he was holding them responsible for putting right the damage. The firm requested the local magistrate to arrange for three independent architects to carry out an inspection. They reported that the arcade's own flimsy foundations were to blame, and that M & M's had done everything possible to avoid causing damage. The arcade-owner's further request, that M & M's stop work until he had carried out major repairs, was also turned down by the authorities: in the interests of public safety, he must carry out repairs immediately, but this need not interfere with M & M's operations.

On 10 September a religious service and blessing with holy water was held on the site to mark the beginning of building. Construction of the iron and steel frame, begun in August, continued throughout the winter, whereas bricklaying stopped with the autumn frosts, to be resumed with the arrival of an early spring. On 1 May 1907 another service of blessing was held, this time to mark the laying of the foundation-stone. A small brass plaque, which has since disappeared, was inserted into the wall above the main entrance at second-floor level. It bore the inscription:

In the year of Our Lord nineteen hundred and seven, on the first day of May, a service was held to commemorate the foundation of the Muir and Mirrielees Trading Company Building, in the presence of the head of the firm Vladimir Vasilyevich Philip, Arkhip Arkhipovich Mirrielees, Vasilii Lvovich Cazalet, of the director of building operations Nikolai Dmitrievich Rodionov, his assistants engineer Nikolai Pavlovich Akimov and Andrei Mikhailovich Bogolyubtsev. This building is constructed according to the design and under the supervision of the architect Roman Ivanovich Klein and his assistant Georgii Andreyevich Shuvalov by the contractor Lazar Borisovich Tsigel and by the St Petersburg Metal Factory Company.

By October the roof was on, the heating was functioning, and work inside the building continued without a break all winter. By 1 August 1908 everything was ready. The building had taken 28½ months to complete, required 177,670 working days (the average daily work force was 260, the largest on any one day, 659) and cost almost 1½ million roubles, or £150,000.

For all M & M's employees – and the management, too – the end of July and beginning of August was a period of intense activity. The move from the nearby Gagarin Building to the new premises began on 24 July. While the firm's joiners and carpenters were dismantling cupboards, counters and stands, and reassembling them, the assistants were busy packing all their stock into boxes, parcels, baskets and bales. Bulky items were not packed and fragile ones were carried round by hand. The Umbrella Department had the lightest task. All their stock went into five packages, whereas the Domestic Appliances Department required 1132. The firm paid out large sums in overtime and special bonuses, and laid on evening meals. By 29 July the first departments in the new building were open to the public. On 1 August, at 2 o'clock, the third and final service of blessing was held. Then followed a celebration meal, prepared and served by M & M's own catering staff. The firm's 800 shop assistants were accommodated in the staff dining-rooms on the fourth floor of the new building, while the 700 craftsmen and workmen had their meal served in the old Gagarin Building. Many of the latter had themselves worked on the new building: all the plumbing, for example, had been carried out by the Technical Department. Both assistants and workmen were served a six-course meal. Whether they had the same menu is not clear, but we know that a distinction was made in the refreshments provided: coffee, tea, lemonade and champagne for the assistants, and for the workmen tea, lemonade, beer and vodka. By 4 August all the departments and the restaurant were open to the public.

The new building contained thirty-seven departments, but in addition M & M's were still renting premises in the Khomyakov Building, which by this time housed all their heavy goods departments, like furniture and carpets. Anyone visiting the new building for the first time in 1908 would have entered by the main doors in the middle of the Petrovka frontage, where the commissionaire was on duty. But first he or she – or more probably, they, since the firm was anxious to appeal to all members of the family – would have stopped to admire the window display. Much thought had been given to the lighting effects, which were based on a system of electric arc-lamps copied from the best department stores in Germany. For young Anastasia Tsvetaeva, being taken at last with her elder sister Marina (Musya) to see the completed shop after the long months of anticipation, it was like looking into a brightly-lit aquarium, in which all sorts of bewitching objects were floating about. Passing through the automatic self-closing doors, they found themselves walking not on Axminster carpeting – the Russian winters ruled that out – but on linoleum, laid by the firm's own staff onto the concrete floors. In siting the Perfume Department to the left of the main entrance, M & M's anticipated Selfridge's in London – another purpose-built department store founded in 1909 – which placed cosmetics just inside the main doors so that the scents should lure the unsuspecting passer-by into the shop. Haberdashery was also placed strategically close to the entrance, for although its turnover was small, it offered an expected service and ladies might then move on to other counters. To reach the Enquiry Desk you had no choice but to go through Novelties. Other small departments on the ground floor were Gloves and Umbrellas, Cupronickel and Nickel, Gold and Silver, and Clocks and Watches; the China department was much bigger, and Office Supplies the biggest of all.

Such prosaic details would have been lost, however, on the Tsvetaeva sisters. Anastasia's first impressions were of all the different floors, the lustre of glass and china, the breathtaking profusion of goods, and the fantastic sweep of the stairs. This grand double staircase towards the back of the ground floor had two bronze torchères with electric lamps, and was one of the most visually striking features of the interior, while at the same time it cunningly contrived to expose the maximum range of goods to the eye of the casual observer.

The first floor was devoted to a wide range of ladies' clothing, but also contained three men's departments – Underwear, Hats and Footwear – tucked away in a corner at the furthest possible remove from Ladies' Underwear, Corsets, Dresses, Skirts, and their attendant fitting-room. Ladies' and Men's Hats, however, were continuous departments, perhaps on the assumption that consultation between the sexes would result in the happiest purchases; but ladies in search of footwear had to go to the floor above, since exposing the foot was that much more intimate. This second floor, too, was biased in favour of the ladies, but included Children's Wear, Menswear and the Sports Department, successor to the Firearms Department in the old building.

In addition to the grand staircase there were two customer lifts, painted in the 'old bronze' colour much favoured both inside and outside the building. Each held eight passengers. The 'slow' lift went from the ground floor to the third floor at a speed of 0.75 metres per second, the 'fast' lift from the basement to the fourth floor at a speed of 1.25 metres per second.

How much talk there had been in Moscow about these lifts! How many fabulous tales had been told about them! Now here at last, Anastasia recalls, they were standing in front of this bright little room, which glided airily up and down, collecting and delivering ladies, gentlemen and children, plunging down fearlessly and re-emerging from the abyss as if protected by a magic spell.

Oh, to stand there and watch forever! But when someone's hand takes a firm grip on mine and we move towards this object called 'a lift', my courage deserts me and I'm about to start howling as usual... But Musya's attitude and expression have a sobering effect upon me: I can see perfectly well she's afraid, she's very pale like when she's feeling sick, but there's a faint smile at the corners of her mouth and she's striding towards the lift. It's like stepping into a boat buoyed up on the waves; and bathed in bright light as if in a mirror, we glide slowly upwards...

For children the third floor was the most exciting of all – that half of it, at least, which was open to the public (the other half housed the administration, including Walter's private office above the Petrovka and the firm's own telephone exchange). From the lift you stepped straight out into the huge Toy Department, with Musical Instruments on one side and the Restaurant on the other. Occupying a slightly smaller area than Toys, the Restaurant had a fine view across Theatre Square, so that tables by the window must have been keenly sought after. Here the decor of the interior was at its most elaborate, with carved oak panels and sculptured ceilings. (Where did Anastasia notice the stuffed bears? In the Restaurant or in Toys? Placed in some eye-catching position on the stairs or landings, or in the 'Sports' Department?) You could also reach the restaurant without entering the shop, by using the semi-circular staircase in the corner tower, which had a waiting-room on the second floor where you could look out for friends coming from either direction; but hard would have been the heart of the parent who chose to leave by the same route without taking a peep into Toys.

The time came, Anastasia concludes, when they had had their fill of walking round the different floors and looking at every department. Their eyes could not take in any more. 'Once again we were conducted to the lift. It was going down. The floor gave way beneath us, sinking with nightmarish smoothness. My body felt weak, my feet were aflame with fear, and to Musya's shame and disgust, I set up a howl that could be heard all over Muir & Mirrielees...'

After that, it seems unlikely that they went on to visit the Basement. Had they done so, they would have found various utility departments: Lamps, Electrical Appliances, a second China Department, and Domestic Appliances, which stretched the whole length of the Petrovka frontage. Customer Deliveries occupied a large area, though not as large as the Mail Order Department on the fourth floor. In a far corner of the Basement, beyond the engine-room, were the boilers, supplied and installed by British firms: two Lancashire boilers by R.Smith & Co., and four smaller ones by Babcock & Wilcox. In general, British firms contributed little to the new building, and even in this instance, Walter's choice was probably determined by the fact that both firms were well established in Moscow. From their foundation in 1856, the Smith Boiler Works had specialized in very large high-pressure boilers, but by this time their market was shrinking fast, and the order from M & M's must have been very welcome.

In designing the new building, careful thought had been given to the needs of staff as well as of customers. The workshops on the fifth floor (for clothing, ladies' hats, clocks and watches, and musical instruments) were spacious and lit by electricity, whereas the departments were almost all lit by gas, although provision had been made for the whole building to be lit by electricity in future, using the firm's own power supply. The staff kitchens were on two floors and separate from the Restaurant kitchen. They were designed to cater for up to 1500 employees, served in five dining-rooms and a refreshment-room on the fourth floor. As in the case of staff cloakrooms, where senior members of staff working on the third floor and above had their own cloakroom while the rest had to use the basement, there were separate dining-rooms for Heads of Department, Salesmen, Saleswomen, Delivery Men, and Female Domestic Staff. The kitchens were supplied with all the most up-to-date equipment, including the latest 'Vortex' dishwashing machines from Germany, which, the manufacturers claimed, were more hygienic, saved manpower, eliminated breakages and reduced to a minimum the number of towels required.

'The meal was very well organized,' the grandmother of Bazilyevich recalled.

The saleswomen, about five hundred of them, were divided into five shifts. When the bell rang for the first shift, we went into the dining-room and each person collected her own serviette and cup from a little cupboard on the wall with her number on. There was bread on the table and everything else required. By the time we sat down, the kitchen maids, wearing aprons and starched white caps, had brought in the soup tureens on rails running from the kitchen to the dining-rooms. We helped ourselves to as much as we liked (the rest stayed on the table), and while we were eating, the maids brought in the main course on individual plates – usually roast beef, sausages, cutlets or veal, all with trimmings of course. They also brought in the teapots. Afterwards we put away our cups and serviettes and went to the rest-room, where the walls were covered with photographs of the latest hairstyles from abroad. Here we could lie down for a short while on the low sofas and arrange our hair in the mirror before going back to our posts to make way for the second shift. On the top floor there was a medical room with a nurse permanently on duty to attend to any member of staff who felt unwell, but the two doctors attached to the firm did not treat employees, they only visited those off work to check they were really ill.

The top floor also housed a staff smoking-room and a porters' room. M & M's did not provide any accommodation for staff in the new building (in England, too, the old living-in system was gradually disappearing), nor did they introduce any extramural staff activities – all those athletics and rowing clubs, musical, choral and dramatic societies, which William Whiteley fostered so diligently and of which he was invariably the patron. The Tsarist secret police would probably have banned them in any case. Yet for all his clubs and societies, Whiteley was not highly regarded as a manager of men, whereas M & M's reputation as good employers seems always to have persisted.

*   *   *

'In the eyes of Muscovites,' a contemporary commentator wrote, 'Muir & Mirrielees is a kind of show-case for everything that the capital deals in to suit the tastes both of rich, fashionable society and of the middle classes of the population.' This reference to fashionable society suggests that the firm was now making a more deliberate effort than in Chekhov's time to attract wealthy customers. It was still the expanding middle classes who were responsible for the steady increase in the firm's turnover: departments like china and domestic appliances, selling goods at reasonable prices, continued to occupy most floor space and to be the backbone of their trade. But with the opening of their sparkling new shop, M & M's must also have felt more confident, especially in their numerous clothing departments, about introducing the kind of goods that would appeal to the tastes of the rich and fashionable. Later generations looked back nostalgically to three retail shops in Moscow. They identified Yeliseyev's with high-class provisions (in the style of Fortnum & Mason), Filippov's with cakes and pastries, and Muir & Mirrielees with top-quality clothes. This increasing emphasis on luxury items would have been consistent with Walter Philip's own tastes, but also conforms to a pattern frequently repeated in the history of department stores, whereby, having once become firmly established, they can begin to introduce more expensive lines without jeopardizing their overall prosperity.

In a book published in 1917 with the title, *Through Moscow*, the authors take the reader on a series of walks through the city, describing its artistic and cultural institutions. Looking across Theatre Square, they note the Bolshoi Theatre, 'a massive building distinguished by a certain ponderousness... but that ponderousness has a majestic grandeur and charm of its own'. To its right stands 'the reinforced concrete and glass building of Muir & Mirrielees, Russia's only universal stores, which is intriguing because it represents the new culture that is engulfing Moscow more and more'.

Russia by this time had begun to look increasingly to the West, but the pace of change was slow: M & M's was still its *only* universal stores. Moscow had always been more traditional than St Petersburg, and to many Muscovites in 1917, and still more so in 1908, the building must have seemed aggressively modern, an uncompromising example of the new culture that was engulfing the city. All that reinforced concrete and glass suggested America, the New World; all the goods inside the shop pointed to Europe, to European style and European living standards. Unlike its predecessor, a modest 19th century building of conventional design, the new M & M's no longer huddled in the shadow of the Bolshoi, either physically or metaphorically. On the contrary, it signalled a direct challenge to that powerful symbol of 19th century Tsarist conservatism and imperialism. Here is progress, it seemed to say, here are exciting new possibilities, here is what life is soon going to be like throughout Russia. Walter Philip, cosmopolitan in background, European in outlook, forward-looking and expansionist, cannot have failed to be aware that his new M & M's was in its way making a powerful political statement. In contrast again to its predecessor, the new building did not fly any flags, nor was the firm's name prominently displayed all round the facades. They may have felt that such trappings would detract from the merits of the building as a work of architecture, and that in any case their location was already sufficiently well known. But this lack of ostentation seems to hint at something more: a certain quiet self-confidence and awareness that this is not just a shop in which to buy things, but a symbol of Moscow – even Russia itself – being drawn into the 20th century.

The size of the crowds flooding the shop in the ten days before Christmas 1908 was unprecedented. M & M's now entered its most successful phase.

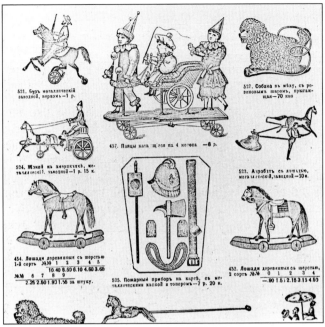

32. A selection of toys

33. A selection of ladies' jackets

34. Walter Philip the Company Chairman

35. Muir & Mirrielees shop, 1909

19

A Reversal of Fortune

Before the opening of the new shop, an important change had been made in the firm's constitution. On 23 October 1907 His Majesty the Emperor formally sanctioned the new Statutes, whereby M & M's ceased to be privately owned and became a joint-stock company. In London Harrod's had taken this step in 1889 and been quickly followed by many of the other large shopkeeping enterprises. For William Whiteley giving up personal control cannot have been easy, and when in 1900 his business empire was finally capitalized at £1,800,000, he kept half of this, in the form of shares, for himself; only the other half, consisting of debentures, was offered to the public, and these were subscribed seven times over. The 68-year-old Whiteley became Chairman of a Board of seven directors, including his two sons. On 24 January 1907, however, the Universal Provider departed from this life in one final blaze of publicity. A young man believing himself to be Whiteley's natural son entered the office from which Whiteley was still controlling the firm's operations, asked him for a loan which was refused, and shot him dead.

M & M's capital was fixed at 3 million roubles or £300,000: ten times more than the amount originally put in by Andrew Muir, Walter Philip and Archy Mirrielees. It was divided into 3000 shares of 1000 roubles each. More proprietorial even than Whiteley, Walter kept three-quarters of these, or 2250 shares, for himself. The remaining 750 were not, however, offered to the public, but only to a carefully chosen group of relations, friends and business associates. This did not include the Muirs. Nine-tenths of the shares were held by British people, the only exceptions being men like Faleyev, managing director of the Oborot Company in St Petersburg. The share certificates, issued in 1908, bore the names of Walter Philip as Chairman, Archy Mirrielees and Willie Cazalet as Directors, Edmond Hawtrey as Bookkeeper and Fred Cazalet as Cashier. Archy retired in 1910; Willie Cazalet later became Managing Director and his brother Fred an Assistant Director. By 1914 there were also two non-British directors.

Archy retired at the age of sixty. Might this not have been the moment for Walter, then sixty-four, to stand down also, thereby enabling Willie Cazalet, highly experienced but fifteen years his junior, to take over? Already a very wealthy man and the owner of a large London house at 5 Portman Square, Walter had surely satisfied all his personal ambitions. Like Whiteley, though, he was psychologically incapable of detaching himself from the flourishing enterprise to which he had devoted his life and with which he felt identified. His future was its future, and he was still driven on by his ambitions for the firm.

The cover of the Autumn & Winter catalogue for 1914-15 continues to describe M & M's as Russia's biggest universal stores and gives the number of departments as 'about 80': similar to Harrod's, but still a long way short of Selfridge's (130) and Whiteley's (159 in 1906). Extra departments must have been created since 1908. Some of these may have been fitted in to the new building, but this could not be enlarged, and it was at the firm's rented shop on the Petrovka that additions and alterations were made in 1911. As well as continuing to sell heavy goods like carpets, this shop was the retail outlet for the Factory's products. Thus, in 1913 the firm announced that because of the huge demand for electric light fittings, they had recently opened their own 'artistic bronze' factory, and customers were invited to inspect its wide selection of products at No.3 Petrovka.

With both retail shops flourishing, Walter turned his attention to the expansion of the Factory. Between 1912 and 1915, following the acquisition of adjoining sites, M & M's rebuilt their main Factory block, once again employing Klein as their architect. His brief was similar to that for the shop: to produce a building that would be functionally very up-to-date, but also have some architectural distinction. Consisting of a long frontage with two wings, it was a solid building of red brick rising to a height of six storeys at the corner towers. A contemporary sketch shows several busy delivery vans, one of which is now motorized, and a chimney of immense height belching forth smoke with an exuberance that might be frowned upon today. Klein again made use of medieval and Gothic decorative motifs. Today, the building houses the *Rassvet* ('Dawn') Machine Works, and its towers, with their white castle-like battlements above red-brick walls, are still a local landmark. Only very recently, the Russian architectural historian, A.D.Vasil'eva, discovered in the archives plans drawn up by Klein, which show that the 1915 building was in fact intended to be only the first stage in a far more ambitious building programme.

The most important part of the Factory remained the furniture factory and showrooms, followed by the printing-house. A complete plumber's workshop served the Technical Department. According to a contemporary advertisement, this was now offering an impressive range of down-to-earth services in areas where even William Whiteley had seldom dared to tread, namely: 'Water-supply of towns and railway stations. Water-pumps, sumps, drains. Sewerage, manuring of fields with sewage. Tiling of floors and walls. Brickwork. Sanitary appliances – English and American. Gas equipment. Gas mains. Gas cookers and ranges. Gas appliances for heating water, baths, etc.' It was this department that left behind the most visible mementoes of M & M's in Moscow. Not far from the front entrance of the old Moscow University building, walked over, stood upon and almost universally ignored by generations of students, there remains to this day a humble M & M manhole-cover (it is not unique). Until they finally succumbed to modernization, many of the city's older hotels had spacious bathrooms and lavatories with tiles bearing the firm's name, while a tile of this kind is still to be seen at the entrance to the Cathedral of Our Lady of Smolensk at the Novo-Devichy Convent.

In addition to the various workshops, the Factory site included accommodation for thirty resident employees, and a hospital and convalescent home. The firm also introduced a medical insurance scheme or 'Sick Fund'. The Tsarist authorities were very suspicious of these schemes, and among the various oppressive measures introduced in 1916 was the prosecution of men taking an active part in them. Early in 1915 the printing-house brought out a 'Sick Fund Report', covering the second half of 1914. Its compiler, probably a doctor associated with the Factory hospital who was concerned about social conditions, had collected some interesting data. During the six-month period the number of contributors to the Fund had gone down from 549 to 457, no doubt as a result of men being called up for active service. Furniture workers had dropped from 233 to 175, printers from 100 to 81, and workers in the nickel, tin and bronze workshops from 64 to 42; plumbers had gone up from 74 to 85; while the number of clerks (45) and workers in the Machine Department and General Administration (29) had remained constant. The employees' total earnings had been 108,000 roubles, representing an average annual wage of about 400 roubles (£40). From this about 6 roubles was deducted as each person's contribution to the Fund, the Company putting in 4 roubles per head. The age of the workforce was low, one-fifth being under 20 and more than half under 30; this was true of Russian factories generally. Three-fifths were married, of whom almost 70% were living away from their families. The level of literacy was exceptionally high: 95%, compared to 51% for factories in the Moscow Region, 40% for the Moscow Region population as a whole, and 23% for European Russia. The majority of workers had been taught in village schools. The clerks and printers were the most stable elements in the workforce, 40% of clerks and 31% of printers having been with the Company for more than five years.

Excluding clerks, over 90% of employees were officially classified as 'peasants', more than half from the Moscow Region. To what extent, asks the compiler, were they peasants sitting on land and making up for deficiencies in their agricultural economy by factory work, and to what extent professional workers closely tied to the factory? The answer was striking. Only one-sixth had severed all ties with the village: here again, it was the clerks (two-thirds) and printers (more than half) who had cut themselves off completely and could be regarded as pure urban proletarians. Of the rest, however, almost 60% were not only owners of land, but also, through their families, land-cultivators. In 75% of cases the land was cultivated by their parents – hence the youthfulness of the factory workforce. These migrants from the village sent home on average 100 roubles a year, or a quarter of their wages. The links between Moscow workers and the countryside were considerably stronger than in the case of workers in Petrograd (as St Petersburg had been renamed on the outbreak of war) or Kiev.

Rather more than a third of employees ate in the factory canteen, which offered two simple inexpensive meals a day and unlimited quantities of sweet rye bread baked on the premises. Those who preferred to be independent and eat in the *traktir* or tavern paid considerably more for food of very dubious quality: sausages, for example, were made from rotting meat and artificially coloured with harmful dyes. About thirty staff, such as watchmen and timekeepers, lived on the premises. Of the rest one-sixth rented flats, where they seldom had more than one room and usually took in lodgers, although this applied less in the case of clerks. The overwhelming majority, however, lived in rooms or dormitories. Here there was gross overcrowding, with more than three people on average sharing a room. Worst off were the 11% in basements, which seldom had sewage or running water, were often cold and damp, and in a few cases even without windows. Moreover, the compiler concludes, the kind of accommodation occupied by contributors to the Fund was not only very unhygienic and insanitary, but also, compared to other European capitals, very expensive.

In 1908-09 M & M's made a modest profit of 265,000 roubles and paid a dividend of 7½%; in 1912-13, their most successful pre-War year, these figures rose to 938,000 roubles and 15%. Turnover in 1914-15 was 13 million roubles (£1.3m.). A 1915 Guide to Moscow states that the firm had 2800 employees, that they might serve as many as 40,000 customers in a day and send off a thousand parcels in response to written orders from all over European and Asiatic Russia, and that they spent a considerable sum on advertising. This took many forms. A photograph from the early years of the century of the massive Moscow Duma building shows in the foreground an appealing little Moscow tram, drawn by two horses. Curving metal stairs at either end lead to the upper deck, which is uncovered, with a wide bench down the middle on which passengers sit back to back. This is obviously popular, even though it has started to rain and one gentleman is sitting under a large umbrella. A long board at the passengers' feet proclaims the name of Muir & Mirrielees to the passers-by. Then, in Whiteley fashion, they also published pocket almanacs with a pencil attached. Among the information included was a list, quite indispensable in Tsarist Russia, of all the fast-days, holidays and saints' days, and another list, for reverence only, of the names and dates of birth of every conceivable member of the Imperial family. Light relief was provided by each month's lucky stone (January – garnet, February – amethyst, etc.) and the allegorical meaning of flowers and plants (aster for inconstancy, balsam for beauty, etc.). Needless to say, full details are also given throughout the year of all the firm's seasonal catalogues, bargain sales, and Easter and Christmas bazaars.

While young Russians were being slaughtered in hundreds of thousands on the Western front in 1914-15, life in the big cities went on with few outward signs of change. As the war progressed, however, increasing numbers of refugees poured into Moscow from the areas invaded by the Germans, making the accommodation problem even more acute and leading to shortages of food. Such changes, while helping to undermine the stability of the Tsarist regime, had little effect on the lives of the monied classes, and M & M's were not the only retailers who did record business during the war years. In 1915 they issued another 750 shares.

The war was no longer a time for national self-effacement, and on the cover of the Autumn & Winter catalogue for 1915-16 M & M's describes itself as a 'Russo-English firm'. Otherwise, almost the only hint that a war is in progress comes from the Gold & Silver department, which is advertising silver-gilt cuffLinks with a choice of seven Allied national flags in enamel. Clothing, mainly women's wear, takes up about half the catalogue's 120 pages. As for furniture, 'more than 200 complete rooms have been prepared for the current season: drawing-rooms, studies, dining-rooms, bedrooms, boudoirs, entrance halls, artistically designed in all styles', while a new Handmade Furniture department has been opened 'in response to the huge demand for furniture at medium and cheaper prices'. The English reader comes upon some familiar names: Jaeger underwear, Gillette safety razors, Froebel building boxes, Burberry mackintoshes. The last four pages and back cover advertise the Book department, especially the children's 'Golden Library', and the Subscription department, now accepting annual subscriptions for all newspapers and magazines printed in Russia.

For the year ending 31 January 1917 the firm's Profit and Loss Account showed a staggering gross profit of over 6 million roubles (£600,000). 'Losses and Expenses incurred in consequence of the War', which one might have expected to be a major item, were negligible (4000 roubles). The net profit was 2½ times that of the most successful pre-War year.

Figures like those were tempting providence.

What happened next is described by Willie Cazalet in the 'Notes on the Position of the English Shareholders in Muir & Mirrielees', which he compiled some time after his return to England:

Within a fortnight of the first successful Russian Revolution, i.e. on 14 March 1917, a minority of the male and female employees of Muir & Mirrielees went out on strike, as did three-quarters or four-fifths of all the factory, mill, warehouse and shop hands, all over Moscow and district. The actual strike might have been averted, but the Chairman of the Board of Directors saw in the coming strike an overt threat to control, even dominate, the Board and therefore set his face against compromise by not conceding the more reasonable demands of the would-be strikers.

A conference was arranged between the Board and half a dozen of its chief advisers on the one hand, and a dozen delegates of the employees with one Trade Union official, a prominent Bolshevik, to instruct them on the other. It was then made clear, not only that the demands for increased pay were excessive, but that further demands for longer annual holidays with full pay were absolutely impracticable. Further the employees, led by three hotheads and acting on Trade Union and revolutionary pressure from outside, demanded the immediate formation of a Control Committee of Clerks and Workmen. The reason for their obduracy was that they knew that if they won this great concession from the leading firm, a little pressure would suffice to bring all other shops and warehouses in Moscow into line and thus the thin end of the wedge in their fight against capitalism would be introduced. At that time everything in Russia hinged on politics, the land question and higher wages, the question of the Great War no longer being of paramount interest.

After futile conferences, journeys to Petrograd to interview the new Ministers by the Managing Director, Mr William Cazalet, and after a weary wait of nearly seven weeks, the Board of Directors was compelled to 'toe the line' and concede practically all the original demands of a *minority* of their employees, and the great strike was over, which might probably have been averted altogether by the timely concession of substantial increases of salary and revision of the holiday terms.

Other employers of labour at once 'caved in' and the employees had won their first revolution. 'Force Majeure', of course, played a great part in these wholesale surrenders of the capitalists and tradesmen, as well in M & M's case, as in nearly all the others.

Walter was no longer alive when these notes were written, and Willie may have been anxious to justify his own position in retrospect. It seems clear, though, that there had been a fundamental difference of opinion at the time between him and Walter on how the threatened strike was to be handled. As Willie writes, 'the Chairman... set his face against compromise by not conceding the more reasonable demands of the would-be strikers', and again: 'the great strike... might probably have been averted altogether by the timely concession of substantial increases of salary and revision of the holiday terms'.

Willie was in no doubt that the Chairman's uncompromising attitude had been inappropriate and shortsighted. What the situation called for, he implies, was a relaxed approach and a willingness to make generous concessions (which the firm could easily have afforded). Willie himself – a genial figure who was to live on, remarkably unembittered by his Russian experiences, until 1953 – could have brought such qualities to bear on the situation, and the outcome might have been very different. Why was Walter unable to do so?

For all Willie's long association with the firm, he was not emotionally involved with M & M's to the same degree as Walter. That Walter's response to the threatened strike was more emotional than rational is suggested by Willie's choice of phrase: the Chairman 'set his face' against compromise. To vary the metaphor, Walter was digging his heels in, as he had done over the boys' dismissal in 1893. Why should they have even to contemplate the possibility of sharing control of the firm with those who were manifestly unqualified to exercise it? And why should they be expected to make concessions when they had always been good employers? To admit the strength of the would-be strikers' case was to admit their own previous shortcomings. Yet here was Willie suggesting that they should start bargaining and striking deals with their employees: to resort, in other words, to low cunning as a means of extricating themselves from the situation. To Walter such an approach was inappropriate and dishonourable.

Why *did* M & M's' workers, albeit a minority of them, come out on strike? By contemporary standards the firm's reputation as good employers was well deserved. After the fire in 1900 they had at once promised to keep on all their staff at full pay, they were genuinely concerned about working conditions, their social welfare policy seems enlightened (witness the Sick Fund, the Factory Hospital and convalescent home), and they were in general associated with the more liberal trends in Tsarist society.

One explanation of the strike is given by G.A.Fokin in his booklet about TsUM, *Flagship of Soviet Trade* (1968). During the years 1908-13, he writes, the foreign office of the Central Committee of the Party smuggled Bolshevik literature into Moscow, including the newspapers *Proletarian* and *Social Democrat*. Among the stores' employees were individuals acting as the Party's confidential agents, who distributed this literature. Then in the summer of 1917, 'a three-month strike of workers, in which more than 3000 people took part, was organized in the stores under the leadership of the Bolshevik group and the trade union of commercial-industrial employees. Alongside their demands for higher wages and better conditions of work the strikers also put forward political demands in support of the striking workers of Moscow's factories and industrial enterprises'.

This account is unreliable: the strike did not last for three months in the summer, but for seven weeks from 14 March, and according to Willie Cazalet, it was supported not by 'more than 3000 people', but only by a minority. The fact remains, however, that the employees of a previously loyal workforce did come out in sufficient numbers and with sufficient conviction to carry the strike through to a successful conclusion. Was this only the result of intense revolutionary pressure from outside, directed against M & M's as the leading firm in Moscow with a workforce known to be relatively stable, or were there other more 'internal' reasons?

M & M's factory workers, as we have seen, had good reason to feel bitter about bad food and bad accommodation, but these complaints could not be laid directly at their employers' door, and they were probably happy enough to be sending home a quarter of their wages. What may have been more critical in their case was something different: the land question. The Revolution gave fresh impetus to the age-old peasant movement to dispossess the landowners and restore the land to its rightful owners: those who tilled it. This revolutionary message must have been sweet music to the ears of all those migrants from the village employed by M & M's.

But what of those employees who were permanently established in Moscow, like the Factory clerks and printers, and especially the shop assistants, many of them female, who formed the majority of M & M's workforce and had little cause for complaint? It is hard to imagine them avidly reading secret copies of *Proletarian* before the War, or later being influenced by political agitation. Active support must have come from others within the firm. Like so many Tsarist institutions, M & M's was a very hierarchical structure, not only as regards pay: everyone knew his or her place; even the staff dining-rooms were socially graded; heads of department looked down upon assistants, while assistants looked down upon delivery men and female domestic staff. After the first Revolution there was a violent popular reaction against the abuse of rank and privilege that had been so characteristic of the Tsarist regime. Support for M & M's strike must have come from those within the firm who had nothing to lose in the hierarchy stakes.

Might Russian history have been different if Walter had not been so inflexible, if M & M's had made timely concessions, and other capitalists and tradesmen had followed their lead? The question is intriguing, though unanswerable. It was not, in any case, in Moscow that the political future of the country was being decided, but Petrograd, where the Provisional Government was nominally running the country, while power was shifting to the workers' councils or soviets.

At M & M's likewise, the Board continued running the firm after the strike, but with the Control Committee breathing down its neck. According to Willie Cazalet, the Committee had gained the right, 'not only of inspecting all the books, including the ledger and the wages sheets, but of being present (two in number) at Board Meetings and even

Auditors' Meetings.' It is not clear whether they were represented at the
tenth Annual General Meeting, held at the Company's offices on 31
May/13 June 1917, when the Board had to decide what to do with the
huge profits made in the previous year. They allocated them as follows:

Dividend at 20 per cent on each share	Rs 750,000
Voluntary Reserve	700,000
For Employees' Needs or Gratuities at the Board's discretion, not exceeding	400,000
Government Tax on Capital and Profits	257,999
Remuneration to Members of the Board	100,000
Statutory Reserve	76,348
Donations for War Purposes	50,000
Balance forward	1,866
TOTAL	Rs 2,336,213

The Voluntary Reserve had been set up by Walter at the beginning of
the war as a means of ensuring that in any lean years a dividend might
still be paid, so that the 700,000 roubles was in effect a further
allocation to shareholders. The 400,000 roubles 'for employees' needs
or gratuities' is carefully qualified ('at the Board's discretion', 'not
exceeding'), but the Board could argue that they were being generous:
this was the rough equivalent of a 20% bonus. The decision to allocate
themselves a further 100,000 roubles (on top of their salaries and
dividends) seems, however, like a deliberate and in the circumstances
provocative assertion by the Board of its own authority. If members of
the Control Committee *were* present and agreed to it, they cannot as
yet have been very confident of the strength of their position.

Some time after the end of the strike Walter's Moscow flat was
requisitioned. Wealthy cosmopolitan Walter Philip had more in
common with other wealthy Europeans and Russians in Moscow than
with his fellow British residents. The latter lived comfortably but
without ostentation in middle-class areas or on their own business
premises. Only the best, however, was good enough for the fastidious
Walter. For some years he had been renting a luxurious flat in the city
centre, just off the Petrovka and close to both M & M shops. Although
he had been living on his own in Moscow since 1914, it is unlikely that

he did much to curb his expensive way of life, or to reduce the size of his staff. As a result, not only was his flat requisitioned, but he was told to reduce his number of servants to one. Accompanied by the elderly Arina, he took over three small rooms at M & M's Factory.

These actions against Walter must have been taken after the firm had been forced to climb down and make so many humiliating concessions to the strikers. Now it was Walter himself who had to be cut down to size, and bearing in mind how the driving force behind his whole career might be seen as the urge to compensate for the shabby gentility of his youth, it seems at first sight a cruel irony that in old age he should have been reduced to living in such humble surroundings. But this is to ignore the strength of his commitment to the firm. The wealthy life-style had never been an end in itself. If for the firm's sake it was now necessary for him to live in three small rooms at the Factory, so be it. Those who thought to break Walter's spirit by these humiliations would have been mistaken.

In an attempt to prevent the accumulated reserves from falling into the wrong hands, the Board decided to authorize a new share issue. Shareholders were informed by letter

that the Government has permitted our Company, on account of the increase in the valuation of Real Estate and also on account of the Reserve Capital, to issue 2500 new shares at Rs1000 each, to be distributed free amongst the Shareholders of our Company. After distribution of the 2250 shares of the new issue to the 3750 shares of the old issue, there will fall to each old share three-fifths of a new share.

The letter was dated 25 October / 7 November 1917, the very day on which the Bolsheviks seized power in Petrograd. The shares were never issued.

Many members of the British community, anxious for the safety of themselves and their families under the uncompromising new regime, now decided to leave Moscow. The Bolsheviks were proposing to nationalize all businesses. If they hesitated to do so straight away, it was because the managers and senior employees were men of skill and experience, who could not easily be replaced. It was also important for public morale that a well-known shop like M & M's should function normally. Its doors remained open and its management soldiered on.

A new wages scale, to take effect from 1 July 1918, was drawn up by the Board in consultation with the Clerks' and Workers' Committee.

Only members of the Board and heads of sections were not included: a concession, perhaps, to what little autonomy the Board still had left. Other staff were divided into thirteen classes, Class13 being for juniors and apprentices. Promotions would be recommended by the Board but had to have the Committee's approval. Pay differentials were drastically reduced. Those in Class 1 (heads of departments with annual turnover exceeding 200,000 roubles, and the chief bookkeeper) were to receive 975 roubles p.a., far less than in the past, while those in Class 12 (timekeepers, watchmen, firemen, lift-attendants, delivery-men, female cleaning staff, kitchen and dining-room staff, etc.) would receive 450 roubles, a considerable improvement. Ordinary shop assistants found themselves in Classes 9, 10 and 11. Knowledge of foreign languages entitled the Company's correspondents to special bonuses. On the other hand, once the new scale was introduced, all the Christmas, Easter and annual bonuses were scrapped as belonging to the bad old days of pre-Revolutionary paternalism.

Turnover for the year ending 31 January 1918 was more than 30 million roubles (£3m.), but because of the strike, there was a small overall deficit. At the A.G.M. on 30 May 1918 the management made a last-ditch attempt to assert itself. Fred Cazalet as a shareholder, seconded by his wife Lucy as an auditor, proposed that the Clerks' and Workers' Committee's two delegates be refused admittance. This was passed by a large majority. The meeting then proceeded to vote a dividend of 10%, in spite of the year's loss. The money was to come from the Voluntary Reserve set up by Walter with just such a situation in mind.

It was a defiant but futile gesture. When the Committee read the Minutes of the Meeting, they protested to the Board and the Minister for Trade & Commerce that the 'hidden' dividend was prejudicial to the employees' interests. Their protest was upheld and an embargo placed on payment of the dividend.

By the early summer of 1918 the British in Moscow were living in a state of constant apprehension. No one knew when their homes might be searched or requisitioned, whether their money was safe and would still buy anything, and above all, where the next meal was coming from. Life was especially difficult for Fred and Lucy Cazalet with two young children, and on 29 June, not long after making their last stand at the A.G.M, they all left Moscow. Before leaving, Lucy hid her priceless collection of Russian china in the cellar of their flat, but it cannot have remained hidden very long, for she had carefully packed everything in wooden crates, and in the desperate winter of 1918-19 people were hunting for firewood in every corner. The Cazalets were members of a party of twenty-seven British people leaving Russia, including their friends, the Smiths and the Whiteheads, and the story of their six-week journey via Archangel and Murmansk is told in detail in *The Smiths of Moscow*. Soon after they had left Archangel, a small British expeditionary force landed there as part of the Allied intervention against the Bolsheviks. In Moscow anti-British reprisals quickly followed. Walter, now seventy-two, and Willie Cazalet were among those arrested without charge. Willie spent thirty-nine days in prison, but was well treated and allowed to receive food from his wife. By November 1918 he, too, was back in England. Walter, he reported, had been released from prison and could have come away at the same time, but had refused to do so.

That decision does not surprise one, even though Walter had not seen any of his family since 1914. (When war broke out, Laura and her daughters were on holiday in Scotland and did not return to Russia, while Terence was caught in Germany and interned there for the duration of the war.) The most sensible course of action would have been for Walter to cut his losses and return to England; no one could have blamed him for doing so in the circumstances. But hardheaded businessmen, as Andrew Muir has already illustrated, do not always do the sensible thing. Had he been considering himself alone, it might have been different, but to abdicate all responsibility towards the firm's shareholders would have seemed to Walter the action of a dishonourable man.

By this sta ge, however, events were quite out of his control. First, the shop was looted, then the business was confiscated in its entirety for the benefit of the Moscow Municipal Supply Committee, and finally on 18 November 1918 the Board of Directors was completely suspended from office and the running of the business handed over to a newly-elected Control Committee. A formal announcement of the nationalization of M & M's appeared in the government newspaper *Izvestiya* in December. For a brief period Walter worked under the new Committee for a small salary – perhaps imagining that he might be able to salvage something from the situation or in some way influence the future course of events – then in January 1919 he received two weeks' salary and was dismissed.

In the following August a former senior employee of M & M's, Sergei Maximov, sent a letter from Lithuania to M & M's former bookkeeper, Edmond Hawtrey, in London. He describes how he had been arrested and kept in prison for six weeks when the business was confiscated, but his letter is mainly concerned with Walter. It makes clear in passing what would otherwise have been in doubt: that Walter was capable, in certain cases at least, of inspiring great loyalty and affection among people who worked for him. One person not so affected, however, was the man who had been in charge of building operations in 1906-08 and compiled the Specification, Nikolai Rodionov. Although, as Maximov writes, Rodionov had been in such great favour with Vladimir Vasilievich (Walter), he went over completely to the side of those who began harassing him in various ways, even in trifles; not only did he fail to stand up for him, but he actively co-operated in depriving the old man of his third room at the Factory. Fortunately, Arina continued to look after her master faithfully until the very end, 'in spite of the various petulances and caprices of the invalid'.

By now the ex-Chairman of Muir & Mirrielees had become a former person. It was a dangerous time for Russians to be associated with foreign capitalists, and no one went to see him, with the exception of Alexander Rodionov (the brother of Nikolai and another senior employee?), a Madame Zanstrem and Maximov himself. Then, at the beginning of June,

he caught a slight chill, which turned to bronchitis. Doctor Levin attended him. The illness, the shattering of his nerves from all he had gone through, all this affected his heart and he began to fade away.

The last time I was with him was on 6 June on the eve of my departure, and already then one could forsee that the end was near, but one wished to believe in the possibility of a miracle. Afterwards I had to live for nearly a month in Minsk and I received the news of his death there.

He died on the night of 27/28 June in Dr Ignatiev's Nursing Home in which he was placed by Alexander Dmitrievich [Rodionov], who was with him nearly all the time and even passed the last night there. He died peacefully – his heart ceased working.

It is a very heavy loss to the business, which finally, sooner or later, must revive.

Personally, I am so shaken by what has happened that I can only compare this loss to the death of my own father, so well was Vladimir Vasilievich disposed towards me, and I towards him.

Communicate all this if possible to his widow, to Vasili Lvovich [Willie

Cazalet], Fyodor Lvovich [Fred Cazalet] and to all whom you think fit.

At our last meeting Vladimir Vasilievich asked me to send off a telegram as follows: 'Royal Bank of Scotland, London. Inform wife am well but feeble longing for news if practicable, Philip.' But now I shall not send it.

Yes, a most honourable, most noble man has died – and died far away from his family. It is very sad and painful!

Walter was seventy-three and had been in Russia from the age of sixteen. He had first gone to Moscow as a very young man in the late 1860's to start building up the wholesale trade of Muir & Mirrielees, never dreaming then that he would one day preside over the opening of Moscow's finest shop. He had been in charge of the firm for forty-four years, longer than his two predecessors put together. They had climbed high, but he had climbed far beyond them, so that his fall, when it came, was bound to be precipitate. What made it even more so was his uncompromising nature, which refused to let him cut his losses or to save his own skin.

Walter's commitment to the firm, filling the vacuum that had been left by the emotional deprivations of his early years, was far more exclusive than that of his predecessors. Archibald Mirrielees owed his first allegiance to God, while in Andrew Muir's life the thinker was always looking over the businessman's shoulder, but in Walter's life there was one theme only: that of the firm. Like William Whiteley, he had identified himself with his business enterprises to such an extent that it is doubtful whether he could ever have brought himself to retire. If it needed a bullet to dislodge Whiteley, it needed a revolution to remove Walter Philip. It was both inevitable and appropriate that his life should come to an end so soon after that of Muir & Mirrielees.

Postscript

Among those due to attend the opening of M & M's new shop in 1908 was Maida Bernard. In the twenty years since Harry's resignation from the Moscow Chaplaincy he and Maida had been very busy. At Haeckel's Zoological Institute in Jena, Harry pursued his studies with all the enthusiasm of a late beginner, but his lack of British qualifications meant that from 1893 to 1907 he had to be content with modestly-paid work writing up the rich collection of corals in the Natural History Museum. He also published more than fifty papers, but was never accepted by the scientific élite. His daughter, Una, writes that his highly developed scientific imagination always led him to make original suggestions and to propose new hypotheses. On one occasion, when he was urging a new view of evolution at a biological conference, the chairman remarked that Mr Bernard's ideas were very interesting, but surely Darwin had settled the whole matter once for all?

For Harry science and socialism went hand in hand, as the title of his book, *The Scientific Basis of Socialism* (1908) indicates. In Streatham he and Maida started a small socialist society. Maida organized a lending library and Harry arranged for visiting lecturers. On Sunday mornings they held meetings on Streatham Common, and on Sunday afternoons, as Maida reminded her daughters in the Family Record, 'Dad used to have men members to tea in our kitchen, he and his visitors doing the washing up unaided'.

There was never any money to spare in the Bernard household, and Maida sometimes wondered how they would have managed without her rich and kind brothers. Since leaving M & M's, Fred had become more and more of an Establishment figure, eventually taking over from his father-in-law as head of the Union Castle Mail Steamship Co. Ltd, and receiving a knighthood in 1910. But he remained loyal to his relations, however much he might differ in outlook from his socialist sister and brother-in-law, and it was he who paid for all three girls to be educated at St Leonards School, St Andrews.

In June 1908 Maida returned to Russia for the first time, accompanied by Austin Birrell's sister, Olive. In St Petersburg they spent three nights at a hostel run by the Y.W.C.A., prompting Austin to comment that it was absurd for two women who were neither young nor Christian to put up at such a place. Maida admitted the first criticism, but not the second. In Moscow Walter and Archy laid on lavish entertainments, and Archy's coachman, who remembered 'Matilda Arkhipovna' well, was proud to point out all the improvements in Moscow since her departure. Olive returned to England at the end of July, but her place was taken by Maida's second daughter, Ida, a medical student. All their plans were turned upside down, however, when on 5 August Maida received a letter from her youngest daughter, Maude, saying that her father was quite different from his usual self and very silent. Maida decided to return at once to England. As a result, she missed what must surely have been intended as a highlight of her visit: the opening of the new M & M building, which took place a week later, on 1 August in the Old Style Russian calendar.

Harry was suffering from Bright's disease, from which he died on 4 January 1909 at the age of fifty-five. An announcement of his death was made to the congregation of St Andrew's Church, Moscow, by his successor, Frederic Wybergh.

In England Maida had not only contributed to the family exchequer by translating German scientific textbooks and by popular scientific journalism, but also continued to act as Harry's secretary. She faced her greatest challenge, however, after his death. Early in 1907 the funds for coral research were diverted to other purposes, and Harry found himself without a job. He took the blow philosophically, reflecting that this would enable him to concentrate on writing up his own most important ideas, but at the time of his death this task was far from complete. There were hundreds of pages covered with corrections, or in Harry's minute handwriting that Maida alone could decipher. 'Often I would go to bed almost in despair over some difficulty, but in the early morning some solution would occur to me, almost as if Dad had helped me.' The result was a book entitled *Some Neglected Factors in Evolution*, published in America in 1911. Although it failed to mark the new epoch in philosophy that Harry had hoped for, its theory of 'Rhythmic Evolution' anticipated many ideas that were popularized much later. It was Maida's last act of support for 'the dear boy', as she and the three girls always called Harry.

Maida's brother, Archy, retired to England in 1910. He had first gone to work for M & M's at the age of seventeen. The choice had not been his, but he was dutiful and conscientious and eager to please, and young men in the 1860's did what was expected of them, especially if they had a father like Archibald Mirrielees and an uncle like Andrew Muir. He spent the next forty years – a lifetime – in the firm's employment, with interruptions for 'ill health'. If nothing else, though, he had become a wealthy man and could look forward on retirement to leading the life of a gentleman of leisure. He bought Templemore House in Hampstead, and then a Highland estate set in the midst of beautiful countryside, where he commissioned a London architect to design him a fine house, Aultmore, as a summer residence for himself and his wife, Annie.

But Archy was not even to be allowed a happy retirement. 'It is strange and sad,' Maida reflects, 'that anxiety about money matters undoubtedly hastened the end of both my rich brothers.' Fred died in January 1914 at the age of sixty-two, and Archy a year later at the age of sixty-four. He enjoyed his Scottish estate – if 'enjoyed' is the right word – for one summer only, the hot summer of 1914, during which the First World War broke out. 'He had never been a strong man,' Maida writes, 'and Fred's illness and death had told on him greatly; also, during the last months he had much worry about financial affairs, owing to being cut off from his Russian resources.' A memorial service for him was conducted in Moscow by Wybergh's successor, the Revd Frank North.

Unlike that of Walter Philip, his close friend and business associate, Archy's life does not contain any dramatic reversal of fortune, yet this uneventful story of a man who never did what he wanted to in life has a Chekhovian poignancy of its own. After his death there was a final touch of irony. Because of the post-War slump in property prices, his widow was unable to sell the Scottish estate until 1924.

Following the deaths of her husband and brothers, Maida remained astonishingly active, both physically and mentally. In 1916 she published *100 Russian Verbs & 1000 of their compound forms*. A leading authority wrote gratifyingly of the book's usefulness to students, but spoiled the effect by assuming that its compiler must be a man. During the 1920's, whenever she had any free time, she worked away at the Family Record, which takes her life up to 1927, typing and correcting it all herself, and tying up its 500 pages of family history and personal memoirs into the kind of 'neat parcel' that would have met with her father's approval. She would have been surprised by the use made of it so many years later.

After her father's sudden death, Maida had reflected that it was a happy ending for such an active man, and hoped that her own end might be similar. Early in 1929 she went to help Ida and her family, who had been struck down by influenza. She, too, had an attack, but seemed to have recovered, and began eagerly to plan for another visit to Una and her family in California. By then she would be seventy-six. One day, as she was writing to ask what sort of shoes would be best for mountain walking, she was interrupted by Maude's arrival from Italy, and they sat up talking cheerfully till late at night. She did not wake the next morning.

* * *

On New Year's Day, 1903, in reply to Meta's Christmas letter giving news of the family, Austin Birrell wrote: 'I think Eva's case is the only *really* sad one. The Boys will do all right and a really *splendid* Spinster like Molly is a better thing to gaze upon than an absorbed Matron.'

The three sisters remained very loyal and devoted to each other for the rest of their lives. Molly continued to lead a busy social life, always fashionably dressed, always visiting or being visited. She never married, although there was at least one 'disappointment', but in August 1904 the unpredictable Eva married Francis Richmond, eldest son of the painter, Sir William Richmond. Emulating her mother, she gave birth to three sons, including twins, when she was over forty, but never quite succeeded in breaking out of the vicious circle of self-pity and psychosomatic illness.

As for 'The Boys', Martin's life took no fresh turn, but Kenneth started a new career after stepping down from the Chemical Works. In 1903 he became deputy manager of the St Petersburg branch of 'The Gramophone & Typewriter Ltd.', later 'His Master's Voice', which had branches all over Europe, and in August 1904 was transferred as manager to Milan. He left them in 1909 and worked for two years with the 'Fonotipia' company. In 1911 he married an Italian girl, Maria von Reiser, by whom he had three children.

Alice Muir lived on for a number of years after Andrew's death. To her London-bred granddaughters, Alison and Margaret Hogg, who went to tea with her every Sunday afternoon, she seemed very Scottish, playing lively Scottish reels on the piano for them to dance to. New Year's Eve was celebrated in traditional Scottish style with shortbread and bun. 'She knitted and sewed,' Alison recalled, 'played patience, and was a great reader. She was rather dreamy and could sit and let the world go by, but if it was a question of a journey, or making marmalade, she would take action.' One such journey, undertaken in 1908 with her daughter-in-law, Laura Philip, was to the Isle of Skye, ancestral home of the clan of McLeod, to which she belonged through her mother. After a rough crossing they were met at the pier by the

Chief and his daughter. The Chief, Alice wrote to Molly, was standing a little apart from the other islanders, who took off their caps and saluted him. 'He is a fine-looking man with white hair, and Laura says looks older than I do, although he is sixty-three and I am eighty-five.' He offered her the use of a donkey chair while she was on the island.

Alice's extraordinary life came to an end on 15 December 1910, when she was eighty-eight. Austin Birrell described her to Meta as one of the few who would always people the gallery of his memory. He wrote of her 'capacity to face the emergencies of this life, in either Zone' (an allusion to Africa and Russia) – a capacity that had stamped itself upon her, though where exactly he could never decide. 'I suppose she had many sorrows and disappointments – who has not? – and had led a life of varied adventures and heroisms and endured many things – but all this sad experience, though it gave her the "stamp" just mentioned, left her face without a stain of trial or temper.'

From Moscow Walter wrote to Meta: 'Now that it is all over I feel so thankful that her end was such a peaceful one, but as you said in your letters, how cold the world seems without her. A strange feeling of loneliness has come over me, for having already for years regarded her as my only link with those happy years in the past, I feel to a certain extent as if I were stranded... It seems to me that no love can exactly replace that of a mother, especially of such a mother as we had. Did you ever know anyone else so guileless?'

By 'those happy years in the past' Walter meant the time before the family quarrel of 1893. In 1912 a reconciliation did, however, take place between him and Kenneth. Walter gave Kenneth generous financial support while the latter was without a job, and agreed to act as his agent in Moscow in negotiations with Lepeshkin Sons for the sale of the Chemical Works. 'You will appreciate,' Kenneth wrote in March 1913, 'the effect likely to be produced upon them when they find that it is you whom I have asked to settle the final terms with them and the adventitious prestige acquired by thus sailing in under the protection of the guns of a Dreadnought.'

For some reason, however, the negotiations fell through, and this led to another dispute over financial matters between the two brothers and their sisters. When Martin complained to Meta that they did not treat him with sufficient respect, she replied that respect must be earned and the days were past when the females of a family looked up to the males merely because of their sex. The comment was true, she reflected later, after Martin's death, but it gave her no satisfaction to think of it. Kenneth was prepared to acknowledge that when he and Martin were sent out to Russia, they were very young men and found themselves surrounded by people of low standards of honour, and that this had been very bad for them, yet he could never reach the point of admitting to himself or others that his actions towards his sisters might have been reprehensible in any way; but as Stuart pointed out, a man will cheerfully admit to any fault under the sun except that of behaving dishonourably. This breach between brothers and sisters was never properly healed, although Kenneth in his will left Molly one-fifth of the principal moneys and interest secured by a first mortgage of the Chemical Works, in recognition of her 'courageous support' in enabling him and Martin to carry on the business.

Martin, like Walter, must have felt stranded after the death of his mother, with whom he had been living since Eva's marriage. Trying to foster an image of himself as a skilful man of business, he became involved in all manner of unsuccessful schemes that sound like parodies of earlier Muir business activities. Among them was the turtle soup venture. Two men in a houseboat on the Swan River in Western Australia were reputed to have taken advantage of the abundant supply of turtles in that area to start a cosy little business producing turtle soup, but as soon as the next gold rush came along, they abandoned the turtles and set off with pick and shovel. They had shown, however, that the soup could be made in bulk, packed in tins or jars, and kept for a considerable time. Why not form a syndicate to import it into Britain? 'Turtles are moving slowly (as is their wont),' Martin wrote to Kenneth in June 1914, 'but, thank goodness, definitely moving.' As soon as enough money had been raised, the syndicate's representative would go out to Australia to prepare samples. But with the outbreak of war soon after, turtles must have stopped moving altogether.

In November 1917 Meta and Stuart heard that Martin was 'in rather a bad way' and invited him to stay with them in the country. 'He has his usual winter cough,' Meta wrote to Eva, 'and I dare say that might impress anyone who did not know him as something alarming and ominous. He looks much better since he came here and has been in a very serene and happy mood.' Apparently, he had been earning a fair amount in some Anglo-Russian undertaking, but she was afraid this source of income would dry up as a result of the disturbances in Russia; he himself, however, said not.

Meta was being too sanguine. When Martin next came to stay with them a year later, he was already in an advanced stage of consumption, and died at the Hoggs' home near Hertingfordbury on 26 December 1918 at the age of fifty-four. It was then that Austin Birrell made his comment about Martin never having been given a fair chance in life. To Kenneth fell the task of going to Martin's lodgings to collect his things. He was shocked by the poor dingy little room in south London where his tubercular brother had been living without even a fire. 'On two pegs,' he wrote to Meta, 'were hanging two old suits completely worn out – the only ones besides the suit he wore when he came to you. The landlady brought me a little old underclothing also worn out. I thanked her and paid her £6 that was owing.' What a contrast, Kenneth reflected, with the 'early life of prosperity and bright, cultured environment' enjoyed by them all at 42.

Kenneth himself, having spent the war as an interpreter and liaison officer with the Scottish forces in Italy, was anxious to rebuild his business career as soon as possible, knowing that he had only ten more years or so of working life in which to lay by enough capital to support his young family. To Meta he confessed that he was 'in a blue funk of falling ill and being incapacitated or dying'. His sense of foreboding may have been justified, for only a month after Martin's death he had what was diagnosed as a slight stroke, but seems more likely to have been a symptom of the sleepy-sickness which slowly incapacitated him, and from which he died in April 1922: a victim of the international epidemic that claimed so many lives between 1916 and 1928.

Molly followed him little more than a year later. 'One contemplates, in gloomy forebodings, many things,' Austin Birrell wrote to Meta, 'but never that one. It carries me back, a long way, to another dim and distant day, but though dim and distant, always unforgettable': to 6 September 1879, when his first wife, Maggie, died. 'Molly was a figure not easily forgotten and impossible to replace. Her vitality was so great and her humour so vivid, that it seems impossible to think of her having so suddenly disappeared. What a blow to you and Eva.'

Eva's husband died in 1933, but she, Meta and Stuart lived on into their eighties. Meta and Stuart are buried in the village churchyard at Hertingfordbury. Today, John Bagenal and his wife, Patience, still live in the cottage beyond the village that John's grandparents first rented as a holiday retreat in 1902 – a quiet place beside the river Lea, though only twenty-three miles as the crow flies from Piccadilly Circus – and it was they who provided the first impetus for the writing of this book.

Afterword, 1994

In February 1994 I returned to Moscow for the launch of the book's Russian version, entitled Muir & Mirrielees: Scots in Russia. *Since its initial acceptance by Moscow Worker almost four years earlier there had been many setbacks. Publishing in Russia, once so firmly regulated from above, had become a chaotic free-for-all. Paper was in chronically short supply; prices rocketed. I sought sponsorship for the book from British firms with business interests in Russia, but the most I ever received from them was their good wishes. I reduced the book's length by a third. Even after the translation was under way, publication seemed far from certain, but in May 1993 the story took an unexpected turn. The state-owned TsUM had shown no interest in their capitalist predecessors, but then the store was privatized and – much to the publishers' delight – the new management agreed to buy the whole edition of 10,000 copies for sale in the shop.*

At Moscow Worker I noticed many changes. In the past they had published a considerable amount of Party literature, but when the Party was dissolved in December 1991 this comfortable source of income dried up overnight. Outside and in, the building looked less impressive than in 1990. A path to the entrance had been hacked crudely out of the snow. The publishing house was now on two floors only: the other four were let. The staff had been similarly reduced, Party people being the first to go. But Moscow Worker had adapted and survived, and in 1993 had brought out 170 titles without resorting to the literary trash then filling Moscow's bookstalls.

On a fine still day I found myself standing once more with my camera in the gardens opposite the Bolshoi Theatre. The bare February trees made it easier to photograph the buildings, but removing one's gloves for any length of time was not a good idea in the sub-zero temperature. Parked cars kept their engines running. One end of the Bolshoi was covered by scaffolding, but in the far corner of Theatre Square the Metropole Hotel, closed in 1990, had been restored to its former glory. Outside the Metro station lurid books and magazines were being sold from folding tables, and the pavement was awash with piles of discarded cardboard boxes.

Going into TsUM was still 'a bit like entering a dungeon', as a seven-year-old Russian girl had put it four years earlier, but whereas in 1990 the assistants in the shoe department almost outnumbered the pairs of shoes for sale, now all the departments looked well stocked and busy, in spite of the high prices. On the last page of Muir & Mirrielees *an advertisement by TsUM*

*invited customers to make purchases in their main shop and three branches,
'where all kinds of goods are on display, from threads and buttons to prestige
furniture and cars'. They certainly caught the eye, those gleaming new cars
not far from the main entrance on the ground floor, and I wondered how
Walter Philip would have reacted to them. Perhaps without raising an
eyebrow. Perhaps he would have said: fine, now show me the threads and
buttons, because on them the long-term prosperity of a store like this depends.
He would not have been surprised in the least – surprising though it seems to
us after all the upheavals from 1917 onwards – to discover that his office
desk, a massive affair likely to have been made to his own specifications in
M & M's Furniture factory, was still being used by the present managing
director in whose office the book was launched.*

I had never imagined that the Russian version of Muir & Mirrielees, *beset
with so many difficulties, would appear first, but finding a publisher for the
English version had its own peculiar problems. It was like watching a game
of snakes and ladders, in which first one version, then the other, seemed to be
edging cautiously towards its goal, only to be ambushed by some
unpredictable disaster. Meanwhile, during the course of those four years, the
whole Anglo-Russian scene was being rapidly transformed. In the 1970's and
80's, describing the Anglo-Russian world of* Miss Emmie and The Smiths of
Moscow *for English readers, I felt like an archaeologist who had stumbled
upon the remains of some deliberately forgotten civilization. Even in 1990,
when that world could be talked and written about freely in Russia as well as
Britain, no one would have guessed that four years later Queen Elizabeth II
would visit Russia, the first ever reigning British monarch to set foot on
Russian soil: a visit that does not so much mark the start of a new phase,
since that has already happened, as symbolize the long-term hope for better
times ahead in the continuing Anglo-Russian story.*

Cromer, October 1994   *H. J.P.*

Bibliography

Adburgham, Alison. *Shops and Shopping 1800-1914*. Where, and in What Manner The Well-Dressed Englishwoman Bought her Clothes (London, 1964).

Aplin, Hugh A. (ed.) 'Yu.V. Lomonosov. "At the Home of L.N.Tolstoy". (An Unpublished Memoir).' *Scottish Slavonic Review*, vol.17, Autumn 1991, pp.147-164.

Baedeker, Karl. *Baedeker's Russia 1914* (first published 1914; reprinted London and Newton Abbot, 1971).

Bible Society Monthly Reporter, vol.x, No.23, April 2, 1877, pp.217-220 (obituary of Archibald Mirrielees).

Birrell, Augustine. *Things Past Redress* (London, 1937).

Birrell, Rev. C.M. *The Life of the Rev. Richard Knill of St. Petersburg* (London, 1859; Special Edition printed by the Religious Tract Society, 1878).

Black, George F. *The Surnames of Scotland* (New York, 1946).

Boa, V.(ed.) *The Clyde Pottery, Greenock, 1816-1905* (Inverclyde District Libraries, Greenock, 1987).

British and American Congregational Church, St Petersburg. Jubilee Commemorative Volume 1840-1890 (St Petersburg, 1891).

Cabot, Harriet Ropes. 'The Early Years of William Ropes & Company in St Petersburg', *The American Neptune*, Vol.xxiii, No.2, April 1963, pp.131-139.

Canton, W. *The Story of the Bible Society* (London, 1904).

Carroll, Lewis. *The Russian Journal and other selections*, ed. John Francis McDermott (New York, 1935).

Cooke, Catherine. 'Moscow Map Guide 1900-1930', *Architectural Design* 1983, No.5/6, pp.81-96.

– 'Shekhtel in Kelvingrove and Mackintosh on the Petrovka. Two Russo-Scottish Exhibitions at the Turn of the Century'. *Scottish Slavonic Review*, vol.10, Spring 1988, pp.177-205.

Darlow, T.H. (ed.) *Letters of George Borrow to the British and Foreign Bible Society* (London, 1911).

Dickson, Mora. *The Powerful Bond.* Hannah Kilham 1774-1832 (1980).

Dukes, Paul *et al.* *The Caledonian Phalanx: Scots in Russia* (Edinburgh, 1987).

Ffolliott, Pamela and Croft, E.L.H. *One Titan At A Time*, The Story of John Paterson of Port Elizabeth, South Africa, and his Times (Cape Town, 1960).

Granville, A.B. *St Petersburgh*, 2 vols (London, 1828).

History of George Square Congregational Church, Greenock 1805-1905. By the Centenary Committee (Glasgow, 1906).

Jacks, L.P. *Life and Letters of Stopford Brooke*, 2 vols (London, 1917).

Jenkins, Herbert. *The Life of George Borrow* (London, 1912).

Johnston, John Octavius. *Life and Letters of Henry Parry Liddon* (London, 1904).

Kohl, J.G. *Russia* (London, 1842).

Lambert, Richard S. *The Universal Provider.* A Study of William Whiteley and the Rise of the London Department Store (London, 1938).

Mason, Griselda Fox. *Sleigh Ride to Russia.* An Account of the Quaker Mission to St Petersburg in 1854 (York, 1985).

Parry, Albert. *Whistler's Father* (Indianapolis and New York, 1939).

Pasternak, Alexander. *A Vanished Present.* The Memoirs of Alexander Pasternak, edited and translated by Ann Pasternak Slater (Oxford, 1984).

Pitcher, Harvey. *The Smiths of Moscow* (Cromer, 1984).

– *When Miss Emmie was in Russia* (London, 1977).

Sayers, Jane E. *The Fountain Unsealed.* A History of the Notting Hill and Ealing High School (1973).

Scott, Richenda C. *Quakers in Russia* (London, 1964).

Swanwick, H.M. (née Sickert). *I Have Been Young* (London, 1935).

Weir, Daniel. *History of the Town of Greenock* (Greenock, 1829).

Witting, Clifford (ed.) *The Glory of the Sons, a history of Eltham College School for the Sons of Missionaries* (London, 1952).

Index

The Mirrielees and Cazalet Families

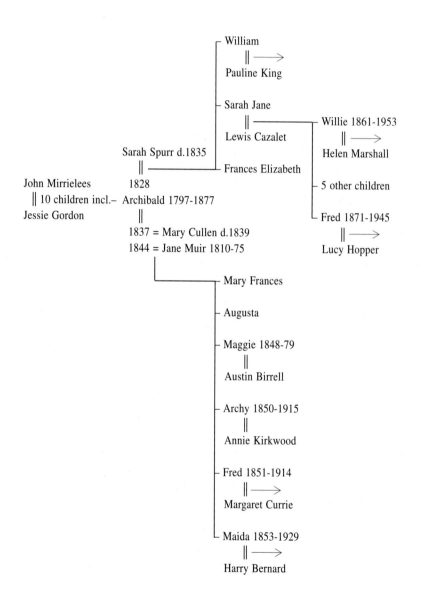

The Muir and Philip Families

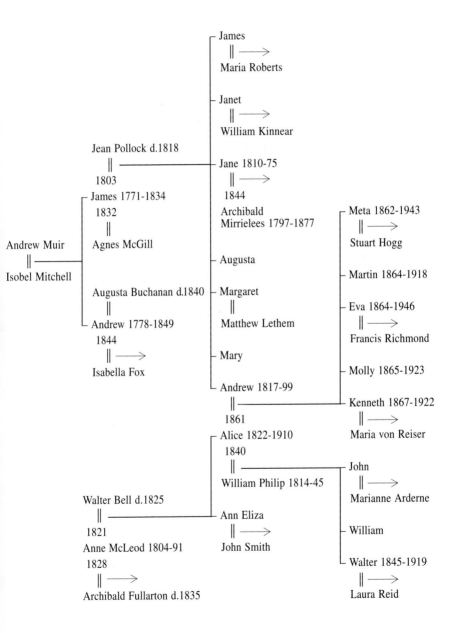

James
‖ ⟶
Maria Roberts

Janet
‖ ⟶
William Kinnear

Jean Pollock d.1818
‖ ——————— Jane 1810-75
1803 ‖ ⟶
James 1771-1834 1844
1832 Archibald   Meta 1862-1943
‖ Mirrielees 1797-1877   ‖ ⟶
Agnes McGill   Stuart Hogg

Andrew Muir   Augusta
‖   Martin 1864-1918
Isobel Mitchell

Augusta Buchanan d.1840 — Margaret   Eva 1864-1946
‖ ‖   ‖ ⟶
Andrew 1778-1849 Matthew Lethem   Francis Richmond
1844
‖ ⟶ Mary   Molly 1865-1923
Isabella Fox
Andrew 1817-99   Kenneth 1867-1922
‖ —————————————— ‖ ⟶
1861   Maria von Reiser
Alice 1822-1910
1840   John
‖ ——————— ‖ ⟶
William Philip 1814-45   Marianne Arderne
Walter Bell d.1825
‖ ——————— Ann Eliza   William
1821 ‖ ⟶
Anne McLeod 1804-91 John Smith   Walter 1845-1919
1828   ‖ ⟶
‖ ⟶   Laura Reid
Archibald Fullarton d.1835

ПАЙ ВЪ ТЫСЯЧУ РУБЛЕЙ.

№2665 №2665

ТОРГОВО-ПРОМЫШЛЕННОЕ ТОВАРИЩЕСТВО „МЮРЪ и МЕРИЛИЗЪ".

Уставъ Товарищества ВЫСОЧАЙШЕ утвержденъ 23 Октября 1907 года.

ОСНОВНОЙ КАПИТАЛЪ 3.000.000 РУБЛЕЙ.

 ВЪ ТЫСЯЧУ РУБЛЕЙ

выданъ на имя Великобританскаго подданнаго
Архипа Архиповича Мерилизъ.

TRADING COMPANY
MUIR & MIRRIELEES, Limited.

The Statutes of the Company were sanctioned by H. M. the EMPEROR October 23, 1907.

Capital 3.000.000 Roubles.

CERTIFICATE FOR
ONE THOUSAND ROUBLE SHARE.

Предсѣдатель Правленія }
Chairman }

Члены Правленія }
Directors }

Бухгалтеръ }
Book-keeper }

Кассиръ }
Cashier }

Москва, 1908, Moscow.

ONE THOUSAND ROUBLE SHARE.

Cover of the Winter Catalogue, 1904